Human resource management in education

OPEN UNIVERSITY PRESS

Management in Education Series

Editor
Tony Bush

Senior Lecturer in Educational Policy and Management
at The Open University

The series comprises five volumes which cover important topics within the field of educational management. The articles present examples of theory and practice in school and college management. The authors discuss many of the major issues of relevance to educational managers in the post-Education Reform Act era.

The five readers are components of The Open University M.A. in Education module *E818 Management in Education*. Further information about this course and the M.A. programme may be obtained by writing to the Higher Degrees Office, The Open University, PO Box 49, Walton Hall, Milton Keynes, MK7 6AD.

Human resource management in education

EDITED BY

Colin Riches and Colin Morgan

at The Open University

OPEN UNIVERSITY PRESS
MILTON KEYNES · PHILADELPHIA
in association with The Open University

Open University Press
12 Cofferidge Close
Stony Stratford
Milton Keynes MK11 1BY

and
1900 Frost Road, Suite 101
Bristol, PA 19007, USA

First Published 1989

British Library Cataloguing in Publication Data
Human resource management in education.
1. Education. Personnel management
I. Riches, Colin R. (Colin Roderick, 1931–) II.
Morgan, Colin III. Open University
371.2'01

ISBN 0-335-09251-9
0-335-09250-0 (paper)

Library of Congress Cataloging-in-Publication Data

Human resource management in education / edited by Colin Riches and
Colin Morgan.
p. cm. — (Management in education series)
ISBN 0-335-09251-9. — ISBN 0-335-09250-0 (pbk.)
1. School personnel management—Great Britain. 2. Leadership.
3. Teachers—Great Britain. I. Riches, Colin R. II. Morgan,
Colin. III. Series.
LB2831.5.H84 1989
371.1'44—dc20   89-38797 CIP

Typeset by Rowland Phototypesetting Ltd
Bury St Edmunds, Suffolk
Printed in Great Britain by Biddles Ltd
Guildford and King's Lynn

Contents

169389

Acknowledgements

All possible care has been taken to trace ownership of the material included in this volume, and Open University Press would like to make grateful acknowledgement for permission to reproduce it here.

1 W. H. Squire (1987). *Education Management in the UK*, pp. 5–30 and 75–6, Aldershot, Gower Publishing Group.
2 P. F. Drucker (1988). *Management*, pp. 131–41, Oxford, Heinemann Professional Publishing.
3 G. Morgan (1988). *Riding the Waves of Change*, pp. 54–68, San Francisco, Jossey-Bass.
4 H. L. Gray (1987). 'Gender considerations in school management', *School Organization*, Vol. 7, No. 3, pp. 297–302, Abingdon, Carfax Publishing Company.
5 H. Furukawa (1987). 'Motivation to work', *Advances in Educational Psychology* edited by B. M. Bass and P. J. D. Drenth, pp. 34–42. Reprinted by permission of Sage Publications, Inc.
6 C. Kyriacou (1987). 'Teacher stress and burnout: an international review', Educational Research, Vol. 29, No. 2, pp. 146–52, Windsor, NFER-Nelson Publishing Company.
7 G. Morgan (1988). *Riding the Waves of Change*, pp. 46–52, San Francisco, Jossey-Bass.
8 P. A. Duignan (1988). 'Reflective management: the key to quality leadership', *International Journal of Educational Management*, Vol. 2, No. 2, pp. 3–12, Bradford, MCB University Press.
9 S. Murgatroyd and H. L. Gray (1984). 'Leadership and the Effective School', *New Directions in Educational Leadership* edited by P. Harling, pp. 39–50, Lewes, Falmer Press.
10 W. W. Savage (1968). *Interpersonal and Group Relations in Educational Administration*, pp. 299–318, Illinois, Scott, Foresman and Company.

11 T. J. Lowe and I. W. Pollard (1988). *Negotiation Skills*, unpublished paper given at *British Educational and Administration Society* Annual Conference 1988.

12 G. Morgan and G. Morris (1989). A revised paper specially prepared for this collection.

13 P. F. Drucker (1988). *Management*, pp. 361–71, Oxford, Heinemann Professional Publishing.

14 C. Morgan (1989). Commissioned for this collection.

15 D. A. Joiner (1984). 'Assessment Centers in the Public Sector', *Public Personnel Management*, Vol. 13, No. 4, Winter 1984. Reprinted with permission of the International Personnel Management Association.

16 R. F. Mager and P. Pipe (1984). *Analyzing Performance Problems*, pp. 6–11 and 60–1, California, Lake Publishing Company.

17 B. Fidler (1988). 'Theory, concepts and experience in other organizations', *Staff Appraisal in Schools and Colleges* edited by B. Fidler and R. Cooper, pp. 1–22, Harlow, Longman Group.

Introduction

Colin Riches and Colin Morgan

Human resource management (HRM) in any organization – educational or otherwise – is part of the process of management in general but is focused on the *people* side of management, seeking to ensure that the objectives of the organization, whether factory, hospital, school or college, are met. Indeed, many see management as the art of getting things done through the key resource – people.

Of all the resources at the disposal of a person or organization it is only people who can grow and develop and be motivated to achieve certain desired ends. The attaining of targets for the organization is in *their* hands and it is the way *people* are managed so that maximum performance is matched as closely as possible with satisfaction for the individuals doing the performing, which is at the heart of HRM and optimum management.

All managerial activity involves action of various kinds: the making of decisions in a number of areas and applying a variety of techniques to carry out each process effectively. The management of personnel does not involve processes which are different in kind from those of management in general; the focus on people distinguishes it. Human resource management embraces all of the core functions of general management wherever practised: *planning* or working out how aims are to be achieved; *organizing* by analysing the activities to be carried out and making decisions to meet objectives; *commanding* through *leading*; *communicating* with people; *co-ordinating* activities so that *targets* are achieved; and *evaluating* the *effectiveness* of all these managerial activities. HRM still has its so-called *operative functions*, which include, for example, recruitment and selection, appraisal, and development, but its scope of activities is even wider in that it is involved in helping to improve human performance within an institution and with the longer-term planning and development of human resources.

Current general management thinking has brought this people focus into prominence for a variety of reasons. Increased legislation with respect to fair employment and health and safety at work has been one impetus; another has been the outcome of technological, economic and demographic pressures represented by the highly competitive global economy. This has been reflected in the UK in the new ideology which has marked government thinking in recent years and has put increasing emphasis on *economy* and value for money as a resource allocation yardstick. Within this thinking it is argued that it is the effective and efficient use of *human* resources which is the key to successful outcomes, that is, optimum performance.

Performance indicators (PIs), or measures for evaluating what is being achieved in institutions – including individual performance – have been seen as increasingly important in British management. Such concepts from *general* management are – quite rightly in our view – seeping through into the way people are now being obliged to view the management of educational institutions. However, the acceptance of such ideas in the British education world have, for a variety of reasons, been slow and subject to a good deal of criticism.

British educationists have generally perceived the links between generic management and the specific management of educational institutions as rather tenuous. There has been a reluctance to identify with, and use, general management concepts. The supposed values of industry and commerce have been seen as utilitarian with educational management set apart from them because it is engaged in educating people rather than in processing products. Our view is that this is a false polarization, for education is equally about achieving objectives of various kinds in the most effective and efficient ways. To use systematic management – and most especially the current approaches to HRM – is not to dehumanize educational processes and products but to ensure that what is most desired is delivered to the recipients of education. Nor does it devalue the contribution made by the people – teachers and managers – who deliver: it is our view that they are given greater professional status by taking the relationship between the means and ends of education rather more seriously than hitherto.

In educational establishments, where people rather than inanimate objects are being 'processed', this focus on HRM is of the utmost importance, but not different in kind from the problems and issues which face personnel elsewhere. You will have noted that our preferred term for managing people is not personnel or staff management but HRM. The use of the term 'staff management' has restrictive connotations in that it is usually applied, in education, for example, to teaching staff and not to people with non-staff status or to the students themselves. The human resource *model* takes a broader and more integrated view of the personnel function than that of just maintaining people in their organizations or engaging in specific personnel activities or keeping records up to date without any noticeable impact on the 'bottom line' of achieving *results* through their contributions. The HRM approach seeks to start from a consideration of what the strategies of an organization might be and then asks how the human resources can help formulate and accomplish those strategies, and what human development and motivation is required to meet those ends.

HRM clearly covers a wide area of activity. One British text on the subject lists: manpower planning, recruitment and selection, appraisal and evaluation, training, wage and salary administration, industrial relations, management development, organizational development, organizational design and welfare (Cowling and Mailer, 1981) – and this is not a full list as, for example, the two vital aspects of leadership and communication are missing. Another volume widens the discussion and chooses to structure its discussion of the subject by linking the effective functioning of an organization with three core elements, each of which has a people focus: (i) mission and strategy, or the organization's reason for existing and the policy for carrying out the mission; (ii) organizational structure, or the way people are organized to do the necessary tasks to achieve this; and (iii) the selection, appraisal, rewards and development of people for performing these tasks (Ferris and Rowland, 1988).

Regarding the range of HRM issues then, we have had in this Reader to be selective because of the limitations of space and to avoid attempting to cover the whole field of HRM in a discursive way. We have therefore tried to represent a discussion of the most important areas of concern by selecting four topics of special coverage. *The external context – key issues for HRM*, where consideration is given to the implications of the core functions of management generally, and HRM in particular, by certain major changing social trends and values. This is followed by three topic sections on: *leadership and motivation*, which is concerned with the way people influence others and build up trust to carry out a mission; *communication and negotiation*, or the way strategies are formulated and conveyed and the vision of the mission is communicated and negotiated; and, finally, *selection, appraisal and development*, or the processes by which competence and performance in an organization are developed.

Within each of the sections we invite the reader to list the *sub-topics* being covered and then to tease out the concepts and *constructs* which are associated with them. This step should be followed by the attempt to establish in one's own mind what are the *implications* of these for HRM and the way they may be *applied* through techniques and policy plans to specific contexts – especially educational ones. Some chapters do in fact discuss applications of HRM precepts. Overall, we would want you when reading to build mental bridges, so to speak, from the concepts and constructs discussed in the readings to precise techniques which are necessary for the application of ideas and intentions.

Section I, The External Context – Key Issues for Human Resource Management reflects the viewpoint expressed earlier in the discussion, namely that HRM in education should be seen as a subset of HRM in management in general, in that the core functions are not different in kind. Also it discusses key trends in the external environment for all management whether in school or factory, and argues that education cannot set itself apart from macro-technological or social change or the wider world of management thought.

The standpoint that a service-type organization, or education specifically, is a special case in terms of thought and managerial practice is questioned in the first two chapters. Squire in 'The Aetiology of a Defective Theory' (Ch. 1) attacks the 'special case' argument, exemplifies how educational practice fits the generic core functions of management anywhere, and argues for an objectives approach. Drucker (Ch. 2) takes up the whole issue of performance in service organizations – a category seen to include schools and colleges. Service organizations do not have a good record of effective performance, argues Drucker, not because of the alibis they offer that they are not businesses or because their output or results are intangible and incapable of definition, but because they are not financed on the basis of results. Much of the direction of educational policy in the UK in 1989 with its devolution of financial control and search for performance indicators seems to have taken Drucker's precepts to heart.

The management of any institution takes place within a context of wider technological and social culture. The two other chapters in Section I confront the proposition that there is radical technical and social change and argue that people have to be managed and developed within this turbulent environment. Morgan (Ch. 3) writes about the importance of 'empowering human resources' in an environment where the information technology (IT) revolution has shifted sources of wealth from those of natural resources from the surfaces, sky and depths of this globe to the resources of *human intelligence* which needs to be released, empowered to perform, and given competence to meet the changes taking place around us. Educational provision or management cannot ignore this turbulence in this IT age. Adaptability to achieve results seems to be a *sine qua non* within the changing scene which has to keep pace with the new technologies, both internal and external to itself.

Another important area of social change concerns the recognition of the need to empower all human resources, female as well as male. This value position is enshrined in equal opportunities legislation, although in practice much discrimination remains. The result of this is that organizations are the poorer for not selecting and developing staff from the widest pool of people but also, as Gray points out in Chapter 4, for not valuing and using feminine qualities in the exercise of educational management. Thus, Section 1 addresses in a variety of ways the issues of managing people in an environment which is changing rapidly, economically, politically, socially and technically with an unprecedented explosion of knowledge. The Education Act 1988 is just one of the landmarks of change with its emphasis on 'competition as a spur to quality' (Maclure, 1988, p. xiv).

Section II, Leadership and Motivation moves from the environment to consider the first of the important HRM functional areas we have chosen. It starts from a position that organizational success depends on motivating staff and that leadership is a vital element in this process. Such notions are not only derived from experience but from a sound research base. Motivation has been defined in general terms as the process by which people are moved to engage in particular behaviours. HRM is only possible if staff are motivated to be developed and therefore a knowledge of the nature and theories of motivation is important. Furukawa in Chapter 5 reviews general research developments in this field and the ways of increasing motivation in work situations. Demotivation by contrast leads to loss of morale which may result in personal stress and burnout. In Chapter 6 Kyriacou provides an international review of studies on teacher stress and addresses the issue of the reduction in stress levels in schools, which has, of course, wider application. Teachers and managers in all types of conditions and situations need to learn to cope with stress and strain and support systems should be developed to assist in this at organizational, interpersonal and individual levels (Freeman, 1987). Organizational commitment, goal setting and the fostering of job satisfaction are key concepts here.

Leadership is central to HRM because it is concerned with motivating and organizing people in certain quality ways which lead to successful outcomes. Leaders are participants in an organization who influence their fellows more than they are influenced by them. We choose to examine leadership as a *process* (see e.g. Hosking, 1988) rather than by identifying positive attributes of individual leaders and also to focus on the *person* rather than the *task* aspects of leadership. Gareth Morgan in Chapter 7 argues that effective leadership needs to exhibit an overarching purpose or vision and the ability and skills to communicate what is termed *mission*. Chapter 8, by Duignan, emphasizes the point already made in this Introduction that leadership is a concept which is about exercising higher-order skills which lead to the effective management of individuals and the overall quality of the leadership practised. These quality skills include the skills of organizing and 'orchestrating' affairs so that the values and interests of an organization are promoted and a climate or ethos is created in which these values are embodied, i.e. 'a cultural view of leadership' (p. 75). Chapter 9 (Murgatroyd and Gray) applies the concept of leadership to school effectiveness. The chapters in this section offer valuable insights for analysing the effectiveness of leadership in specific educational cases, based on the general contention that sound leadership is vitally important for increasing motivation and reducing stress among people in organizations and involves the exercise of quality decision-making in a satisfactory network of interpersonal relations at all levels, based on clear goals and sound vision.

In *Section III, Communication and Negotiation*, we consider the import-ance of communication skills and negotiation. Effective communication is central to establishing interpersonal relationships. It is a process which may be defined as sorting, selecting, forming and transmitting symbols between people to create meaning. The major hurdles to effective communication are problems of perception, language, organizational structures, networks and channels, which form the setting for communication, as is analysed by Savage in Chapter 10. Such barriers give rise to many misunderstandings and the HRM manager needs to be able to diagnose these and to develop strategies for countering them (Farr, 1987). Effective communication takes place in a multiplicity of contexts including interviewing (see below), leading and motivating (see above) and in negotiating. In Chapter 11 Lowe and Pollard set out the conditions for effective negotiation and begin to apply them to educational cases. 'What the Teachers Say' (Ch. 12) provides some empirical data from a TVEI pilot project in Wales on the connection between the way leaders communicated with their colleagues to meet certain educational aims and what was achieved in terms of certain measured outcomes. The communication responsibility of top management is substantially evidenced by the data in this chapter.

Section IV, Selection, Appraisal and Development, emphasizes, as we have already seen, the importance of developing competence and performance as a central concern of HRM. Performance is viewed as the central linking concept to these three personnel activities; and in Chapter 13 Drucker sets out what he and we ourselves see as the essential characteristics of 'the spirit of performance' whereby 'ordinary human beings' are enabled 'to do extra-ordinary things' (p. 161). Staff selection is seen to be essentially about picking people to use their skills, abilities and knowledge to achieve a desired performance.

In Chapter 14 Colin Morgan demonstrates the often-tenuous nature of the selection criteria used by selection panels in education drawn from empirical research into secondary headteacher selection. Much more valid and reliable selection methods have been advocated in recent years via the assessment centre approach. In Chapter 15 Joiner describes the way assessment centres operate in the public sector in the USA and gives an important view of their predictive validity.

While job selection is about predicting performance, appraisal and development are about controlling performance. Chapter 16, by Mager and Pipe, centres on the notion of *performance discrepancy* or the difference between *actual* and *desired* performance. This is a useful basis for the discussion which follows on appraisal and development. In Chapter 17 Fidler distinguishes between the latter two terms but, like us, does not see them in contra-distinction. He takes our view that the processes are the same in education as in general management. The whole section deals with some fundamental HRM problems which are receiving increasing attention in the world of education where the formal appraisal of teachers is now on the agenda and where more intensive monitoring of performance is likely to increase.

As was stated earlier in this Introduction we do not offer this Reader as providing coverage of the full range of human resource development (HRD) issues, but to present some of the key topics of human resource management and to set out a philosophy and practice for HRM which we consider is vital in education, especially within the new environment of imposed and/or inevitable change. In our view the world of education has been very good at the rhetoric of human resource management but less effective in its actual practice. All this is now changing in response to the new external statutory demands. In the UK we are moving into an era when more precise judgements on school and college performance will be made as the basis of resourcing. We believe that all the issues discussed in this book have relevance and applicability to the achievement of performance through the better management of all the people who work in schools and colleges.

References

Cowling, A. C. and Mailer, C. J. B. (1981). *Managing Human Resources*. London, Edward Arnold.

Farr, R. (1987). 'Misunderstanding in human relations: a social psychological perspective', *Educational Management and Administration*, 15(2), 129–40.

Ferris, G. R. and Rowland, K. M. (1988). *Human Resources Management: Perspectives and Issues*. Boston, Allyn & Bacon.

Freeman, A. (1987). 'The coping teacher', *Research in Education*, 38, Nov., 1–16.

Hosking, D. M. (1988). 'Organizing, leadership and skilful process', *Journal of Management Studies*, 25(2), March, 137–66.

Maclure, S. (1988). *Education Re-formed*. London, Hodder & Stoughton.

Section I

The external context – key issues for human resource management

1

The aetiology of a defective theory

W. H. Squire

The nature of education management

This chapter will first offer a taxonomy of the mainstream of management theory, in comparison with which the nature of education management can be defined and certain of its deficiencies made clear. It will then be argued that these are serious deficiencies of theory, doctrine and attitude and that their effects are damaging to the management of education in the UK. A study of the literature will be made to reveal particular difficulties in the appreciation, in the context of education management, of certain major concepts in management theory.

Fayol has observed,[11] 'All organisations require planning, organisation command, coordination and control, and in order to function properly all must observe the same general principles. We are no longer confronted with several administrative sciences but one which can be applied equally well in public and private lives'. Nor is management exclusive to the head or seniors in an organization but is spread in some degree between the head and all members of the organization.[12]

The Fulton Committee on the Civil Service[13] saw managers as responsible for 'organisation, directing staff, planning the progress of work, organising and commanding, setting standards of attainment, measuring results, reviewing procedures and quantifying different courses of action'.

Brech[14] identifies the activities of management as those of planning, control, co-ordination and motivation; Drucker[15] refers to the definition of purpose and mission so as to make work productive, Argenti[16] to deciding how to do it and checking results, Albers[17] to planning, organizing, directing, controlling, Liston[18] to identifying objectives, securing and deploying resources and monitoring results, and Stewart[19] to planning, setting objectives, forecasting, analysing problems and making decisions; Morgan,[20] not surprisingly, finds a high degree of agreement on the main elements of management among the major writers.

A further feature has emerged comparatively recently into its own right from subsumption in Fayol's 'commanding', Drucker's 'motivating' or the AASA's[21] 'stimulating' and that is the function of leadership in management.

In comparing and contrasting education management with other types of management under his chosen three key concepts in considering organizations – organizational goal, bureaucracy and professionalism – Morgan aims at displaying the arguments rather than at arriving at a conclusion as to whether education management differs decisively from other types of management. He did find, however, that the classical definitions of the core functions[22] 'showed similarity rather than dissimilarity in relation to educational organisations', and he does point[23] to the problems of engaging in a congruence–dissimilarity discussion in regard to education management when so few people have work experience which encompasses educational, industrial and commercial organizations. Here he is supported by the recent relevant reports from the University of Birmingham and the University of Leicester.

One who does possess such experience is likely to be struck, as the present writer has been, by the similarities of the management process in these spheres insofar as they require to define goals and then to engage energies and to measure progress in the pursuit of those goals. It is only in the nature of the goals, and hence in the nature of the process of their pursuit, that dissimilarities arise.

At first sight, it may seem to the educator unserviceable as well as repugnant to liken a school to a factory or 'conversion box' into which flows 'raw material' which, after a period as 'work in progress', emerges as a 'finished product'. However, a consideration of this model shows the curriculum clearly to be the vitally important mode of production but to be nothing more than that. Such a comparison can be useful to the educator without committing him to any confusion between a human being and a piece of pig-iron.

[. . .]

Educators need to understand a body of management theory which has its provenance largely in industrial and commercial activity only in order to adapt it to their own purposes, to use it in practice and then in turn to contribute their own distinct formulations to the body of theory, to modify and develop it.

Developments in operations management may provide a useful meeting-ground if we accept, for instance, Monks's[25] proposition that productive systems of any kind transform input resources into outputs of a higher value, that the inputs are typically classified as human, material and capital and that 'outputs range from assembled products, such as automobiles, to all manner of services, such as medical and educational services'.

Analogies such as this, between education management and what will be defined as mainstream management theory are legion. The necessary transfer is easily made but it will only be made if the educator's mental set is right and he or she is ready and willing to regard management theory as relevant to his or her needs as a manager of education. The evidence adduced herein is that this is far from being the case, currently, in a UK education service which is being managed by the largely managerially unaware who, it is fair to suggest, are unaware also of any pressing need to cure their unawareness.

One of the major barriers to any change in such attitudes is the conviction that the management of education is not related to either the theory or the practice of managing any other sphere of activity. The conviction is supported in the literature, inviting the critical examination which follows.

Is education management a special case?

[. . .]

The classic division of management, conceptually and operationally, into the functions of finance, marketing, production and personnel holds good for education management as it does for every mode of management, although their interrelationship and relative importance will be determined by differing objectives. The correspondence of the financial function in education to that of, say, manufacturing industry is clear, although sources of finance, process and accountability may differ. The market for education spreads outwards from pupil to parents, through local communities to the life of the nation and of the world, both present and future. The marketing of education in the independent and further education sectors is often very clearly analogous to non-educational modes. As to the product, much thought is devoted by educators to the results of the educative (or production) process in terms not only of learning but also of character qualities and behaviour, as well as to fitting their product to its market (or environment), including its potential to change that environment. In education management the personnel function is, again, clearly analogous to that function in other modes of management, differing only in the emphasis which it gains from the central position accorded, in education, to human quality and human values.

However, perceptual blindness to such comparisons is conditioned by attitudes formed and reinforced by allegiance to existing defective theory and practice. It will therefore be useful now to examine such attitudes more closely.

Attitudes to management theory in the education service

Having listened carefully to a plain statement of MBO [management by objectives] theory, an experienced grammar school deputy head responded, in 1980, 'I was appalled'. Appalled, she explained, not by the theory *per se* but by the grossness of the proposition that it could and should be applied to education. There was, she continued, too startling an incongruity between the overt positiveness of MBO and the occult uncertainties of the learning process. Most of this very able lady's apprehensions yielded in the event to the 10 hours of argument, explanations, discussion, demonstration and reflection which appear to represent the learning time for MBO‾ in the education service, but her reservations are entitled to examination. Is there any sense in which systematic management and its strategies are fundamentally inappropriate to the activity of education?

The principal arguments for this proposition appear to be as follows:

1   Management theory is derived from profit-oriented practice and is, for that reason, unfitted to direct a service which is concerned with the development of people rather than the processing of goods and services. A good deal of the emotional charge is removed from this argument when it is recognized that both pecuniary profit making and the education of a person share, importantly, the concept of 'value added'. For a person, this is for social, vocational and individually personal purposes; for a raw material, it is by means of a process which will fit it for use by a particular market. Further, it is clear that both processes are teleological. They are purposive, even accepting – in the case of education – Russell's[33] view of the pursuit of knowledge as an end sufficient in itself.

2   Management theory is mechanistic where the proposed processes of education are organic. Such a statement as Gilbreth's[34] that 'It is the aim of scientific management to induce men to act as nearly like machines as possible' would be fastened upon to demonstrate a basic incongruity of purpose. To answer this by placing Gilbreth in the post-Victorian pre-Hawthorne studies context, writing as he was in a year in which armies (backed by scarcely less disciplined national work forces) were being trained to walk into machine-gun fire at the blast of a whistle, would be only part of a legitimate refutation. What is being alleged is that management is to be rejected as part of Forster's[35] 'world of anger and telegrams', to which education is foreign and what is temporarily out of mind is that every mode of existence is the meat of education management and that every mode of existence can be managed with advantage. Further, this is likely to be an argument out of the sort of ignorance which puts the lay view a generation behind the professional, since the major feature of the development of management theory and practice in the last 50 years has been precisely in its assimilation of sociological and psychological theory. This emphasis upon the importance of the human resource in organizations in itself demonstrates the adaption of management theory to emergent realities, in the shape of new findings about human nature and of changes in the social and political orders. Insofar as a theory exists in order to explain observed facts, it is bound to be adapted to them and a theory of education management will accordingly be adapted to the facts of education as they exist at any given moment.

3   Management strategies are necessarily inimical to creativity. This can imply both that creativity thrives on chaos and that management con-

notes rigidity, conservatism and opposition to novelty and initiative. Indeed, a serious case can be made for organizing educational institutions as anarchies, so as to promote desired turbulence since, as Turner[36] for example has maintained, educational institutions operate with a degree of uncertainty which makes them classifiable as anarchies (after the definition of Cohen *et al.*[37]), within which teachers operate as free-ranging autonomous decision makers. Whether this doctrine is regarded as beneficial or not, it constitutes, paradoxically, a model for management. Even (and perhaps especially in an environment of organizations striving for creativity and predictability) anarchy needs to be organized. So does creativity, as any research establishment will show. Nor does that conclude the rebuttal, for it can fairly be claimed that a working structure which is concerned with classifying aims and appraising results is, at worst, neutral to creativity and, at best, highly congenial to it when, as part of its operation, resources are deployed and appropriate motivation provided, with initiative and innovation encouraged, recognized and rewarded.

4   Systematic management entails appraisal of performance against set goals and that teacher performance should not be so appraised because educational aims are too diffuse to allow measurement of performance and because the direct observation of teacher performance would attack a traditional class- or lecture-room freedom, essential to the educative process.

The first argument is to be heard, in some degree, whenever it is proposed for the first time to define jobs and to set clear targets. Yet few managers would claim to be aimlessly occupied and almost everyone would seek to justify his efforts in terms of the results of his work and, if an aim is capable of being pursued, it is capable of being defined.

Furthermore, it has been amply shown that, however large or ramified, any job can be intelligibly defined upon one side of a sheet of A4 paper.

In fact, the protest is likely to originate in other factors, such as fear of taking up an exposed position in relation to success or failure, or sheer conservatism, the dislike of the disturbance inevitably connected with the introduction of new ways of working, and, for the lazy or incompetent, fear of detection.

When it is realized, however, that work targets are to be a matter for discussion and agreement with colleagues and that appraisal by hearsay has its dangers, especially when used as a basis for professional reporting, attitudes change and an overt objective adult approach to performance appraisal is preferred to obscurity and paternalistic allocation of praise and blame in the work-place.

As to the sacredness of teachers' class-room privacy, this cannot be seriously defended. Their work takes place always before an audience of pupils who sit in continuous judgement on their efforts. How can they uniquely deny the right of senior colleagues, representing their employer and paymaster, to judge their efficiency in their appointed work? How much better that appraisal should be based upon direct observation, with its results openly communicated with the aim of recognizing the merit of offering training and development in the case of any shortfall between target and achievement. Baker and Ballinger,[38] for example, have shown how pedagogy and class-room management can be assessed together. Teacher performance appraisal must follow the increased rigour of educational–institutional performance assessment, and it must be practised for the benefit of both individual teachers and the organization which they and their jobs exist to serve.

[. . .]

Management and administration

A recognizable tendency among educators, as among others, is to define 'management' almost entirely in terms of 'administration'. The dictionary makes little distinction between these terms but usage does in that, although the terms are interchangeable as they refer to some levels of activity, it is the term 'management' which, alone, includes reference to comprehensive strategies such as MBO or OD [organization development] within which administration is conducted.

In the education service the term 'administration' is more often heard, referring, as it does, to a collection rather than an integration of fragmented systems. This usage is significant, suggesting neglect of strategy in favour of tactics.

A leading educator[39] of 'education administrators' said that '. . . we begin to notice how, in the absence of a central discipline, the vagueness of either multi-disciplinary or multi-ethological or even multi-logical approaches to the idea of education administration emerge . . . There is no satisfactory composite theory, let alone practice of educational administration which can match the problems being faced.' The same writer, in a position to make an informed judgement, adds, 'The vast majority of occupants of senior posts in educational institutions or administrative services have no formal training before or after appointment in educational management.' This is the equivalent of a statement that the senior officers of the British Army have no formal training in strategy or tactics or that the majority of surgeons operate on hunch and experience. It may be added that both the latter categories are, like all other professions, educated in institutions managed by the former.

Jones[40] is categorical: 'There is a world of difference between administration and management, although too often the words are thoughtlessly interchanged. Administration is a much more passive task than management and does not carry the same authority. It excludes policy making. The administrator makes possible what has been planned: the manager plans the policy.'

'Administration', too, is bound to have a more familiar ring to the educator in terms of his experience. Its use conveniently excludes a world of 'management' which is outside that experience and may in addition be felt to threaten.

Morgan,[41] after reviewing the authorities from Cicero onwards, finds the two terms interchangeable in usage, with 'administration' more often deployed in relation to government and the Civil Service but with 'management' in the ascendency to describe chief or senior executive functions. For him, 'management' is the preferred term because it is more comprehensive and does not exclude directing, policy making or a separation of powers as 'administration' does. 'Management' then is the more powerful term, more relevant in its reference and more prevalent in usage.

This question of nomenclature, minor in itself, is far from academic in its implications. The still wide use of 'education administration' in place of 'education management' often indicates an unawareness of or, worse still, a reluctance to recognize the existence of a highly developed theory of management, together with its accompanying practice. [. . .]

The education service and the 'non profit' paradigm

[. . .] Drucker[46] has defined eight key areas in business in which it is necessary to set performance objectives.

1 Market standing.
2 Innovation.
3 Productivity.
4 Physical and financial resources.
5 Profitability.
6 Manager performance and development.
7 Worker performance and attitude.
8 Public responsibility.

Holroyde[47] has shown how these areas could be re-defined in educational terms as the basis of the overall aims for the comprehensive school of which he was head.

1 Reputation: with the community; with pupils; with parents; with staff; with the teaching profession; with colleges and universities; with the LEA; with employees; nationally.
2 Innovation: curriculum development; pupil assessment; learning methods; community projects; school community integration; management.
3 Productivity: whether the teaching group size is right; whether the staff are doing what they are best at; use of time; use of buildings and equipment; application of educational technology; contributions from all agencies.
4 Resource acquisition: generating income; fund raising; voluntary help; finding resources from other agencies; economy and conversation.

5   Effectiveness: identifying and satisfying the real needs of the people that
    we serve.
6   Staff development: individual development programmes; team work
    and in-house training; motivation and delegation of responsibility;
    communication and participation.
7   Community relationships (pupils and others): counselling and help;
    participation in planning; recognition and reward; building cooperative
    attitudes.
8   Public responsibility: care of public property; good neighbours.

Bush *et al.*[48] recognized such differences between industrial and educational contexts but they do so in ascribing the lack of interest in management
shown by British teachers to the failure of most management courses to
recognize[49] 'the very special nature of the educational context' and go on to
conclude that[50] 'a management course for people concerned with schools
must relate to schools and their staffs and clients first and foremost'. This
statement remains unexceptionable only until it is perceived that a management course should relate first and foremost to management principles and
practice at large and then to their applications in the educational context. To
hold otherwise is to risk moving permanently out of the mainstream of
management practice, as management trainers are required to be, first and
foremost, practitioners in education will possess limited insight into developments in management theory and practice in other spheres and their value for
the education service.

[. . .]

Under such conditions, it is not at all surprising to find that relatively
subtle theories of the management of the 'non-profit' organization have been
neglected and their usefulness denied to the education service. This is one
more example of the way in which unawareness of management theory as it is
developing has worked to perpetuate the skew from the mainstream in which
education management is at present proceeding.

A further important example, now to be examined, is to be found in the
way in which neglect and, it will be argued, misconceptions of major
concepts such as MBO and OD have operated to the disadvantage of
education managers in their roles as leaders.

Management by objectives, organization development and their implications for leadership

Management leadership can be found[52] to possess the four interdependent
characteristics of initiative, influence, intelligence and acceptability which the
leader is bound consistently to practise. Initiative should be first to produce or
cause to be produced successful new ideas, applications and solutions to
problems.

To influence, he or she must possess power of command, linked with
power of self-expression. Intelligent awareness of the environment and

applied reasoning ability are required, together with quickness of perception, and the leader must find acceptance through temperamental stability and social skills, since there can be no leadership without the ability to command a following.

These are testing requirements indeed and sufficient to daunt an educational institutional head trained in leadership by his or her own experience alone. It will not be surprising if he or she has resort to the various resources of uncertainty, such as incessant activity, the cultivation of an inflated persona, reluctance to delegate, Nias's[53] 'Bourbonism' with autocratic remoteness or, in contrast, the excessive passivity or paternalism described by Coulson.[54] The educational leader in the public sector of education is being forced to lead heroically, that is without either a strong tradition of leadership such as his or her military equivalent inherits to inform the explicit training in leadership which his or her industrial or commercial equivalent has to hand. Gray[55] has noted the insecurity of head teachers when confronted with new management ideas as opposed to new educational ideas and that the head is often forced into an autocratic style of leadership. To this the writer would add his own observations of heads led, by insecurity and lack of a theory for their managerial role, into the ignominy of inconsistency and equivocation which arises from the conflict between a democratic ideal and the need to hug power for want of knowledge of the means to share it.

Courageous and intelligent open-mindedness can achieve a great deal as Watts's[56] Countesthorpe experiments demonstrated, but not every head is able to deduce good practice from first principles, nor is there any need for him or her to do so. The framework which he or she requires is ready to hand in strategies such as MBO, known and practised widely outside the education service. Whilst still *primus inter pares* retaining the initiatives which constitute his or her office, the head is able, within a framework of agreed objectives and delegated responsibilities, to exercise leadership in a way which recognizes the nature of leadership as a necessary and inevitable function of and for the group.

Comments have been made to refute the misconception of MBO as antagonistic to creativity and to show how MBO is likely, on the contrary, to promote it. Schmuck[57] has allocated a leading role in the encouragement of creativity to the techniques of OD defined, after Bennis,[58] as 'a planned and sustained effort to apply behavioural science to system improvement, using reflexive self-analytical methods' and describes the beneficial efforts of OD interventions in (inter alia) establishing goals, defining roles and improving group processes.

Typically, however, no link is indicated between MBO and OD. OD is presented as an autonomous strategy. Yet, when diverse OD practice in some 50 organizations is searched for a common factor, this would emerge as[59] 'any strategy intended to link individual feeling with corporate aims'. In other words, OD is concerned with process, presupposes the existence of corporate aims and is best considered as offering means to extend the interpersonal dimension of MBO. Otherwise, an organization can commit itself to a study of role conflict without a definition of the roles concerned, even by way of a bare job description or, at corporate level, can try to measure attitudes to organizational goals which do not yet exist.

Such failure in practical logic is bound to occur in a service whose managers are not being equipped by either training or experience to relate sometimes complex and sophisticated concepts of management either to other concepts or to whether they work out in practice. The literature of education management reflects and perpetuates such defects.

[. . .]

A view of the literature

Systems management

What appears often to be either forgotten or even, sometimes, not fully grasped is that MBO is a system within which to carry out one's intentions. The major part of its scope concerns the implementation of decisions arrived at on a corporate level, while also concerned with the study, through an appraisal system, of past results which, together with other data, will inform fresh decisions. The system, therefore, does not decide the nature or, more important, the quality of the decisions of whose implementation it is the agent. What it can do (inter alia) is to confer additional clarity upon the formulation of what is to be attempted and upon the evaluation of outcomes.

Contrary to the misgivings of many educators, for example Apple,[88] a curriculum which is designed to accept the ambiguity and uncertainty of human knowledge is not reduced to terms of brash positivism merely because it is managed by objectives.

Polanyi[89] uses the analogy of the physician's need to know his patient in terms of both general human perceptions and scientific rationalism, to illustrate his concept of 'personal knowledge'. The analogy of the educator and his pupils is no less apt.

[. . .]

An educational philosopher on management

It is the reverse of cheering to find a leading educational thinker engaged in perpetuating if not error, then certainly unawareness, in his field. In his editorial introduction to a distinguished collection of monographs,[93] Peters describes what seems to him to be the dilemma of the modern head teacher, the head teacher that is who is rationally minded enough to reject the 'very authoritarian and paternalistic way'[94] of a Thring (celebrated head of Uppingham School) who is 'supreme here and will brook no interference'. For Peters, 'there is no case for authoritarianism'.[95] Yet he is clearly appalled by what he sees as the only alternative role for his anxious head teacher, namely that of the manager which, he seems to conclude,[96] would be 'more damaging to education than the paternalism which is being rejected'.

However, for Peters,[96] management is identified with 'business-like efficiency' and what is to happen to the educational institution's role as a place of learning if its organization is 'just regarded as ways of promoting particular objectives'.

Peters shows no awareness of the possibility of a form of MBO exactly adapted to these sensitive requirements. For him, all management must be 'business-like', even when what it is proposed to manage is patently not a business, and thus the head is left suspended, deprived of paternalism and denied a strategy of participative management which is ready to hand and from whose use and adaptation to his own educational purposes the head is debarred by the ignorance and suspicion fathered by perhaps unconscious, certainly unexamined, prejudice transmitted to him or her by those to whom he or she looks for open-minded clarification of his or her difficulties.

Still less happily, Peters refers to the Arnoldian concept of the 'hidden curriculum' in schools, that is what is taught by climate, inference and suggestion. Again, he fears the ethos of 'the business manager' in this connection but is apparently content to leave the pupil to gather that management theory and good managerial practice is for the businessman from whom the educator has nothing to learn.

The true dilemma is Peters's own. There must be 'a rational system'[96] but never that of the manager who would 'run a school as if it was a modern industry'.[96] Such are the symptoms of the nundinophobia (to give a name to this morbid fear of the market-place and its ethos) which blinds so many academics and scholastics to the sanity and usefulness of management theory. Taylor,[97] writing in the same symposium, displays similar fears and his contribution is stated as 'an attempt to set out the grounds for my unease'. One of these lies in the fear that training in management will lead educators to think about relationships 'in business terms'. Why should they do so, any more than a surgeon might in managing a case or an abbot in managing a monastery?

Taylor recognized the efficacy of management theory but fears that educators may take it up with[98] 'uncertain enthusiasm, with possibly unforeseen and illiberal consequences that are inimical to the values embodied in the broader educative task of the school'. 'There is', Taylor concludes, 'so much that is important that cannot adequately be described in management terms'; in doing so, he clearly shows the lack of faith in the ability of his education manager colleague to understand the provenance of management theory and to adapt it to his own purposes which is apparently so widespread among educational theorists.

[. . .]

Conclusion

This study has sought to establish the existence, in the theory of education management, of an important and damaging skew from the mainstream of management theory, to describe its nature by reference to significant texts and to refer to certain attitudes to management theory and practice which have both conditioned and been conditioned by the literature and the research. In proceeding to examine the practice of education management, in some of its more important aspects, the discovery of a corresponding skew could be reasonably anticipated and this is indeed the picture which emerges.

References

[. . .]
11   H. Fayol (1949), *General and Industrial Management*, Pitman, London, p. xii.
12   H. Fayol (1949), op. cit., p. 6.
13   DES (1968), CMD 3638, HMSO, London.
14   E. F. L. Brech (1975), *The Principles and Practice of Management*, Longmans, London.
15   P. Drucker (1974), *Management*, Heinemann, London.
16   J. Argenti (1972), *A Management System for the Seventies*, Allen and Unwin, London.
17   H. H. Albers (1969), *Principles of Management*, Wiley, New York.
18   D. J. Liston (1971), *The Purpose and Practice of Management*, Hutchinson, London.
19   R. Stewart (1981), *The Reality of Management*, Pan, London.
20   C. Morgan (1976), *Open University Course E321, Management in Education, Unit 1*, Open University, Milton Keynes, p. 20.
21   *Staff Relations in School Administration*, AASA, Washington, DC, Chapter I.
22   C. Morgan (1976), op. cit., p. 20.
23   C. Morgan (1976), op. cit., p. 25.
[. . .]
25   J. G. Monks (1982), *Operations Management*, McGraw-Hill, New York, p. 1.
[. . .]
33   B. Russell (1925), *On Education*, Allen and Unwin, London.
34   F. J. Gilbreth (1917), *Primer of Scientific Management*, Van Nostrand, New York.
35   E. M. Forster (1910), *Howards End*, Edward Arnold, London.
36   T. M. Turner (1976), 'Organising education institutions as anarchies', *Coombe Lodge Study Conference, July 1976*.
37   T. M. Cohen, J. G. March and J. P. Olsen (March 1972), 'A garbage can model of educational choice', *Administrative Science Quarterly*, vol. 17, no. 1, pp. 1–25.
38   K. Baker and L. Ballinger (1982), in R. Bolam (ed.), *School-focussed In-service Training*, Heinemann, London, pp. 42–3.
39   G. E. Wheeler (1974), 'Speculations on teaching in the field of educational administration', *International Education Management Intervisitation Programme, 1974*.
40   R. Jones (1980), *Primary Schools Management*, David and Charles, Newton Abbot.
41   C. Morgan (1976), op. cit., p. 14.
[. . .]
46   P. Drucker (1974), op. cit., p. 100.
47   G. Holroyde (1976), 'Staff handbook – Sidney Stringer School', in *A Case Study*

in Management: Sidney Stringer School and Community College, Oxford University Press, Oxford, 1976.

48 A. Bush, R. Glatter, J. Goodey and C. Riches (eds) (1980), *Approaches to School Management*, Harper and Row, London.

49 Bush *et al*. (1980), op. cit., p. xv.

50 Bush *et al*. (1980), op. cit., p. xvi.

[. . .]

52 W. H. Squire, S. Poppleton and D. N. D. Roberts (1977), *Educational Heads Conference, Himley, 19 January 1977*.

53 J. Nias (1980), 'Leadership styles and job satisfaction in primary schools', in A. Bush, R. Glatter, J. Goodey and C. Riches (eds), *Approaches to School Management*, Harper and Row, London, pp. 255–73.

54 A. A. Coulson (1978), 'The role of the primary head', in R. S. Peters (ed.), *The Role of the Head*, Routledge and Kegan Paul, London, pp. 92–108.

55 H. L. Gray (1974), 'The head as manager', *Education 3–13*, vol. 2, no. 2, pp. 81–4.

56 J. Watts (1978), 'Sharing it out! The role of the head in participatory government', in R. S. Peters (ed.), *The Role of the Head*, Routledge and Kegan Paul, London, pp. 27–136.

57 R. A. Schmuck (1974), *Creativity of the School. The Centre for Educational Research and Innovation*, OECD, Paris, pp. 104–26.

58 W. G. Bennis (1968), 'Beyond bureaucracy', in W. G. Bennis and P. Slater (eds), *The Temporary Society*, Harper and Row, New York.

59 W. H. Squire (1976), *Himley Organisation Development Reference Workshop, 23 January 1976*.

[. . .]

88 M. W. Apple (1975), 'The adequacy of systems management procedures in education', *Journal of Education Research*, vol. 66, no. 1, pp. 11–18.

89 M. Polanyi (1962), *Personal Knowledge*, Routledge and Kegan Paul, London.

[. . .]

93 R. S. Peters (ed.) (1976), *The Role of the Head*, Routledge and Kegan Paul, London.

94 R. S. Peters (1976), op. cit., p. 6.

95 R. S. Peters (1976), op. cit., p. 3.

96 R. S. Peters (1976), op. cit., p. 7.

97 W. Taylor (1979), 'The head as manager', in R. S. Peters (ed.), *The Role of the Head*, Routledge and Kegan Paul, London, pp. 37–49.

98 W. Taylor (1979), op. cit., p. 37.

[. . .]

2

Why service institutions do not perform

P. F. Drucker

Making the service institutions perform

The service institution does not differ much from a business enterprise in any area other than its specific mission. It faces very similar challenges to make work productive and the workers achieving. It does not differ significantly from a business in its social responsibility. Recent events have shown that the service institutions face the same problems in their relationship with the environment and with society as do businesses. The worst polluters today are, after all, governments – local governments with inadequate sewer plants. Discussion of social impacts and social responsibilities [. . .] applies with little modification to all institutions, public or private.

But the service institution is fundamentally different from business in its 'business'. It is different in its purpose. It has different values. It needs different objectives, and it makes a different contribution to society. Performance and results are quite different in a service institution from what they are in business. Managing for performance is the one area in which the service institution differs significantly from a business.

[. . .]

There are three popular explanations for the common failure of service institutions to perform:

- their managers aren't businesslike;
- they need better people;
- their objectives and results are intangible.

All three are alibis rather than explanations.

How businesslike are they?

The service institution will perform, it is said again and again, if only it is managed in a businesslike manner.

The service institution has performance trouble precisely because it is not a business. What characterizes a business is control by performance and what 'businesslike' means in a service institution is control of cost, a measure of efficiency. But it is *effectiveness and not efficiency which the service institution lacks*. Effectiveness cannot be obtained by businesslike behaviour as the term is understood – that is, by greater efficiency.

To be sure, efficiency is necessary in all institutions. Because there is usually no competition in the service field, there is no outward and imposed cost control on service institutions as there is for business in a competitive market. But the basic problem of service institutions is not high cost but lack of effectiveness. Some are very efficient, but they tend not to do the right things.

The need for better people

The cry for better people is probably even older than the belief that being businesslike will save the service institution. It can be found in the earliest Chinese texts on government. It has been the constant demand of all American reformers, from Henry Adams, shortly after the Civil War, to Ralph Nader today. They have all believed that the one thing lacking in the government agency is better people.

Service institutions can no more depend on supermen or lion tamers to staff their managerial and executive positions than can businesses. There are far too many institutions to be staffed. It is absurd to expect that the administrator of every hospital in the world be a genius or even great. If service institutions cannot be run and managed by administrators of normal capability, they are indeed unmanageable. If, in other words, we cannot organize the task so that it will be done adequately by men and women who only try hard, it cannot be done at all.

There is no reason to believe that the people who staff the managerial and professional positions in our service institutions are any less qualified, any less competent or honest, or any less hard-working than those who manage businesses. On the other hand, there is also no reason to believe that business managers, put in control of service institutions, would do better than the 'bureaucrats'. Indeed, we know that they immediately become bureaucrats themselves.

In World War II large numbers of American business executives who had performed very well in their own companies moved into government positions. Many of them rapidly became bureaucrats. The individuals did not change, but whereas they had been capable of obtaining performance and results in a business, in government they found themselves producing mainly procedures and red tape – and deeply frustrated.

The tangibility of goals

The most sophisticated and, at first glance, the most plausible explanation for the failure of service institutions to perform is the last one: the objectives of service institutions are 'intangible' and so are their results. This is at best a half-truth.

The definition of what 'our business is' is always intangible, for a business as well as for a service institution. To say, as Sears, Roebuck does, 'Our business is to be the informed buyer for the American family' is intangible. To say, as Vail did at Bell Telephone, 'Our business is service to the customer' may sound like a public relations slogan. At first glance these statements seem to defy any attempt at translation into operational terms, let alone quantitative ones. To say, 'Our business is electronic information', as Sony of Japan does, is equally intangible; so is IBM's definition of its business as data processing. Yet as these businesses have shown, it is not too difficult to derive measurable goals and targets from such intangible definitions.

Specific targets can also be derived from the apparently even less tangible goals of service institutions.

'Saving souls' as the definition of the objectives of a church is intangible. At least the bookkeeping is not of this world. But church attendance is measurable. And so is 'getting the young people back into the church'.

'The development of the whole personality' as the objective of the school is, indeed, intangible. But 'teaching a child to read by the time he has finished third grade' is by no means intangible. It can be measured easily and precisely.

Achievement is only possible against specific, limited, clearly defined targets, in business as well as in a service institution. Only if targets are defined can resources be allocated to attain them. Only then can priorities and deadlines be set, and somebody be held accountable for results. But the starting point of effective work is the definition of purpose and mission of the institution, which is almost always intangible.

'What is our business?' is as ambiguous and as controversial a question for a service institution as it is for a business. There will surely be dissent and controversy before a workable definition is found. Service institutions have many constituents. The school is of vital concern not only to children and their parents, but to teachers, to taxpayers, to the community at large. Similarly the hospital has to satisfy the patient, but also the doctors, the nurses, the technicians, the patient's family – and again taxpayers or, as in the United States, employers and unions who together provide the bulk of the support of most hospitals through their insurance contributions.

Misdirection by budget

The one basic difference between a service institution and a business is the way the service institution is paid.

Businesses (other than monopolies) are paid for satisfying the customer. They are paid only when they produce what customers want and what they are willing to exchange purchasing power for. Satisfaction of the customer is, therefore, the basis for assuring performance and results in a business.

Service institutions, by contrast, are typically paid out of a budget allocation. This means that they are not paid for what taxpayer and customer mean by results and performance. Their revenues flow from a general revenue stream that depends not on what they are doing but on some sort of tax.

This is as true for the service institution within a business as it is, for instance, for the state school. The typical staff department is not paid for its results. It is, as a rule, not even paid according to the extent to which its customers, that is, the managers, use it. It is paid out of an overhead allocation, that is, out of a budget. The fact that the service institution within a business tends to exhibit the same characteristics and to indulge in the same behaviour as service institutions in the public sector indicates that it is not business that makes the difference. It is the method of payment.

The typical service institution – including most service staffs in business – also has monopoly powers. The intended beneficiary has no choice. Most service institutions have power beyond what the most monopolistic business enjoys.

If I am dissatisfied with the service of the local power company or of the telephone company, I have no other place to go for electric power or telephone service. But if I choose to do without either power or telephone, I do not have to pay for it. This option is not available, however, to customers dissatisfied with a service institution. There the customers pay whether they want to use the service or not.

The American household pays school taxes whether it has children of school age or not. Parents may choose to send their children to a private or a parochial school but they still pay taxes for the state school, even though they do not use it and consider it inappropriate or unsatisfactory for their own children. Behind the school, or any government service institution, stands the police power of the state, which exacts payment, not for services rendered but for the support of a governmental agency.

Most service staffs in business have this monopoly power too. Operating managers know that they are judged in some measure by how well they cooperate with the staff services; and only rarely are they permitted to go outside their own company for advice or expertise in a staff service's area.

Being paid out of a budget allocation rather than for results changes what is meant by performance. Results in the budget-based institution are measured by the budget size. Performance is the ability to maintain or to increase one's budget. Results in the usual sense, that is, contributions to the market or achievement towards a goal and objectives, are secondary. The first test of a budget-based institution and the first requirement for its survival is to obtain the budget. And the budget is not, by definition, related so much to contribution as to good intentions.

When efficiency is a sin

Efficiency and cost control, however much they are preached, are not really virtues in the budget-based institution. The importance of a budget-based institution is measured essentially by the size of its budget and the size of its staff. To achieve results with a smaller budget or a smaller staff is, therefore, not performance. It might actually endanger the institution. Not to spend the entire budget will only convince the budget maker – whether legislature or the budget committee of a company – that the budget for the next fiscal period can safely be cut.

Thirty or forty years ago it was considered characteristic of Russian planning that Soviet managers, towards the end of the plan period, engaged in a frantic effort to spend all the money allocated to them. This usually resulted in total waste. Today the disease has become universal as budget-based institutions have become dominant everywhere. End-of-year pressure on the executive of a budget-based institution certainly accounts for a good deal of waste in the American defence effort. The practice of 'buying-in', that is, getting approval for a new project by grossly underestimating its total cost, is also built into the budget-based institution.

Efficiency loses out when the acid test of performance is budget size. This standard of success subtly discourages administrators from trying to do a job cheaply and efficiently and may even penalize them for doing so.

A confusion of goals

But effectiveness even more than efficiency is endangered by reliance on the budget allocation. It becomes dangerous to raise the question as to what the business of the institution should be. The question is always controversial. The controversy is likely to alienate support and is therefore shunned by the budget-based institution. At best the institution may achieve effectiveness by deceiving the public and itself.

The US Department of Agriculture, for instance, has never been willing to ask whether its goal should be farm productivity or support of the small family farm. It has known for decades that these two objectives are not identical, as had originally been assumed. In fact, they are becoming increasingly incompatible. To admit this, however, would have created controversy that might have endangered the Department's budget. As a result, American farm policy has frittered away an enormous amount of money and human resources on what might be called a public relations campaign, that is, on a show of support for the small family farmer. Its effective activities, however – and they have been very effective indeed – have been directed towards eliminating the small family farmer and replacing him by the far more productive 'agribusiness'. These large, highly capitalized and mechanized farms are run as businesses, not as a 'way of life'. Favouring agribusiness may have been right, but it was not what the Department was founded to do, nor what the legislators, in approving the Department's budget, expected it to do.

The American community hospital is not governmental but private, though nonprofit. Yet, like hospitals everywhere, it presents the same confusion of missions and objectives, with the resulting impairment of effectiveness and performance. Should a hospital be, in effect, a physician's plant facility, as most older American physicians maintain? Should it be a community health centre? Should it focus on the major health needs of a community or try to do everything and be abreast of every medical advance, no matter how costly and how rarely used the facility will be? Should it focus on preventive medicine and on health education for the community? Or should it concentrate on the repair of health damage that has already been done?

Each of these definitions of the mission of the hospital can be defended. Each deserves a hearing. The effective hospital is a multi-purpose institution that strikes a balance between various objectives. What most hospitals do, however, is pretend that there are no basic questions to be decided. The result, predictably, is confusion and impairment of the capacity of the hospital to serve any function and to carry out any mission.

[. . .]

Being dependent on a budget allocation discourages an institution from setting priorities and concentrating efforts, yet nothing is ever accomplished unless scarce resources are concentrated on a small number of priorities.

A shoe manufacturer that has 22 per cent of the market for work shoes may be a profitable business. If the business succeeds in raising its market share to 30 per cent, especially if the market for work shoes is expanding, the company is doing very well indeed. It need not be concerned too much with the 70 per cent of the users of work shoes who buy from somebody else. And the customers for ladies' fashion shoes are of no concern at all.

Contrast this with the situation of an institution on a budget. To obtain its budget, it needs the approval, or at least the acquiescence, of practically everybody who could possibly be considered a constituent. Where a market share of 22 per cent might be perfectly satisfactory to a business, rejection by 78 per cent of the constituents – or even by a much smaller proportion – would be absolutely fatal to a budget-based institution. It might survive without the active support of 22 per cent of its constituents but it certainly should consider itself in serious danger. And this means that the service institution cannot concentrate; it must instead try to please everyone and offend none.

Finally, being budget-based makes it even more difficult to abandon the wrong things, the old, the obsolete. As a result, service institutions are even more encrusted than businesses with the barnacles of unproductive efforts. No institution likes to abandon anything it does. Business is no exception. An institution paid for its performance and results stands, however, under a performance test. The unproductive, the obsolete, is sooner or later killed off by the customers. In a budget-based institution, no such discipline is enforced. On the contrary, what a service institution does is always virtuous and likely to be considered in the public interest.

The temptation is great, therefore, to respond to lack of results by redoubling efforts. The temptation is great to double the budget, precisely because there is no performance. The temptation, above all, is to blame the outside world for its stupidity or its reactionary resistance, and to consider lack of results a proof of one's own righteousness and a reason in itself for keeping on with the good work.

The tendency to continue unproductive efforts is not confined to service institutions in the public sector. It is just as common in staff services within large business enterprises. The organization planner, the computer specialist, or the operations researcher all tend to argue that the resistance of operating managers to their wares is itself evidence of the need for their services and reason for doubling the 'missionary effort'. Sometimes this argument is, of course, valid. But more often it makes impossible concentration of efforts on important areas where results are attainable.

All service institutions are threatened by the tendency to cling to yesterday and to put their best and ablest people on defending what no longer makes sense or serves a purpose. Government is particularly prone to this disease, believing that present policies and projects will be equally valid forever. It might better realize that conditions and needs change and that every programme should be reviewed often.

Earned revenue or deserved

Human beings will behave as they are rewarded – whether the reward is money and promotion, a medal, an autographed picture of the boss, or a pat on the back. This is a lesson the behavioural psychologist has taught us. A business or any institution that is rewarded for its performance in such a way that the dissatisfied or disinterested customer need not pay has to earn its income. An institution which is financed by a budget – or which enjoys a monopoly that the customer cannot escape – is rewarded with what it deserves rather than what it earns. It is paid for good intentions and for 'programmes'. It is paid for not alienating important constituents rather than for satisfying any one group. It is misdirected by the way it is paid into defining performance as what will produce the budget rather than as what will produce contribution.

This is a built-in characteristic of budget-based institutions. Amazingly enough, it has escaped the attention of the economists – perhaps because few of them seem to be aware of the fact that more than half of the gross national product these days does not go to businesses, that is, to institutions paid for performance and results, but rather to service institutions paid for promises or, at best, for efforts.

Being budget-based is not necessarily bad or even undesirable. Self-supporting armies, for instance, such as the armies of the fifteenth century or the traditional armies of the Chinese warlords, had to engage in continual warfare, terrorize the citizens of their own nation, and depend on plunder for their support. Civilian control and defence budgets paid out of taxes were instituted precisely to stop free enterprise in warfare.

Similarly, most service staffs in business should be on a budget allocation. To pay a research laboratory for results, for instance, in the form of a royalty on the sales of the new products and processes it produces (as has been tried in several businesses) is almost certain to misdirect the research laboratory even more than the budget allocation does. It is likely to divert resources from research into gadgetry. But there is also no question that budget allocation induces research directors to inflate the research staff, to come up with an impossible list of projects, and to hang on to projects that are unlikely to produce results.

Summary

There are three common explanations for the lack of performance in service institutions: their managers aren't businesslike; the people are not as good as they should be; results are intangible and incapable of definition or measurement. All three are invalid and are pure alibi. The basic problem of the service institution is that it is paid for promises rather than for performance. It is paid out of a budget rather than for (and out of) results.

3

Empowering human resources

G. Morgan

I want to find the way to unleashing creativity and innovation – to give individuals the freedom to make a full and effective contribution to my organization.

How do you encourage people to let your organization become flexible, to face the issues, so that you can approach a competitive situation competitively? How do you do it? I think it's critical. We're facing a future where we'll see changes all the time. How do we organize our corporations to face change? How do you get that through to people? It's not just a communications exercise; it's a mindset. It's a different way of thinking. How can we address this issue?

[. . .]The development of creative, innovative organizations that 'go with the flow' and remain competitive in a highly competitive world was a challenge facing most of the executives involved in my research. Indeed, unleashing the power and creativity of our people and our organizations – even if this means only realizing and tapping the considerable potential already there – was regarded as one of the most pressing issues facing the modern manager. Many of our organizations have difficulty in doing their best. Although they show considerable promise, they fall short in their actions.

What can managers do to change this?
How can they make innovation the life blood of their organizations?
How can they promote an ability to learn and change on a continuous basis?

The development of proactive mindsets, outside-in management, and appropriate leadership and vision all have a role to play here; however, many more specific practices and policies are needed. This chapter discusses issues relating to human resource management: the importance of viewing people as a key resource, encouraging people to relish change, blending specialist and generalist qualities, managing in an environment of equals, and making education a continual process. [. . .]

People as a key resource

It all boils down to one thing: people, people, people, people, people. I don't care what country, or what organization, or what team you are in – it is the people and whether you can organize those people to achieve an end result that count.

If you have the right people in all your key sectors, and all of your people are keen, then you will *make* it happen.

You have to have people that get right to the important issues. Two organizations can agree to go through the same process and get the same consultant to help them, but the difference in effectiveness rests in the ability of those present to get into the issues that need to be discussed.

I want all my people to be excellent. In today's competitive environment that's exactly what has to happen. Everyone has to be damn good, and we have to make it all pull together. It's no use if the person in marketing is damn good and the person in production is damn good if they can't talk to each other. We, as chief executives, have to ensure that they all function together.

Popular opinion often leads us to conclude that money is the most scarce and most valuable organizational resource. Every organization understands the importance of money, and as every manager knows, there is precious little one can do without it. But in most organizations, especially those that are not in immediate financial difficulty, the truly key and scarce resource is *excellent people*. The executive who has excellent people in all the key places is probably the exception rather than the rule. Many organizations find it relatively easy to commit a million dollars to a particular line of development, but much more difficult to get the right people to produce the desired results.

The importance of the human element in an organization is increasing along with the pace of change. Change demands innovation, and innovation demands that we unleash the creative potential of our people. In a more stable world one could organize in a mechanistic way – establish and design one's organization, direct and control it from the top, and rely on middle managers of fairly average ability to 'fill slots' with workers and oversee operations.

Now, much more is required. Bureaucracy is giving way to new approaches that require people to exercise discretion, take initiative, and assume a much greater responsibility for their own organization and management. The need to remain open and flexible demands creative responses from every quarter, and many leading organizations recognize that human intelligence and the ability to unleash and direct that intelligence are critical resources. Traditional economics has taught us that the main factors of production are land, labor, and capital. However, as we move into an 'information society' where the ability to create value through human enterprise grows increasingly important, the principles of economics need to be revised to include such factors of production as knowledge, information, creativity, opportunity seeking, interpersonal skills, and entrepreneurship. Without an adequate supply and good management of these human factors, it simply is not possible for an organization to keep abreast of the changes in its environment with any degree of competence. Future managers will thus need to pay more attention to attracting the right people to their organization, developing human potential and fostering conditions that make this relevant and effective, and positioning and repositioning people so that they always contribute where they are most needed.

These competencies are not new. Indeed, personnel managers have long emphasized their importance. The challenge of the future, however, is to break free of the idea that human resource management skills can be delegated to specific individuals or departments and to make them an 'on-line' aspect of every manager's role, in short, to make them an integral part of the mindset through which managers manage.

Relishing change

How do you get people to be adaptive, and flexible . . . in a manner that they will relish and enjoy, and through that, get better results? And how do you position a group of people so that they enjoy change? Because a lot of people don't enjoy change. They enjoy knowing what the parameters are, so that they can leave at 5 p.m.

I have found that the key ingredient for competent management is somebody who loves change – not just copes with it, but *loves* it. Change is so much a part of our daily menu that you must really thrive on it, and get your kicks from it. The counterpressure, and I think that is what our organizations are struggling with to a large degree, is the great value that is being put on stability. And that clash is one that competent management has to cope with.

Simplicity, clarity, and security, that's what people often want . . . [helpful] words that allow them to deal with fuzzy ill-structured problems – in a procedural way. But we're into situations with the growth of technology and the rapidity of change where we don't have the ability to deal with these needs for clarity and security.

These remarks highlight a major dilemma. Organizations desperately need people who are able to cope with change, even if they don't quite enjoy it. Historically, the trend has been toward creating a sense of stability and certainty. Many people have come to see themselves as having a clear place in their organizations, whether in terms of their immediate job or career path, and this has been encouraged by organizational and union policies that stress the need for clearly defined responsibilities and routes to seniority. Now, this trend needs to be reversed to create a situation in which people recognize and accept change, and rise to meet the challenges it brings. Debate on this issue quickly focuses on the ability and motivation of people to cope with new situations. In my research, some executives expressed great optimism:

> You'd be surprised at the ingenuity of people in coping with new situations. [They] rise to the occasion. One of the problems is that for a long time [they] haven't had enough occasions to rise to.

> People, if they believe they are part of a change process, will be on their mettle; they usually do their best.

Others were more cautious, emphasizing 'the rigidities arising from unionization' and the resistance from 'bureaucratic attitudes' and 'fear of technology'.

[. . .]

Blending 'specialist' and 'generalist' qualities

There has been long-standing debate about the merits of 'generalists' and 'specialists' and the profile of the ideal manager. The executives involved in my research heavily favored generalist abilities, but they tended to reject the either–or character of the generalist–specialist distinction. Instead, they felt that the modern executive needs *both* qualities. Complete specialism was seen as a problem in view of the diverse nature of the modern corporate environment. And generalism – 'a good manager can manage anything' – was thought to ignore the fact that in today's environment there is absolutely no substitute for an intimate knowledge of the nature of one's business. One CEO [Chief Executive Officer] expressed the situation in relation to his role:

> You have to know your business in terms of *detailed* understanding. You have to have this. The generalist stuff is crap. Most executive skills may be generic, but to be effective you must know the details of the business with which you are dealing.

On balance, there was a feeling that specialist abilities are often over-developed and generalist abilities underdeveloped, and that to enrich the human resource base of our organizations, these abilities must be blended to achieve a broadening of skills and perspectives; a better appreciation of the relationship between the human and technical aspects of the manager's role; and a greater emphasis on the entrepreneurial and creative aspects of the management process.

[. . .]

Improving relations between the human and technical aspects of the manager's role

The development of technical specialization has had a tendency to downgrade the importance of the human element in organizations. People are frequently appointed for their technical skills, with the *hope* that they also have good interpersonal skills. In the view of many executives involved in my research it is high time to redress the imbalance by making people critically aware of the importance of integrating the technical and human factors in management. The basic problems and some possible solutions were expressed in many ways:

> Motivating people – but we've got to find a better expression – has to be part of a manager's job description. Instead of saying this fellow is a good accountant, and to boot, he's good with people, we have to say there are two sides to this job – you have to be a class accountant or sales manager and a crack motivator. It will then emerge as a competency, not just as icing on the cake.

> I'm not suggesting that accountants are not important, that finance types are not important, or that computer specialists are not important. But, beyond that, to make the whole system work, you've got to have people who are people oriented, who are trying to understand humans, be they customers, workers, foreigners, the government, or whatever. Number crunching [is not enough]. It is the human side that [makes all the] differences these days.

> As more and more of the physical and technical aspects of a manager's role are routinized or removed through automation, the proportion of time in which skills associated with the subjective side of life are required increases. Dealing with people as people, getting the most out of them, and helping them to do their jobs [becomes more and more important]. Automation has made many jobs less routine. Machines now have the routine jobs. There is an enormous need for nurturing the management competencies that allow people to handle the nonroutine. There is no manual for this, except that of human relations. It's not just a question of technical skills.

Such comments send a clear message about the importance of the human side of a manager's job. The manager of the future will be expected to stretch beyond the bounds of technical competence and develop people skill as an essential ingredient of the managerial role.

[. . .]

Here is how some of the executives involved in my research described the skills and abilities required by the new style manager/orchestrator/facilitator. He or she must be able:

- 'To help people on a day-to-day basis without supervising their work;

[meaning] you have to have some method of being helpful at the generic level, without keeping track of the details'

- To act as 'a resource person rather than a controller, cultivating relations so that staff will call you in when you are required'
- 'To create and communicate a sense of vision and make decisions only when necessary, for example, as a troubleshooter, arbitrator, or hatchet man'
- To orchestrate, facilitate, and network – 'to create conditions that allow things to happen, by finding opportunities, dislodging roadblocks, or acting on focal points that lead to desired action'
- To exercise 'influencing skills' including those of conflict management and negotiation
- To engage in 'team building' and develop other participative and collaborative skills
- 'To work laterally and to launch and sustain joint ventures'
- 'To deal with uncertainty and ambiguity at a fast speed'
- 'To be sensitive to the soft as opposed to the hard, finite, technical sides of an issue'
- 'To be intuitive and sensitive to nondeductive problem-solving methodologies'
- 'To remain open and flexible, yet act decisively when required'
- 'To motivate', 'to inspire', 'to turn people on', and 'to avoid turning them off'
- 'To make personal contact and empathize with employees so a bonding takes place'
- 'To communicate key norms and values' and to nurture an appropriate sense of identity and corporate culture
- To lead *and* to participate: 'to shape direction while remaining open to influence from others'

We find in this list, [. . .] a strong sense of the direction in which management may continue to move into the twenty-first century. Increasingly, organizations are dealing with new kinds of employees using new technologies and requiring new forms of management. Many of these required skills are more 'female' than 'male', perhaps signifying great opportunity for women in organizations. We have been through a phase of 'macho management' in which a highly analytical, directive, 'top-down' approach has dominated. Now we seem to be moving into a phase where more empathic, relationship-oriented approaches, based on cooperation rather than competition, are often more appropriate. Here, women often have the better record.

[. . .]

4

Gender considerations in school management: masculine and feminine leadership styles

H. L. Gray

[. . .]

There has been no significant discussion in educational writing of the implications of gender considerations in the study of schools as organizations. Even in mainstream management thinking, the gender issues in management – beyond a study of feminist concerns – have only just begun to surface (Boydell and Hammond, 1985). Yet, once a consciousness of gender and its implications for management has been raised, it is a short step to considering gender issues in the management of educational institutions because gender-related matters play a much larger part in their organization than is often realized. In fact, many gender issues in education have been staring us in the face for a long time without our recognizing them.

I will try to use the word 'gender' in this context carefully. Gender is the preferred word in the literature of women's (and men's) studies to refer to sex *roles*; the various patterns of behaviour exhibited by a person who is of male or female 'physical' sex, and the psychological dispositions that lead to gender concepts and self images. Its use facilitates the avoidance of sex stereotypes and helps us to explore the wide variety of sex-linked behaviour. Most of us tend to think in terms of sex stereotypes and occasionally must do so to clarify sex roles but we need to take care not to confuse gender expectations. If we are to improve our understanding of maleness and femaleness, masculinity and femininity, we need a word less emotionally charged and ambiguous than 'sex' or 'sexual', so 'gender' has become a useful word in this context. Behaviour and dispositions described in gender terms may or may not be 'sexual' but 'gender' covers the wide variety of behaviour possible for both men and boys and women and girls.

In the popular imagination, there are two sex or gender stereotypes of considerable persistence. We tend to expect men to behave according to the male stereotype which includes aggressiveness, ambition, assertiveness, competitiveness, domination, forcefulness, being good at sports, self-confidence, ability at making decisions and independence. We tend to expect women to be affectionate, emotional, gentle, fond of children, tender, warm and understanding (Archer and Lloyd, 1982). Consequently, any behaviour associated with the paradigm for the opposite sex is considered inappropriate and sometimes unacceptable. However, few of us see ourselves as fitting totally the simple paradigm and we all recognize ourselves in each item of each list. In fact, the better adjusted we are emotionally the easier it is for us to accept this 'fully androgynous' duality – we see it simply as a full description of a mature person, whether male or female being of little relevance.

But social pressures can make this acceptance quite difficult, especially when we are forced into social roles, particularly self-determined roles, as at school or work. Schools tend to expect boys and girls to fulfil each paradigm but not that for the alternative sex. This is equally true of adults – e.g. women secretaries and men bosses – and there is confusion when roles commonly held to be appropriate to one sex are assumed by members of another – e.g. women bosses and men secretaries. This is especially true of headteachers, with the added complication that some headship positions are considered appropriate for one sex rather than the other – nursery, infant and primary schools 'should' have women heads, secondary schools (but not all-girl schools) and Further Education Colleges 'should' have men heads. The reality is that headship, like any managerial role, requires appropriate be-haviour from both sex paradigms but in the normal exercise of duties most of us become conscious of behaviour that is considered sex appropriate or imappropriate and that consequently presents certain difficulties because we feel expected to behave in a maner to which we are not inclined. This has implications for our proper gender (sexual) identity.

Organizationally, schools have been historically more sex conscious than almost any other form of organization, except prisons. Other organiz-ations may have overt sexual bases (strip shows, men's clubs) or claim to acknowledge significant sex differences (the army, the police) and some may have excluded one sex (the Church and exclusive women's organizations) but only schools have tried to cope with males and females equally, while consistently treating them differently. Single-sex schools raise gender issues as well as sexual ones (Davies, 1985). Single-sex schools seem to have stereotyped sex role (gender) behaviour even more than mixed schools and yet they might have been expected to exploit the differences within each sex role more fully rather than repress them.

Schools have tended to hold severely separatist and stereotyped views of sex differences. Children are monolithically 'boys' or 'girls' and schools require naïvely normative behaviour, albeit some self contradictory. Only recently have traditional boys' subjects (e.g. metalwork) been made available to girls, and girls' subjects (e.g. cooking) to boys. But these concessions to antisexist pressures are usually cosmetic and superficial; they are concerned with public patterns of behaviour not the sense of self with its attendant consciousness of sexual identity. Schools seem to acknowledge only two stereotypes, 'feminine' girls and 'masculine' boys, without acknowledging the variety of behaviour engaged in equally by boys and girls let alone the psychological dispositions that exist on the basis of an individual's clear personal identity as 'male' or 'female'. There are many ways of being a boy and many ways of being a girl and they seldom fall into clear stereotypes. Schools have always been confused about sexuality, and sexual identity and what can be permitted in the stereotyping of sex roles. Only by reflecting on the concept of 'gender' will a sorting out process be possible and the biases and imbalances of sexual prejudice be laid aside.

One of the axioms of good management practice is that it should relate to organizational needs (the basic culture) of the institution. Good management derives from an understanding of the organization; it is not an ideal universal system imposed from without. It is, however, 'systematic' in that good management practice is coherent and not self contradictory. By and large, schools fail in consistency and compatibility because too much of what passes for management is simply imposed administration arising from a confused perception of the nature of schooling. The contradictions appear everywhere: an expressed regard for individual needs against limited choice in the types of examination permitted; a declared concern for children to learn independence of thought against rigidly prescriptive teaching; a high regard for loyalty while discouraging loyalty to anything but the school, and so on.

But the biggest contradiction is in the general principles of school management. If schools are 'nurturing' institutions encouraging children to find their skills and talents and develop them fully; if schools are about respect for individuals, individuality and an acceptance of differences; if schools are about self-respect, openness and honest dialogue, one must look for organizational behaviour (i.e. management) that clearly reflects and fosters these qualities. Of course, some people do not believe that this is what schools are for; they see them as machines that mould and define people to be what a greater power has decided we should all become (like the basis of military training). But the issue of compatability still arises even if it requires different treatment. If schools are perceived as needing to be caring, nurturing, maintaining, supportive, understanding, etc., they will be seen to require a form of management that for many is essentially a stereotype of femininity. If they are believed to be thrusting, competitive, confrontational, individualized, etc., they will be believed to require a form of management that is considered essentially masculine. On this polarity, if schools are to be the one they cannot be the other because the contradictions become dysfunctional. A dominating, authoritarian management régime, it will be believed, cannot encourage warm, considerate, caring and intuitive behaviour by pupils. If individual heads think of their schools on this paradigm with these stereotypes, they will encounter personal difficulties in terms of their own self image and consequent behaviour.

It is, of course, difficult to make every organization fit neatly into one or other of two types, whether they be good and bad, ageing and young, authoritarian and democratic, but the polarizing of ideal types is always a useful way of clarifying and understanding. The neatness of gender polarity is that it relates to the two socially defined genders ('sexes') and immediately points to their ambiguity in experiential terms – personal experience. Few of us believe ourselves to be totally masculine or feminine and many of us recognize, in some way or another, our own psychological androgyny. If psychological androgyny is a personal quality, surely it is also manifest in organizations. No one expects a secondary-school head to have the personal qualities of a lumberjack, or a primary-school head to behave like an opera singer. For most of us, our behaviour is more subtly varied. We have these expectations, however, because we each have a set of gender expectations that, for that most part, lie unacknowledged and certainly muddled deep in our consciousness. In any case, the terms used to describe school régimes or values fall neatly into the same category as the terms we use to describe individual behaviour. We seem to *expect* organizations to behave with the characteristics of people.

There are extant two ideal types of school which derive from generally accepted views of primary and secondary schools. Broadly speaking, a primary school will be

caring
nurturing
creative
intuitive
aware of individual differences
non-competitive
tolerant
subjective [. . .]
informal [etc.]

Broadly speaking, a secondary school will be

highly regulated
conformist
normative
competitive
evaluative
disciplined
objective
formal
rule bound etc.

These are extreme types but they will be readily recognized by anyone looking at broad differences between primary and secondary schools. There is considerable evidence that, by and large, head teachers of primary schools have the personal values that characterize their type of school. Those who train primary heads in management find them collaborative, creative, open and tolerant, willing to experiment, reflective and intuitive. In other words, there is considerable evidence that successful management styles for primary schools fit the basic culture and this is perceived by many people to be essentially 'feminine' rather than 'masculine' (Leary, 1985). With secondary heads, the position is different. Many secondary heads are perceived as normative, require general conformity, encourage competition, are highly evaluative through examinations and school organizations, behave formally, tend to be punitive and eschew intuition. In other words, they display the characteristics stereotypically considered 'masculine'.

If it is believed that organizational culture must be matched with a compatible management style and if the essential culture of schools is perceived to be 'feminine', there are problems for some heads as managers. Some primary heads – especially men – with a traditional masculine self concept will find difficulty in adopting the appropriate nurturing behaviour because they perceive it as contrary to their stereotype of appropriate men's behaviour (though many find it possible to do so through a 'parental', i.e. father-figure, role). Men heads may feel a tension between what they view as an essentially 'feminine' school and their view of themselves as men and, as a consequence, may be confused when they compare themselves with secondary heads, seeing the managerial behaviour demanded of them as less 'male'. Secondary heads may experience even greater difficulty because the nurturing ('feminine') qualities of the school are overlaid by 'masculine' regulating/control mechanisms. Secondary schools tend to value rules highly and it may be difficult to be a father-figure in such a large 'rule-bound' family. Heads with a strong ('macho') male image find themselves behaving in ways unrelated to the needs of the school as perceived by others and so become increasingly ineffective. Heads who relax the discipline and control needs may feel threatened by colleagues who demand the authoritarianism of 'strong' headship. Yet many secondary schools find themselves moving towards nurturing behaviour, in spite of the traditional expectations for firmness and control and heads find themselves having to re-evaluate their own management styles and question their own self-image with its gender stereotyping imperatives.

Perhaps the biggest difficulty for male heads is the acceptance that gender issues are involved at all; women seem to find the proposition less threatening. When gender explanations of behaviour are introduced to teachers, there is usually a strong separation between the men and the women in their ability to accept that there are such concerns as gender or sex-based issues. Women teachers invariably find the idea of gender issues in school *organization* easy to accept while men sometimes ridicule it. To face male heads, especially of secondary schools, with the proposition that their job requires much more of the 'feminine' side of their nature than the 'male' is to leave them in a state of shock. Historically, secondary headship is a very male vocation, i.e. most secondary heads are men. To realize that one is required to use some of the 'weaker' qualities in oneself may be seen as an affront to one's sexuality. Since many men are afraid of their sexuality (homophobia), a gender-based analysis of headship is very threatening indeed. A head with secret uncertainties about his masculinity will be uncomfortable when he feels himself called to draw on his more 'feminine' attributes. If the culture of the school can be described in gender terms and if this has consequences for understanding the nature of managerial behaviour for heads, it follows that the same managerial requirements relate to the classroom and the teacher. Does this mean the 'feminization' of the teaching profession? To believe so is to miss the importance of the gender perspective. A gender perspective helps us to see that we all have 'masculine' and 'feminine' characteristics albeit in a unique balance for each of us (Metcalf and Humphries, 1985). 'Masculine' and 'feminine' represent coherent, consistent 'ideal types', which none of us are. Gender is not defined by physical sex so an individual may have a very clear identity as a man (male) while having a largely 'feminine' behaviour repertoire. A male ballet dancer may have a self-image as a man as clear as that of a footballer. So a gender analysis of headship does not question the sexuality of a head, it merely indicates the qualities of behaviour. It is the confusion of sexuality and gender that is the problem for most men and some women. Perhaps some men teachers are secretly insecure in their job, especially men primary-school teachers because of the nurturing require-ments of primary-school children.

There are also implications of gender for students. One reason why a more largely 'feminine' style of management may be appropriate for schools may be that 'feminine' styles are more accepting of differences than male. Male styles are strongly conformist and peer related while female styles are much more tolerant of deviance. Since there is no single best form of sexuality for boys or girls and no one best kind of gender behaviour, schools must be not only tolerant of differences but accepting of them. It is remark-able how intolerant schools are when compared with Further Education colleges, universities, polytechnics, youth groups etc. In many ways, a school's attitude to clothes (and uniform) epitomizes its gender (and sexual) values. Schools usually have strong gender expectations because they are very conscious of sexual issues. One way of diffusing sexual sensitivity is to view issues from a gender perspective because an understanding of gender leads to a greater understanding of sexuality. The horror at the idea of a boy wanting to be a nurse probably arises from a sexual fear that such a vocation is not 'manly'. But, since a gender perspective does not ascribe simple mascu-line/feminine normative paradigms, it becomes easier to understand personal life choices for what they are – simply facets of a personality.

The gender perspective allows us to take a more creative view of the management role. If we define management as dealing with areas of uncer-tainty, crisis, policy and negotiation and administration as the continuance of practice, following of procedures, implementation of other people's de-cisions, and maintenance of routines, we see that management requires a balance of 'feminine' and 'masculine' skills. The problem for many heads, especially secondary ones, is that they are drawn to administration rather than management because this is their 'male' side and they avoid the 'feminine' qualities necessary to function completely. Many heads are ineffective at management because they fear the feminine qualities this draws on: intuition, calculated risk taking, aesthetic considerations, dependence on colleagues, messiness and incompleteness. The resistance to being a manager may well have a greater gender basis than is thought and there is probably an element of sexual confusion too, since 'real' men do not make mistakes!

It may seem somewhat extreme to attribute management failure of heads to their sense of sexual identity but the further one looks the more evidence there is. For example, in the 1960s and 1970s, there was a fashion for populist, aggressive, ideological heads. There was a circus of successful heads going the rounds of meetings, courses and conferences. They saw education as largely political and were concerned to bring about large social changes quickly. They have now largely disappeared and one reason is that they were never really successful. They were concerned with quick, complete and fundamental structural change in schools, but, in the event, the changes did not really happen. Such heads were often replaced with heads who had the job of *nursing* the school back to health – people with counselling skills. The qualities of nursing are undoubtedly 'feminine' in the popular imagination. Indeed all the qualities of nursing, reconciliation, acceptance, forbearance, tolerance, gentleness are 'feminine' qualities and it requires some effort of will for a newly appointed head not to see the need to put matters right in the school in an aggressive, detached, authoritarian, patriarchal way, thus fulfilling the common expectations of masculinity.

The problem for schools is that they are under pressure to encourage pupils to conform to sex stereotypes and this requirement has strong implications for teachers and heads. Effeminate men and macho women as teachers present enormous problems that few schools could cope with. The expectation of heads, therefore, is that they should not present any gender ambiguities: they must be centrally and conventionally either 'masculine' or 'feminine'. A man head who teaches dancing while his woman deputy takes football is usually suspect, even though there is no good reason. The pressures of sexual stereotyping on heads are probably greater than anywhere else. Yet if students are to be taught in an environment and atmosphere that encourages them to grow up and develop as they truly are – in that common psychological androgyny that all adults share – the styles of management must show that there is no single 'masculinity' or 'femininity' in being an adult and no single gender model for managerial behaviour. To be a man or to be a woman allows us to be a distinct personality without regard to sex stereotyping and this should also be true of school heads.

There is a lot more work to be done on gender issues in schools, let alone management. There is little material on the topic because, although there is much feminist writing on sexist issues, there is little from the more objective position of gender studies. In the meantime, heads may well ponder on how their own sense of gender and sexual identity influences how they choose to manage their schools.

Acknowledgements

I am grateful to Carolyn Stone also of the Department of Educational Research, University of Lancaster for helping me to clarify some of my ideas. Any confusion that remains is mine not hers.

References

Archer, J. and Lloyd, B. (1982) *Sex and Gender* (Penguin, Harmondsworth) pp. 36–48.

Boydell, T. and Hammond, V. (Eds) (1985) Men and women in organisations. *Management Education & Development* Vol. 16, No. 2.

Davies, L. (1985) *Pupil Power, Deviance and Gender in Schools* (Falmer, London).

Leary, M. (1985) Men and women: what are the differences and does it matter. *Management Education & Development* Vol. 16, No. 2, pp. 140–154.

Metcalf, A. and Humphries, M. (Eds) (1985) *The Sexuality of Men* (Pluto Press, London).

Leadership and motivation

5
Motivation to work

Hisataka Furukawa

This chapter covers studies that have been published [. . .] since 1980 and begins with a discussion of some of the antecedents of work motivation and organizational commitment such as goal setting, employee expectancies, and their cognitive evaluations. Here the aim is to review current research on motivation to work and such related variables as performance and satisfaction. Then strategies for increasing work motivation such as behavior modification, participation, and job redesign are introduced. Following this, attention is turned to the use of small group activities in Japan, and finally future research needs are addressed.

Antecedents of motivation to work

Despite the continuing lack of agreement on one standard, reliable, and valid way of measuring commitment (Cook and Wall, 1980; Ferris and Aranya, 1983; Gordon, Philpot, Burt, Thompson and Spiller, 1980; Meyer and Allen, 1984), several studies examined the antecedents of organizational commitment measured in somewhat different ways. Welsch and LaVan (1981) revealed, as might be expected, that role conflict and ambiguity are detrimental, while a participative climate, teamwork, satisfaction with work, and promotion are positively related to commitment. Oliver (1984) stressed the necessity of a close match between goals of the members and what the corporation provides. Gould and Werbel (1983) compared the degree of commitment between dual and single wage-earner families and found that commitment was lower among male subjects whose spouses were employed. Culture, as such, could not account for these kinds of results, for Luthans, McCaul, and Dodd (1985) presented data to reveal that Japanese workers are not always more committed to the organizations than are their US counterparts.

The major antecedents of motivation to work are employees' goal setting, their expectancies, and their cognitive evaluations.

Goal setting and motivation to work

Motivation to work is enhanced by having specified goals toward which to work. Goal setting theory has evoked a number of questions about this, mainly in laboratory experiments (Locke, Shaw, Saari and Latham, 1981) and has become one of the most influential theories on motivation to work. Recently, however, some field research results are also available in support of laboratory-based explanation. In a review of the goal setting research literature, Campbell (1982) concluded that both situational and personality factors affect an individual's preference to work on easy or hard goals. Situational factors include such variables as prior success or failure on the task, monetary and verbal incentives, feedback, participation, and competition. Personality factors include need for achievement [. . .], self-assurance, and maturity.

A positive relationship between previous performance and difficulty of the goal chosen has been confirmed consistently (Garland, 1982). Thus Locke, Frederick and Bokko (1984a) reported that experimental subjects tended to choose more difficult goals if their earlier assigned goals had been easy, and to choose easier goals if their previously assigned goals had been difficult. The subjects' performance was heavily influenced by their self-set goals. At the same time, Erez and Zidon (1984) revealed that goal acceptance moderated the relationship of goal difficulty to task performance.

Several studies examined why goal setting works. Campion and Lord (1982) proposed and confirmed a control system model of motivation in which a goal is considered a referent or desired state by which performance is compared. Then the discrepancy between the goal and actual performance creates a corrective motivation. Again, Locke, Frederick, and Bokko (1984b) introduced the concept of self-efficacy and suggested the possibility of integrating goal setting and social learning theory approaches to task performance. Also attempted has been the effort to relate the goal setting theory with the job characteristic approach (Jackson and Zedeck, 1982) and with expectancy theory (Garland, 1984; Matsui, Okada and Mizuguchi, 1981; Mento, Cartledge and Locke, 1980). For example, a job with clear instructions and rewards may generate goals set with more confidence, hence contribute more to task motivation than a job with ambiguous instructions and uncertain rewards.

Goal setting combines well in its effects with feedback appraisals. Ivancevich (1982) conducted a field experiment to compare the effectiveness of three appraisal interview conditions (feedback only, feedback plus assigned goal setting, and assigned goal setting) with a control group. Results indicated that the appraisal interventions were superior to the control group with regard to subordinates' reactions. Training also made a difference. Ivancevich and Smith (1981) showed that the goal setting training relying on role playing and videotaping had a positive effect on increasing salespersons' productivity. At the same time, Saari and Latham (1982) stressed the necessity of union acceptance if productivity improvement through goal setting is to be achieved.

Expectancy and motivation to work

While expectancy theory has been widely accepted in contemporary organizational psychology, the number of studies using this theory as their basis seems to have decreased compared with the 1970s. As for the validity of the expectancy model, Kennedy, Fossum, and White (1983) and Teas (1981) examined within-subject and between-subject predictions. As predicted by the model, within-subject predictions were of greater magnitude than between-subject predictions. In predicting work effort using expectancy theory, the role of its components of expectancy, instrumentality, and valence were investigated (Ilgen, Nebeker and Pritchard, 1981; Shiflett and Cohen, 1982). Effects tended to be modest. Clarity of linkages contributed to the observed efforts. Thus in a 32-week field experiment to study the effects of participative decision making, Neider (1980) found that increments in productivity and effort levels occurred only when the participation process clarified the effort–performance linkage and when valued outcomes were attached to high-performance levels.

Cognitive evaluation and motivation to work

Cognitive evaluation theory has recently been receiving increased attention from organizational psychologists. The impetus for concern seems to stem mainly from the practical possibility that the introduction of extrinsic rewards for a behavior may decrease intrinsic motivation rather than add to it, because the extrinsic rewards decrease the perception of intrinsic causation (Deci, 1975). In a comprehensive review of cognitive evaluation theory, Furukawa (1982) suggested that, for extrinsic rewards to have an inhibitory effect on intrinsic motivation, the task needed to be inherently interesting, and the reward had to be administered in a contingent and salient manner under the strong situational norm of nonpayment for work. Suggesting that industrial work settings do not provide fundamentally those necessary conditions, Furukawa concluded that more research is needed to test the detrimental effect of extrinsic rewards on work motivation in actual organizational settings. A variety of other task and situational factors affect the impact of extrinsic on intrinsic motivation (Daniel and Esser, 1980; Freedman and Phillips, 1985; Pearce, 1983; Porac and Meindl, 1982). Also important are such individual differences as need for achievement (Vecchio, 1982). Moreover, a number of the studies failed to find support for the theory (Boal and Cummings, 1981; Phillips and Lord, 1980).

Programs for increasing motivation to work

So far, we have looked at the important elements in the motivational process as goals, expectancies, and combining of extrinsic and intrinsic rewards. Now we turn to specific programmatic interventions that have been seen to have an impact on motivation to work.

Behavior modification and feedback programs

The theory and application of behavioral techniques in work settings also has received renewed attention. Luthans, Paul, and Baker (1981) conducted a field experiment to investigate the effect of reinforcement technology on service employee performance. Both experimental and control groups were informed of the specific standards against which they would be measured, but only the experimental group was told of and received the contingent reinforcement, which consisted of paid time off, equivalent cash, and a chance for a paid vacation. Results showed that the experimental group had a significant improvement in performance behavior, whereas the control group's behavior remained the same.

Komaki, Collins and Penn (1982) examined the role of performance antecedents and performance consequences. The safety performance of employees of a processing plant was monitored three times a week over 46 weeks as a baseline period. Following this, the antecedent condition was introduced involving frequent supervisor interaction and presentation of photographs on safety. Then the performance consequence (feedback) condition was followed. The results strongly confirmed that in the antecedent period there were no improvements in safety performance. However, during the consequential conditions, safety performance improved over the baseline and antecedent conditions.

The impact of the scheduling of feedback was investigated by Chhokar and Wallin (1984) who assessed the effect of varying the frequency of feedback on safety performance. The results indicated that more frequent feedback (once a week) did not always contribute to more performance improvement than less frequent feedback (once every 2 weeks). Also dealing with the feedback schedule, Saari and Latham (1982) examined employee performance and reactions to a monetary incentive administered on continuous and variable ratio schedules of reinforcement.

Participation and motivation to work

Employee participation in decision making is believed to be a strategy to increase their motivation to work and job satisfaction. Research on whether, when, why, and how participation works have been accumulated. Schuler (1980) found support for his prediction that participation is associated with employee satisfaction when it reduces role conflict and role ambiguity, and clarifies the expectancy from performance to reward. Similarly, Neider

(1980) and Lee and Schuler (1982) revealed that participation worked when it could make clear the employees' perception of effort-performance linkage.

Job redesign and motivation to work

The job redesign model has become a dominant research area in enhancing work motivation. This approach generally includes: (1) measuring employee perceptions of task attributes in terms of skill variety, task identity, significance, autonomy, and feedback, (2) associating these perceptions with relevant outcomes such as motivation, and (3) examining certain hypothesized moderating variables. Besides those paradigms, researchers aided by the work of Terborg and Davis (1982), who proposed and evaluated a retrospective method of assessing job change, have recently begun to investigate the effects of job change caused by advanced technology. Some fundamental questions are involved. For example, incumbents' job perceptions are often assumed to reflect the objective characteristics of the job. However, when both characteristics and outcomes are addressed by an incumbent, a within-person consistency problem may arise. Algera (1983) used both independent objective assessments and incumbents' perceptions of jobs. His results showed a reliable convergence in the patterns of correlations between job characteristics and outcomes in the two forms of assessment. But, O'Brien and Dowling (1980) reported that job satisfaction was more strongly associated with congruency between desired and perceived job attributes than with perceived job attributes alone.

While it has been continuously shown that job attributes have significant influences on incumbents' performance, motivation, and satisfaction (Bhagat and Chassie, 1980; D'Arcy, Syrotuik and Siddique, 1984; Griffeth, 1985; Griffin, 1982), studies have emerged that advocate that the causality may actually be reversed. For instance, Adler, Skov and Salvemini (1985) found that subjects given satisfaction feedback, as compared with those given dissatisfaction feedback, rated the physical environment and task characteristics as being more positive. Keller and Holland (1981) also reported that increases in performance and job satisfaction were reflected in higher ratings of job variety and autonomy. Several studies confirmed growth need strength (Griffin, 1982; Jackson, Paul and Wall, 1981) and job longevity (Kemp and Cook, 1983) as moderators of the job complexity–satisfaction relationship.

Buchanan and Boddy (1982) examined the impact of word processing technology on the typing job. Interviews with typists revealed that the new technology had reduced task variety, meaning, control over work scheduling, feedback of results, and communication with authors. These changes were determined more strongly and directly by management decisions than the technology itself. Recently, Brass (1985) investigated the relationships among technology, job characteristics, and employee performance and satisfaction. Job characteristics influenced satisfaction and performance to the degree that appropriate matches were made with technology and job characteristics.

Small group programs: The Japanese experience

It is widely known that such small group activities as quality control (QC) circles, zero-defect (ZD) program groups, organizations of semi-autonomous groups, and suggestion system groups have been contributing to enhancing workers' commitment and motivation to work in many Japanese organizations of the participating rank and file employees. The overall success of small group activities in Japan, supported by such factors as Japan's strong tradition of group importance, of lifetime employment, of promotion and wage based on seniority, of vagueness of job content, and of labor unions within the company, has led organizations in the United States, Europe, and Asian countries to introduce these activities without the present necessity of these Japanese culture-based traditions (Japanese Industrial and Vocational Training Association [JIVTA], 1982; Ross and Ross, 1982).

It was soon after the end of World War II that group dynamics, as a small group behavioral science, was introduced into Japan (Misumi, 1985). In 1949, the Japanese Group Dynamics Association was established at Kyushu University in Fukuoka. Since then, many laboratory experiments and field researches on the effectiveness of leadership and of participative decision making upon employees' motivation to work have been accumulated (Misumi, 1985). Small group activities like QC circles and ZD groups that have current popularity in Japan, however, are not necessarily matched by the available basic research on the subject. Nevertheless, the past five years have seen the publication of a variety of interesting suggestive findings. Thus Onglatco and Matsui (1984) investigated the effect of QC circle involvement upon performance effectiveness of the branch office, and work motivation and satisfaction of employees in a commercial bank. The analysis by cross-lagged correlation suggested that a high level of quality circle involvement led to improved performance at branch and section levels. And, for higher circle involvement, such factors as a cooperative atmosphere among members, a high level of performance orientation, appropriate behavior of the circle leader, and management attitudes toward circle activities were needed. It was also revealed that the effect of circle involvement on work motivation and satisfaction was moderated by circle members' growth needs.

Onglatco (1985) also contrasted 149 QC circles of a commercial bank in Japan and 66 circles of a manufacturing company in the Philippines. Circle activity had been ongoing at an average of more than 6 and 1.25 years for the Japanese and Filipino samples, respectively. Both Japanese and Filipino managers tended to see a positive contribution of circle activity towards the attainment of organizational goals. As for employees, Japanese members evaluated favorably the circle activity as a chance for work review, as enhancing thinking and judgment, and as self-beneficial. On the other hand, a majority of these same Japanese workers regarded participation in circle activities outside the scope of their work and expressed as their opinion that these activities were not voluntary, but compulsory. This was contrary to the widespread belief that activities with respect to quality circles are voluntary activities. At the same time, the majority of Filipino members were more favorably disposed toward QC activities. They preferred to continue being engaged in circle activities that were seen to be self-beneficial and interesting. The clear differences in attitudes toward QC activities between Filipino and Japanese can be interpreted in terms of the shorter duration of circle activity among the Filipinos and the higher discretion they had on whether or not to participate.

Onglatco's work points to some of the problems with small group activities in Japan. The first problem concerns the self-effacement of the individual that the small group activities may have. Continued group activity brings accumulated work improvements that lead to the optimization of the work procedures and to minimum costs. As improvement approaches near the maximum level, the room for further improvement disappears.

The mannerism and formality in their activities (JIVTA, 1982) is another problem which contributes to the loss of vitality as time elapses. The clear differences of attitudes toward group activities between the Japanese and Filipino samples seems to have emerged partially as a consequence of this.

A further problem involves compulsory attendance. As noted before, Japanese members tended to consider the activity as compulsory. Employees stated that they were forced to engage in the activity only for the sake of the requirement from management. As a result of compulsory implementation, Onglatco (1985) warned that mental health problems among members have begun to appear.

Another problem has to do with the rewards distributed by a company as a return for employees' contribution through small group activities. Employees make an effort in activities that often leads to enormous cost savings on the part of organizations. In Japan, however, employees are seldom provided any kind of financial rewards for their contribution. This is likely to make employees less motivated to engage in QC and related activities in the long run. [. . .]

Comments for future research

Motivation theory has tended to focus on individual processes. The performance of organizations, however, is frequently misunderstood, not for lack of study of individual motivation, but for lack of study of motivation at the group level. Major emphasis of future research should go into investigating how specific individual motivation combines to create collective motivation at the group level. Lawler (1982) made one step in this direction and suggested that collectively oriented behavior is motivating if it contributes to organizational performance that, in turn, is linked to intrinsic and extrinsic rewards received by the individual. Then, we may also be able to acquire useful suggestions from social psychological studies of altruistic behavior (Rushton and Sorentino, 1981), social facilitation (Zajonc, 1965), and social loafing (Latane and Harkins, 1979).

References

Adler, S., Skov, R. B. and Salvemieni, N. J. (1985) 'Job characteristics and job satisfaction: when cause becomes consequence', *Organizational Behavior and Human Decision Processes*, 35, 266–78.

Algera, J. A. (1983) '"Objective" and perceived task characteristics as a determinant of reactions by task performers', *Journal of Occupational Psychology*, 56, 95–107.

Bhagat, R. S. and Chassie, M. B. (1980) 'Effects of changes in job characteristics on some theory-specific attitudinal outcomes: results from a naturally occurring quasi-experiment', *Human Relations*, 33, 297–313.

Boal, K. B. and Cummings, L. L. (1981) 'Cognitive evaluation theory: an experimental test of processes and outcomes', *Organizational Behavior and Human Performance*, 28, 289–310.

Brass, D. J. (1985) 'Technology and the structuring of jobs: employee satisfaction, performance and influence', *Organizational Behavior and Human Decision Processes*, 35, 216–40.

Buchanan, D. A. and Boddy, D. (1982) 'Advanced technology and the quality of working life: the effects of wordprocessing on video typists', *Journal of Occupational Psychology*, 55, 1–11.

Campbell, D. J. (1982) 'Determinants of choice of goal difficulty level: a review of situational and personality influences', *Journal of Occupational Psychology*, 55, 79–95.

Campion, M. A. and Lord, R. G. (1982) 'A control systems conceptualization of the goal-setting and changing process', *Organizational Behavior and Human Performance*, 30, 265–87.

Chhokar, J. S. and Wallin, J. A. (1984) 'A field study of the effect of feedback frequency on performance', *Journal of Applied Psychology*, 69, 524–30.

Cook, J. and Wall, T. (1980) 'New work attitude measures of trust, organizational commitment and personal need non-fulfilment', *Journal of Occupational Psychology*, 53, 39–52.

Daniel, T. L. and Esser, J. K. (1980) 'Intrinsic motivation as influenced by rewards, task interest, and task structure', *Journal of Applied Psychology*, 65, 566–73.

D'Arcy, C., Syrotuik, J. and Siddique, C. M. (1984) 'Perceived job attitudes, job satisfaction and psychological distress: a comparison of working men and women', *Human Relations*, 37, 603–11.

Deci, E. L. (1975) *Intrinsic Motivation*, New York, Plenum.

Erez, M. and Zidon, I. (1984) 'Effect of goal acceptance on the relationship of goal difficulty to performance', *Journal of Applied Psychology*, 69. 69–78.

Ferris, K. R. and Aranya, N. (1983) 'A comparison of two organizational commitment scales', *Personnel Psychology*, 36, 87–97.

Freedman, S. M. and Phillips, J. S. (1985) 'The effects of situational performance constraints on intrinsic motivation and satisfaction: the role of perceived competence and self-determination', *Organizational Behavior and Human Decision Processes*, 35, 397–416.

Furukawa, H. (1982) 'Intrinsic and extrinsic work motivation: a review of definitions and interactive relationships', *Japanese Journal of Experimental Psychology*, 22, 69–80.

Garland, H. (1982) 'Goal levels and task performance: a compelling replication of some compelling results', *Journal of Applied Psychology*, 67, 245–8.

Garland, H. (1984) 'Relation of effort–performance expectancy to performance in goal-setting experiments', *Journal of Applied Psychology*, 69, 79–84.

Gordon, M. E., Philpot, J. W., Burt, R. E., Thompson, C. A. and Spiller, W. E. (1980) 'Commitment to union: development of measure and an examination of its correlates', *Journal of Applied Psychological Monograph*, 65, 479–99.

Gould, S. and Werbel, J. D. (1983) 'Work involvement: a comparison of dual wage earner and single wage earner families', *Journal of Applied Psychology*, 68, 313–19.

Griffeth, R. W. (1985) 'Moderation of the effects of job enrichment by participation: a longitudinal field experiment', *Organizational Behavior and Human Decision Processes*, 35, 73–93.

Griffin, R. W. (1982) 'Perceived task characteristics and employee productivity and satisfaction', *Human Relations*, 35, 927–38.

Ilgen, D. R., Nebeker, D. M. and Pritchard, R. D. (1981) 'Expectancy theory measures: an empirical comparison of an experimental simulation', *Organizational Behavior and Human Performance*, 28, 189–223.

Ivancevich, J. M. (1982) 'Subordinates' reactions to performance appraisal interviews: a test of feedback and goal-setting techniques', *Journal of Applied Psychology*, 67, 581–7.

Ivancevich, J. M. and Smith, S. V. (1981) 'Goal setting interview skills training: simulated and on-the-job analyses', *Journal of Applied Psychology*, 66, 697–705.

Jackson, P. R., Paul, L. T. and Wall, T. D. (1981) 'Individual differences as moderators of reactions to job characteristics', *Journal of Occupational Psychology*, 54, 1–80.

Jackson, S. E. and Zedeck, S. (1982) 'Explaining performance variability: contributions of goal setting, task characteristics and evaluative contexts', *Journal of Applied Psychology*, 67, 759–68.

Japanese Industrial and Vocational Training Association (1982) 'Research reports on the actual conditions and practices of small group activities in Japan' (in Japanese), *Industrial Training*, 28(10), 22–37.

Keller, R. T. and Holland, W. E. (1981) 'Job change: a naturally occurring field experiment', *Human Relations*; 34, 1053–67.

Kemp, N. J. and Cook, J. D. (1983) 'Job longevity and growth need strength as joint moderators of the task design–job satisfaction relationship', *Human Relations*, 36, 883–98.

Kennedy, C. W., Fossum, J. A. and White, B. J. (1983) 'An empirical comparison of within-subjects and between-subjects expectancy theory models', *Organizational Behavior and Human Performance*, 32, 124–43.

Komaki, J. L., Collins, R. L. and Penn, P. (1982) 'The role of performance antecedents and consequences in work motivation', *Journal of Applied Psychology*, 67, 334–40.

Latane, B. W. K. and Harkins, S. (1979) 'Many hands make light work: the causes and consequences of social loafing', *Journal of Personality and Social Psychology*, 37, 822–32.

Lawler, E. E. III (1982) 'Increasing work involvement to enhance organization effectiveness', in P. S. Goodman (ed.) *Change in Organizations*, San Francisco, Jossey-Bass.

Lee, C. and Schuler, R. S. (1982) 'A constructive replication and extension of a role and expectant perception model of participation in decision-making', *Journal of Occupational Psychology*, 55, 109–18.

Locke, E. A., Frederick, E. and Bokko, P. (1984a) 'Effect of previously assigned goals on self-set goals and performance', *Journal of Applied Psychology*, 69, 694–9.

Locke, E. A., Frederick, E. and Bokko, P. (1984b) 'Effect of self-efficacy goals and task strategies on task performance', *Journal of Applied Psychology*, 69, 241–51.

Locke, E. A., Shaw, K. N., Saari, L. M. and Latham, G.P. (1981) 'Goal setting and task performance: 1969–1980', *Psychological Bulletin*, 90, 125–52.

Luthans, F., McCaul, H. S. and Dodd, N. G. (1985) 'Organization commitment: a comparison of American, Japanese, and Korean employees', *Academy of Management Journal*, 28, 213–19.

Luthans, F., Paul, R. and Baker, D. (1981) 'An experimental analysis of the impact of contingent reinforcement on salespersons' performance behaviour', *Journal of Applied Psychology*, 66, 314–23.

Matsui, T., Okado, A. and Mizuguchi, R. (1981) 'Expectancy theory prediction of the goal theory postulate, "The harder the goal the higher the performance"', *Journal of Applied Psychology*, 66, 54–8.

Mento, A. J., Cartledge, N. D. and Locke, E. A. (1980) 'Maryland vs. Michigan vs. Minnesota: another look at the relationship of expectancy and goal difficulty to task performance', *Organizational Behavior and Human Performance*, 25, 419–40.

Meyer, J. P. and Allen, N. J. (1984) 'Testing the "side-bet theory" of organizational commitment: some methodological considerations', *Journal of Applied Psychology*, 69, 372–8.

Misumi, J. (1984) 'Decision making in Japanese groups and organizations' in B. Wilpert & A. Sorge (eds) *International Yearbook of Organizational Democracy 2*, Chichester, Wiley.

Misumi, J. (1985) *The Behavioral Science of Leadership*, Ann Arbor, University of Michigan Press.

Neider, L. L. (1980) An experimental field investigation utilizing an expectancy theory view of participation', *Organizational Behavior and Human Performance*, 26, 425–42.

O'Brien, G. E. and Dowling, P. (1980) 'The effects of congruency between perceived and desired job attributes upon job satisfaction', *Journal of Occupational Psychology*, 53, 121–30.

Oliver, N. (1984) 'An examination of organizational commitment in six workers' cooperatives in Scotland', *Human Relations*, 37, 29–46.

Onglatco, M. L. U. (1985) 'Socio-psychological dynamics of quality circle involvement: research findings based on Japanese and Filipino samples', (Tech. Rep.), Tokyo, Rikkyo University Graduate School of Applied Psychology.

Onglatco, M. L. U. and Matsui, T. (1984) 'Organizational and motivational correlates of quality control circle involvement: a case study in a Japanese bank', *Journal of Applied Sociology* (Rikkyo University), 25, 155–78.

Pearce, J. L. (1983) 'Job attitude and motivation differences between volunteers and employees from comparable organizations' *Journal of Applied Psychology*, 68, 646–52.

Phillips, J. S. and Lord, R. G. (1980) 'Determinants of intrinsic motivation: locus of control and competence information as components of Deci's cognitive evaluation theory', *Journal of Applied Psychology*, 65, 211–18.

Porac, J. F. and Meindl, J. (1982) 'Undermining overjustification: inducing intrinsic and extrinsic task representations', *Organizational Behavior and Human Performance*, 29, 208–26.

Ross, J. E. and Ross. W. C. (1982) *Japanese Quality Control Circles and Productivity*, Virginia, Boston Publishing Company.

Rushton, J. P. and Sorrentino, R. M. (eds) (1981) *Altruism and Helping Behavior*, Hillsdale, NJ, Erlbaum.

Saari, L. M. and Latham, G. P. (1982) 'Employee reactions to continuous and variable ratio reinforcement schedules involving monetary incentive', *Journal of Applied Psychology*, 67, 506–8.

Schuler, R. S. (1980) 'A role and expectancy perception model of participation in decision making', *Academy of Management Journal*, 23, 331–40.

Shiflett, S. and Cohen, S. L. (1982) 'The shifting salience of valence and instrumentality in the prediction of perceived effort, satisfaction and turnover', *Academy of Management Journal*, 27, 877–85.

Teas, R. K. (1981) 'A within-subject analysis of valence models of job preference and anticipated satisfaction', *Journal of Occupational Psychology*, 54, 109–24.

Terborg, J. R. and Davis, G. A. (1982) 'Evaluation of a new method for assessing change to planned job redesign as applied to Hackman and Oldham's job characteristic model', *Organizational Behavior and Human Performance*, 29, 112–28.

Vecchio, R. P. (1982) 'The contingent–noncontingent compensation controversy: an attempt at a resolution', *Human Relations*, 35, 449–62.

Welsch, H. P. and LaVan, H. (1981) 'Inter-relationship between organizational commitment and job characteristics, job satisfaction, professional behaviour, and organizational climate', *Human Relations*, 34, 1079–89.

Zajonc, R. B. (1965) 'Social facilitation', *Science*, 149, 269–74.

6

Teacher stress and burnout: an international review

Chris Kyriacou

[. . .]

In the mid-1970s studies of occupational stress and burnout amongst schoolteachers were generally few and far between (see Coates and Thoresen, 1976; Keavney and Sinclair, 1978; Kyriacou and Sutcliffe, 1977). In the decade since then, the number of studies reported has mushroomed, and the international concern with teacher stress and burnout is reflected in recent studies conducted in countries as far afield as the UK (e.g. Kyriacou and Pratt, 1985; Pont and Reid, 1985), the United States (e.g. Farber, 1984; McIntyre, 1984), Israel (e.g. Kremer and Hofman, 1985; Smilansky, 1984) and Australia (e.g. Docking, 1985; Laughlin, 1984). Indeed it has also featured prominently in a recent report on teachers' working conditions published by the International Labour Organization (1981). In addition, there is a burgeoning list of reports published by unions of teachers (e.g. Armes, 1985) and articles in magazines and journals aimed at teachers (e.g. Gmelch, 1983a). Moreover, such published studies reflect only the tip of the iceberg in terms of current interest worldwide in this topic, as evidenced by the large number of courses/conferences dealing with this topic, and the massive international correspondence taking place.

A definition of teacher stress and burnout

Teacher stress may be defined as the experience by a teacher of unpleasant emotions, such as tension, frustration, anxiety, anger and depression, resulting from aspects of his work as a teacher (see Kyriacou and Sutcliffe, 1978a). Teacher burnout may be defined as the syndrome resulting from prolonged teacher stress, primarily characterized by physical, emotional and attitudinal exhaustion (see Cunningham, 1983). [. . .]

Models of teacher stress and burnout

Kyriacou and Sutcliffe's (1978a) model of teacher stress argued that the experience of stress resulted from the teacher's perception that (1) demands were being made upon him, (2) he was unable to or had difficulty in meeting these demands and (3) failure to do so threatened his mental and/or physical well-being. The key element in this model is the teacher's *perception of threat.* The demands made upon the teacher could be self-imposed or imposed by others. The most potent threats to well-being range from a fear of losing face or esteem to oneself, or in the eyes of others, to a fear of dismissal for incompetence. While a number of models of stress have been elaborated, the role of the teacher's perception of his circumstances and the degree of control he perceives he has over them seem to be widely acknowledged as crucial (see Phillips and Lee, 1980; Payne and Fletcher, 1983; Tellenback, Brenner and Löfgren, 1983).

Why the concern?

The international concern with teacher stress and burnout stems from (1) the mounting evidence that prolonged occupational stress can lead to both mental and physical ill-health, (2) a general concern to improve the quality of teachers' working lives and (3) a concern that stress and burnout may significantly impair the working relationship a teacher has with his pupils and the quality of teaching and commitment he is able to display. There has also been a recent increase in the number of teachers claiming early retirement pensions on grounds of ill-health precipitated by stress and attempts by teacher unions to include an element in their salary claims to cover stress.

Measuring the extent of teacher stress and burnout

Attempts to estimate how widespread and how severe are teacher stress and burnout have been plagued with problems of measurement. [. . .]

Each type of measure has its own strengths and weaknesses, but overall self-report measures have proved to be the most useful. Kyriacou and Sutcliffe, for example, in a series of studies of comprehensive (secondary) school teachers in England, found that about 25 per cent of the teachers responded to their survey question by using the categories 'very stressful' or 'extremely stressful' (Kyriacou, 1980a). Studies worldwide typically indicate that a large proportion of teachers report experiencing stress or burnout (Cunningham, 1983; Farber, 1984; Fletcher and Payne, 1982; Smilansky, 1984). Similar survey-type data which have compared teachers with other professions have typically found that schoolteachers reported one of the highest, and often *the* highest, levels of occupational stress (Cox and Brockley, 1984; Nerell and Wahlund, 1981). In addition, self-reported teacher stress has also typically correlated with indices of mental ill-health (Fletcher and Payne, 1982; Galloway et al., 1984; Kyriacou and Pratt, 1985). In this respect it is interesting to note that, despite this, there is no evidence generally of greater stress-related ill-health (either mental or physical) amongst school-teachers compared with other professions (Kyriacou, 1980b). This may mean that they tend to 'over-report' stress, although a more likely explanation is that the school holidays provide a recovery period which pre-empts or mitigates the development of such illnesses; this is indeed a claim often made by teachers themselves (e.g. Fletcher and Payne, 1982).

Another anomaly is that self-reported teacher stress is negatively associated with job satisfaction only to a moderate extent (Galloway et al., 1984; Kyriacou and Sutcliffe, 1979a; Laughlin, 1984; Smilansky, 1984). As such, it appears that some teachers report both high stress and high job satisfaction. The explanation here may be that stress is only one of a number of determinants of job satisfaction (and vice versa), and that some teachers may find teaching satisfying in spite of stress, or even because of it. Of particular interest is Blase's (1982) study which indicates that a number of teachers lower their level of job involvement (i.e. the time and energy they devote to their work) as a result of experiencing stress, but that such action tends to *increase* (rather than decrease) their likelihood of future burnout.

Two other frequently discussed correlates of teacher stress are absentee-ism and a desire to leave teaching. In fact correlations between self-reported teacher stress and absenteeism are typically low or non-significant (Galloway et al., 1984; Kyriacou and Sutcliffe, 1979a). This probably reflects the fact that absenteeism is subject to a number of social factors, and not least to the possibility that absenteeism may reduce stress for some teachers. Intention to leave teaching is typically associated with self-reported teacher stress (Kyriacou and Sutcliffe, 1979a), although actual resignations or early retire-ments are influenced by too many other factors for a consistent relationship to be identified.

Sources of stress

There has now been a vast number of studies identifying the main sources of stress facing teachers (e.g. Dunham, 1984; Farber, 1984; Galloway et al., 1984; Kremer-Hayon and Kurtz, 1985; Kyriacou and Sutcliffe, 1978b; Moracco, Danford and D'Arienzo, 1982; Pratt, 1978; Schwab, 1983; Smilansky, 1984). Most people unfamiliar with the literature may expect disruptive pupils to be the main source of stress, and indeed many books dealing with disruptive pupils now have a chapter explicitly devoted to teacher stress (e.g. Galloway et al., 1982; Laslett and Smith, 1984). As such, it is surprising to find that pupils' poor attitudes towards work, and too heavy a workload, have been generally found to be the main sources of stress, and not disruptive behaviour by pupils *per se* (although in a few studies disruptive behaviour did appear highest). In part, this reflects the fact that it is the insidious day-to-day sources of stress with their cumulative effect, and not the less frequent but occasionally intense sources of stress, which teachers are most concerned with. It would however be somewhat simplistic and naïve to attempt to list the main sources of stress indicated by these studies in some sort of order since each study must be placed in its own context. What can be said is that there are a large number of sources of teacher stress which include relationships with colleagues, aspects of working conditions, pupil mis-behaviour, salary, status and role conflict. The main sources of stress for any individual teacher or generally for staff in any particular school varies greatly. Overall it is perhaps the general level of alertness and vigilance required by teachers in meeting the potentially threatening variety of demands made upon them that constitutes the essence of why the experience of stress and burnout is so prevalent.

Personality factors

A number of studies have sought to explore the relationship between teacher personality and stress/burnout. Two factors have made such research dif-ficult: first, that teachers are in part a self-selecting group of those who chose to enter the profession, and secondly, that those teachers currently in post represent a survival propulation of those who have remained as a result of a complex set of factors.

Biographical characteristics such as sex, age, length of teaching experi-ence and post held in the school have received a great deal of attention. Overall such differences do not appear to be related to stress and burnout in a consistent manner (see Kyriacou and Sutcliffe, 1978b; Laughlin, 1984). Nevertheless, such biographical characteristics are certainly important re-garding the sources of stress reported, and in moderating the association between other variables.

Given the importance of the teacher's perception of threat and control regarding the experience of stress, the personality dimension of 'locus of control' has been widely explored. This dimension refers to a continuum ranging from those who believe that things in one's life are largely within one's control (a belief in internal control) and those who believe they are generally outside one's control and primarily influenced by luck, fate or powerful others (a belief in external control). There is some evidence to indicate that teachers with a belief in external locus of control report more stress and may be more stress-prone (McIntyre, 1984; Kyriacou and Sutcliffe, 1979b).

A recent study by Kremer and Hofmann (1985) interestingly reported a significant negative correlation between teacher burnout and the teacher's strength of professional identity. However, it is unclear whether strength of identity may act as a barrier to burnout or whether its gradual decline may constitute part of the burnout syndrome.

Specialist studies

A number of studies have now focused on specialist samples of teachers such as teachers in special schools (e.g. Pont and Reid, 1985), teachers of retarded children (e.g. Beck and Gargiulo, 1983), teachers of particular subjects (e.g. Burke and Dunham, 1982), teachers at one school (e.g. Coldicott, 1985), student teachers (e.g. Preece, 1979), teachers in their first few years (e.g. Bashford, 1982) and teachers in a particular post or position, including heads of department (e.g. Dunham, 1978), deputy heads (e.g. Knutton and Mycroft, 1986) and headteachers (e.g. Brimm, 1983; Tung and Koch, 1980). In addition, some studies have explored somewhat neglected aspects such as comparisons of stress amongst teachers in different countries (Dunham, 1980) and the influence of school environments (Ahrentzen *et al.*, 1982).

Coping with stress and burnout

Particular attention has been paid to coping with stress and burnout (Dunham, 1983; Gmelch, 1983a, 1983b). Coping appears to involve two main strategies. The first is direct action, which involves positively dealing with a source of stress (e.g. devoting more time to marking to more easily meet assessment deadlines, changing the curriculum so that pupils are more motivated). Direct action is the more desirable strategy if such action can be effective. The second strategy is to use palliative techniques, which essentially accept the source of stress but attempt to mitigate the emotional experience of stress which follows. Palliative techniques fall into two groups: mental techniques that alter the teacher's perception of his circumstances (e.g. putting things in perspective, trying to see the humorous side) and physical techniques (e.g. relaxation exercises, alcohol, playing squash after school). While palliative techniques can be effective, if the source of stress remains present, then some stress will inevitably be experienced.

A number of studies have surveyed the actions teachers take in order to cope with stress (Dewe, 1985; Dunham, 1983; Kyriacou, 1980c, 1980d). Kyriacou (1980c) used a factor analysis to group coping actions into three categories labelled: 'express feelings and seek support', 'take considered actions' and 'think of other things'. He found that the most frequently used actions reported by a sample of comprehensive school teachers in England were 'try to keep things in perspective', 'try to avoid confrontations' and 'try to relax after work'. Dewe (1985) in a study of primary schoolteachers in New Zealand used a factor analysis to identify five categories of coping strategies, which he labelled: 'attempts to ride the situation', 'rational task-oriented behaviour', 'adopt a conservative approach to teaching', 'utilising colleague support' and 'putting things into perspective'.

In discussion of coping with stress increasing recognition has been paid to the importance of social support within the school from colleagues, and to some extent at home from one's family or friends (Fletcher and Payne, 1982;

Kyriacou, 1981). Unfortunately the culture of the school and a reluctance to admit to colleagues that one is having difficulties often means that many teachers are unable to make use of such support.

Studies which have looked at the effectiveness of in-service courses for teachers to enable them to deal more effectively with sources of stress have yielded equivocal results (Docking, 1985; Woodhouse, Hall and Wooster, 1985). In general, strategies aimed at improving teachers' professional skills and competencies to meet the demands of being a teacher have proved more successful than those aimed at developing psychological techniques reducing the experience of stress, but not consistently so. As such, most discussion of coping with stress calls for developing professional skills and understanding to identify sources of stress and deal with the demands of being a teacher, and utilizing effective coping strategies and techniques (Iwanicki, 1983; Riccio, 1983; Sparks, 1983).

Finally, it is important to note that discussion of coping has tended to focus on what teachers can do to mitigate stress as individuals. However, much attention still needs to be given to how schools can reduce stress for their staff by the adoption of those management practices, organizational and administrative arrangements, staff relationships, working conditions and curriculum processes that minimize those sources of stress within the school's control.

In discussion of how schools may reduce teacher stress and burnout (e.g. Fletcher and Payne, 1982; Dunham, 1984; Kyriacou, 1981) the most frequently advocated changes are giving teachers more preparation time during each school day, reducing the size of classes, better organization and communication within the school, an improved climate of social support, more effective programmes of staff induction and professional development, more recognition of teachers' efforts and a clearer description of job tasks and expectations.

Conclusions

Over the past decade our understanding of teacher stress and burnout has become much clearer. The priority now is to explore how such understanding can be channelled into fostering the reduction of stress levels in schools. This may enable guidelines to be developed concerning those individual actions and managerial and organizational practices which will promote lower and more acceptable levels of teacher stress.

In addition, however, it is evident that there are still a number of unresolved questions concerning the nature and causes of teacher stress. Of particular interest is the relationship between the experience of stress and those factors and circumstances which increase or decrease the likelihood of a stress-related illness being precipitated. A number of such questions deserve attention not only in their own right, but also because they will inevitably have implications for the relative effectiveness of coping actions used by teachers and for other strategies employed to reduce levels of teacher stress and burnout. Two types of study can be recommended here for further research. The first could usefully focus on the managerial and organizational practices adopted in a particular school in order to highlight more clearly how such practices can influence the nature of teacher stress experienced. The second could usefully focus on individual teachers' attempts to reduce stress from an unacceptably high level for them. Such studies could make a useful contribution to the consideration of how best to reduce levels of teacher stress in schools.

References

Ahrentzen, S., Jue, G. M., Skorpanich, M. A. and Evans, G. W. (1982). 'School environments and stress.' In: Evans, G. W. (Ed) *Environmental Stress*. Cambridge: Cambridge University Press.

Armes, D. (1985). *The Unhappiest 'Profession'*. Report for the Teachers' Joint Committee (AMMA, NAS/UWT, NUT) (available from author: 5 Ambleside Avenue, Bradford BD9, 5HX).

Bashford, H. (1982). *A Study of Stress amongst Younger Teachers in the First Five Years of Teaching*. Centre for the Study of Comprehensive Schools, University of York.

Beck, C. L. and Gargiulo, R. M. (1983). 'Burnout in teachers of retarded and nonretarded children', *Journal of Educational Research*, 76, 169–73.

Blase, J. J. (1982). 'A social-psychological grounded theory of teacher stress and burnout', *Educational Administration Quarterly*, 18, 93–113.

Brimm, J. L. (1983). 'What stresses school administrators', *Theory into Practice*, 22, 64–9.

Burke, E. and Dunham, J. (1982). 'Identifying stress in language teaching', *British Journal of Language Teaching*, 20, 149–52.

Coates, T. J. and Thoresen, C. E. (1976). 'Teacher anxiety: a review with recommendations', *Review of Educational Research*, 46, 159–84.

Coldicott, P. J. (1985). 'Organisational causes of stress on the individual teacher', *Educational Management and Administration*, 13, 90–3.

Cox, T. and Brockley, T. (1984). 'The experience and effects of stress in teachers', *British Educational Research Journal*, 10, 83–7.

Cunningham, W. G. (1983). 'Teacher burnout – solutions for the 1980s: a review of the literature', *Urban Review*, 15, 37–51.

Dewe, P. J. (1985). 'Coping with work stress: an investigation of teachers' action', *Research in Education*, 33, 27–40.

Docking, R. A. (1985). 'Changing teacher pupil control ideology and teacher anxiety', *Journal of Education for Teaching*, 11, 63–76.

Dunham, J. (1978). 'Change and stress in the head of department's role', *Educational Research*, 21, 44–7.

Dunham, J. (1980). 'An exploratory comparative study of staff stress in English and German comprehensive schools', *Educational Review*, 32, 11–20.

Dunham, J. (1983). 'Coping with organizational stress.' In: Paisey, A. (Ed) *The Effective Teacher*. London: Ward Lock Educational.

Dunham, J. (1984). *Stress in Teaching*. London: Croom Helm.

Farber, B. A. (1984). 'Stress and burnout in suburban teachers', *Journal of Educational Research*, 77, 325–31.

[. . .]

Fletcher, B. C. and Payne, R. L. (1982). 'Levels of reported stressors and strains amongst schoolteachers: some UK data', *Educational Review*, 34, 267–78.

Galloway, D., Ball, T., Blomfield, D. and Seyd, R. (1982). *Schools and Disruptive Pupils*. London: Longman.

Galloway, D., Panckhurst, F., Boswell, K., Boswell, C. and Green, K. (1984). 'Mental health, absences from work, stress and satisfaction in a sample of New Zealand primary school teachers', *Australian and New Zealand Journal of Psychiatry*, 18, 359–63.

Gmelch, W. H. (Ed) (1983a). *Coping with Stress. Theory into Practice*, 22, 1 (whole issue).

Gmelch, W. H. (1983b). 'Stress for success: how to optimize your performance', *Theory into Practice*, 22, 7–14.

Hiebert, B. and Farber, I. (1984). 'Teacher stress: a literature survey with a few surprises', *Canadian Journal of Education*, 9, 14–27.

International Labour Organization (1981). *Employment and Conditions of Work of Teachers*. Geneva: International Labour Office.

Iwanicki, E. F. (1983). 'Toward understanding and alleviating teacher burnout', *Theory into Practice*, 22, 27–32.

Keavney, G. and Sinclair, K. E. (1978). 'Teacher concerns and teacher anxiety: a neglected topic of classroom research', *Review of Educational Research*, 48, 273–90.

Knutton, S. and Mycroft, A. (1986). 'Stress and the deputy head', *School Organization*, 6, 49–59.

Kremer, L. and Hofman, J. E. (1985). 'Teachers' professional identity and burn-out', *Research in Education*, 34, 89–95.

Kremer-Hayon, L. and Kurtz, H. (1985). 'The relation of personal and environmental variables to teacher burnout', *Teaching and Teacher Education*, 1, 243–9.

Kyriacou, C. (1980a). 'Sources of stress among British teachers: the contribution of job factors and personality factors.' In: Cooper, C. L. and Marshall, J. (Eds) *White Collar and Professional Stress*. Chichester: Wiley.

Kyriacou, C. (1980b). 'Stress, health and schoolteachers: a comparison with other professions', *Cambridge Journal of Education*, 10, 154–9.

Kyriacou, C. (1980c). 'Coping actions and occupational stress among schoolteachers', *Research in Education*, 24, 57–61.

Kyriacou, C. (1980d). 'Occupational stress among schoolteachers: a research report', *CORE*, 4, 3.

Kyriacou, C. (1981). 'Social support and occupational stress among schoolteachers', *Educational Studies*, 7, 55–60.

Kyriacou, C. (1986). *Effective Teaching in Schools*. Oxford: Blackwell.

Kyriacou, C. and Pratt, J. (1985). 'Teacher stress and psychoneurotic symptoms', *British Journal of Educational Psychology*, 55, 61–4.

Kyriacou, C. and Sutcliffe, J. (1977). 'Teacher stress: a review', *Educational Review*, 29, 299–306.

Kyriacou, C. and Sutcliffe, J. (1978a). 'A model of teacher stress', *Educational Studies*, 4, 1–6.

Kyriacou, C. and Sutcliffe, J. (1978b). 'Teacher stress: prevalence, sources and symptoms', *British Journal of Educational Psychology*, 48, 159–67.

Kyriacou, C. and Sutcliffe, J. (1979a). 'Teacher stress and satisfaction', *Educational, Research*, 21, 89–96.

Kyriacou, C. and Sutcliffe, J. (1979b). 'A note on teacher stress and locus of control', *Journal of Occupational Psychology 52*, 227–8.

Laslett, R. and Smith, C. (1984). *Effective Classroom Management*. London: Croom Helm.

Laughlin, A. (1984). 'Teacher stress in an Australian setting: the role of biographical mediators', *Educational Studies*, 10, 7–22.

McIntyre, T. C. (1984). 'The relationship between locus of control and teacher burnout', *British Journal of Educational Psychology*, 54, 235–8.

[. . .]

Moracco, J., Danford, D. and D'Arienzo, R. V. (1982). 'The factorial validity of the teacher occupational stress factor questionnaire', *Educational and Psychological Measurement*, 42, 275–83.

Nerell, G. and Wahlund, I. (1981). 'Stressors and strain in white collar workers.' In Levi, L. (Ed) *Society, Stress, and Disease. Volume 4, Working Life*. Oxford: Oxford University Press.

Payne, R. L. and Fletcher, B. C. (1983). 'Job demands, supports and constraints as predictors of psychological strain among schoolteachers', *Journal of Vocational Behavior*, 22, 136–47.

Phillips, B. N. and Lee, M. (1980). 'The changing role of the American teacher: current and future sources of stress.' In: Cooper, C. L. and Marshall, J. (Eds) *White Collar and Professional Stress*. Chichester: Wiley.

Pont, H. and Reid, G. (1985). 'Stress and special education: the need for transactional data', *Scottish Educational Review*, 17, 107–15.

Pratt, J. (1978). 'Perceived stress among teachers: the effects of age and background of children taught', *Educational Review*, 30, 3–14.

Preece, P. F. W. (1979). 'Student teacher anxiety and class-control problems on teaching practice: a cross-lagged panel analysis', *British Educational Research Journal*, 5, 13–19.

Riccio, A. C. (1983). 'On coping with the stresses of teaching', *Theory into Practice*, 22, 43–7.

Schwab, R. L. (1983). 'Teacher burnout: moving beyond 'psychobabble''', *Theory into Practice*, 22, 21–6.

Smilansky, J. (1984). 'External and internal correlates of teachers' satisfaction and willingness to report stress', *British Journal of Educational Psychology*, 54, 84–92.

Sparks, D. (1983). 'Practical solutions for teacher stress', *Theory into Practice*, 22, 33–42.

Tellenback, S., Brenner, S. and Löfgren, H. (1983). 'Teacher stress: exploratory model building', *Journal of Occupational Psychology*, 56, 19–33.

Tung, R. L. and Koch, J. L. (1980). 'School administrators: sources of stress and ways of coping with it.' In: Cooper, C. L. and Marshall, J. (Eds) *White Collar and Professional Stress*, Chichester: Wiley.

Woodhouse, D. A., Hall, E. and Wooster, A.D. (1985). 'Taking control of stress in teaching', *British Journal of Educational Psychology*, 55, 119–23.

7

Sharing the vision

Gareth Morgan

[. . .] It is crucial that members of an organization be united through some shared understanding of the organization and its mission. This point was a clear and consistent theme in many discussions, carried out in my research on the response of Canadian managers to societal changes:

> It's absolutely crucial to have a good understanding – call it whatever you want – of why you are in business and what you are doing. The rapidity of change makes it all the more important. I think this is what the great successful organizations have in the key places.
>
> [. . .]
>
> There must be a philosophy in action – a philosophy of where we're going and of the way we treat our customers, employees, and other people, [a philosophy that emphasizes] that we work for the organization as a whole, not for individual bosses.

Sustaining this overarching sense of corporate direction was seen as one of the most important tasks – and given the turbulence of the modern world, an extremely difficult task – facing senior management. For as the world grows more uncertain, it becomes difficult to find and communicate that coherent point of reference that simultaneously energizes and focuses the efforts of the wide range of actors typically found in the modern organization.

> A vision!
> A mission!
> A corporate philosophy!
> A sense of identity!'

A set of core values!

A symbolizing presence!

Different executives expressed the nature of the focus in different ways, but in general agreed that corporate leaders need (1) to provide their organizations with an overarching sense of vision to help frame and direct the organization's efforts, and (2) to communicate that sense of vision in an actionable form.

Vision as a frame for action

There is an old adage that if you don't know where you are going, any old path will get you there. An innovation can be wonderful. But it can have absolutely nothing to do with where my firm is going. You have to have a vision of what you are opting into.

This point is crucial. [. . .] Proactive management can create a vibrance that allows an organization to recognize and exploit opportunities and challenges; however, this vibrance must have a reference point. Innovation and opportunity seeking cannot be ends in themselves, or they will lead to haphazard development.

The problem presents top management with a major paradox. They often need to encourage flexibility and innovation. Yet to develop in a coherent and ordered way, they need a clear sense of where they are going, which, when taken to an extreme, can stifle or constrain innovation.

It is thus no accident that so many executives chose to discuss development of a corporate vision in terms of the creation of a 'sense of identity', 'corporate personality', 'philosophy', or 'set of values'. These formulations allow a degree of openness in the way a sense of the future is formulated. They create a frame within which other things can happen.

When people have a good sense of what their organization stands for and where it is going, they can determine the course and appropriateness of their behavior and judge whether a particular innovation will resonate with broader aims. Through this framing process innovation can be encouraged and actively developed, yet managed so that balance is achieved between opportunism and realism. Employees can develop an instinctive feel for what is appropriate. [. . .]!'

Communicating an actionable vision

You can't communicate enough times and in enough ways why we are going where we're going. [In our organization] we discuss [this] so much . . . that we end up on the same wavelength. You can't do that with a job description.

[. . .]

It is often not enough to explain . . . you also have to define specific actions that will make future issues more tangible.

It is one thing for top management to develop a sense of vision. It is quite another to communicate that vision in an actionable manner so that the vision becomes a reality. This ability is a critical managerial competency.

Many organizations attempt to formulate and communicate their view of the future through a 'mission statement'. These statements have an important role to play, because they can be used to communicate the importance of key values, for example, commitment 'to innovation', 'to quality products', or 'to customer service'. But, as a number of executives noted, the danger is that these statements can become 'empty vessels' or rituals.

The attempt to couch mission statements in terms suitable for general consumption often makes them ineffective within the organization. They become like motherhood.

Hence the view of many executives: Mission statements may be important, but certainly are not sufficient to 'get people on the same wavelength' or let them 'hear what's being said', 'absorb the essence of the company's philosophy', and 'know what they have to do without being told' and with 'a strength of conviction and sense of common responsibility to make it happen'.

The really important competency lies in the ability to get employees enthused and fully absorbed with the corporate philosophy, rather than to follow instructions in a mechanical way.

[. . .] A number of specific aspects of the leadership process were identified as particularly crucial.

The leader as symbol and symbol maker

Leaders inevitably come to represent their organizations.

Their credibility and image are crucial. People watch and judge everything they do.

Like politicians and other public figures, their words and actions have a far-reaching effect, of symbolic as well as practical value. It is thus crucial that leaders ensure that their presence and actions send appropriate messages. For example, it is very difficult for staff to take innovation seriously if the Chief Executive Officer (CEO) exudes conservatism, even if the mission statement declares innovation a high priority.

Leadership and empowerment

You have to generate an 'optimism' and 'sense of the possible'. You have to be positive.

There are organizations in which a status quo 'holding pattern' philosophy may be appropriate. But most situations that require strong leadership call for some kind of transformation. Thus, it is important that the leader communicate the possibility of this transformation and move his or her followers toward the achievement of concrete results. Methods must be found to nudge the organization in the right direction, without dictating a detailed course of development and thus creating too much dependence on the leader. Leadership that *empowers* seems to be an important emerging competency.

Broadening the leadership process

Finally, there is the question of openness. How widespread should debate about an organization's mission be? In some organizations, central figures who are able to develop and communicate a corporate philosophy that is very much their own emerge as leaders. The leader symbolizes the organization and inspires employees through his or her presence. Vision and direction emanate from the top; the rest of the organization is concerned with interpretation and implementation. This type of organization can be extremely effective, but its success usually rises and falls with the leader. There is often a 'vacuum', 'succession problem', or 'lack of continuity' when the leader leaves.

In other organizations the process is more widely spread. Although the leader may be very strong and responsible for many initiatives, open debate is a corporate norm. This approach was well illustrated by a number of CEOs who described their attempts to create an atmosphere in which strategy evolves through debate and self-questioning. One CEO described his attempt to make strategic planning a process that mobilizes the inputs of line managers and creates a strong sense of shared ownership:

> [I believe in making] strategic planning a line function. There is a lot of value in this because it completes the circle of a bottom–up and top–down process where you're trying to be both reactive and pro-active in relation to situations. You can get more people involved in the process. You push in the direction you're working at together without saying 'Here is my vision', which is one opinion and may be wrong. The people who really know the business are the people on the line who are servicing the customer, producing the product, and so on. So I think that there is much of value in a group approach to strategic management. [. . .] One of the imperatives is to involve people in the process so that 'we think it's ours' rather than 'I think it's mine'! This participative action that creates a direction is important.

Other CEOs described the importance of cultivating an atmosphere that encourages people to think in an open and challenging manner and to exert an ongoing influence on the direction followed by their organization:

> I think that one of the great strengths of my organization is that of self-questioning – it is encouraged . . . and it makes us a stronger

company. It is a dynamic, driving factor [especially when] you have a group of people who learn that anything can be questioned, including the basic structure of the business.

[. . .]

This openness can broaden the leadership process and greatly facilitate an organization's ability to evolve. Nevertheless, the executives making these points were careful to emphasize that it is important to cultivate an atmosphere where self-questioning is constructive rather than destructive. Open questioning and criticism can provide the basis for learning and change; however, it can also be the emotional outlet for griping and allocation of blame. The line between the two is often fine. The latter must be avoided at all costs.

An important distinction was also made between openness and democracy.

> [The aim is not to create] a democracy. It is not a question of nosecounting. It is not a question of [asking] 'All those in favor?' [Rather], it is a question of [cultivating] the rigorous examination of [an] idea that will produce a clear vision – the right answer. That's not democracy . . . [it] is [more] analytical.

Leadership style is often very much a matter of personality rather than choice. As is well known, different leaders are effective in different situations. The views of executives involved in my research reflected this ambiguity, but they all converged on the importance of understanding the leadership process in terms of the development of *shared values, shared direction,* and *shared responsibility* for the future of the organization. These issues are likely to be the basis on which many important managerial competencies are developed in the future.

8

Reflective management: the key to quality leadership

Patrick A. Duignan

Introduction

The nature and quality of leadership in institutional settings is the subject of much discussion in recent literature on management and educational administration. Recent books by Peters and Waterman[1] and Bennis[2] point to the fact that, while business organizations recognize the need for 'leadership', many do not have effective 'leaders' at their helm. In fact, Bennis, in drawing a distinction between managers and leaders, decries the fact that most American companies are bankrupt when it comes to leadership. He argues that America is full of managers, but has very few leaders. This distinction between managers and leaders deserves some further discussion.

[. . .]

Recent literature on leadership in educational administration also tends to preserve this division between manager and leader. [. . .]

In this article, it will be argued that the maintenance of a distinction between leadership and management functions at the conceptual and/or practical level is counter-productive to our search for a practical theory of educational leadership. [. . .] What is generally referred to in organizations as management structures, functions and processes are best seen as mechanisms for the expression of leadership. These structures and mechanisms can be stifling and constraining, or they can be facilitating and enabling (due, either way, to the nature of power relationships in the organization or to the attitudes and/or behaviour of those in administrative positions). Leadership within an organization is filtered, transacted and transformed through the myriad brief, fragmented, everyday routines or 'chores' that are part and parcel of complex organizational life [9,10,11]. It is the way in which the filtering, transaction and transformation take place that determines whether the organization is vibrant, alive, successful and an exciting place to work, or whether it is dull, frustrating and a place to be tolerated only because it provides security and/or a salary or pay cheque.

[. . .]

A cultural view of leadership

The view of leadership taken here differs from the traditional perspectives presented in texts on educational administration over many years [. . .] Educational managers, like managers in most other organizations, are usually faced with 'complex problematic situations which are puzzling, troubling and uncertain'[14] (p. 40). Specialized management knowledge and techniques are usually inadequate in a context of uncertainty. When means as well as ends are problematic in an organizational setting, there is often no 'one best way' to manage or to lead. [. . .]

Ends are never clear-cut; they must be interpreted. Means are never content free. Those who espouse a management science philosophy tend to view organizational ends as 'givens' and management practice as primarily concerned with the rational selection of the 'best' means to achieve these ends. In their search for the science of management, they regard the practice of management as merely the application of standardized, value-free techniques in the pursuit of efficiency. However, as Fay[15] points out, efficiency itself is not a value-free term. In attempting to choose the most efficient means we have to ask 'efficient in terms of what? – monetary cost? human labour? suffering? time?' (p. 50).

Management practices are as much concerned with values as are so-called leadership activities. In a dynamic cultural context, all organizational members are engaged in culture building through their daily activities. Trying to distinguish between management and leadership activities is as pointless as trying to separate means and ends.

In this view, management is more of an art and less of 'a science' as is suggested in some management textbooks. Through this *art of management*, which Schon[16] refers to as *professional artistry*, managers make sense of, and respond to, their dynamic and uncertain organizational cultural environments.

It will be argued in this chapter that, by using a cultural framework to understand the dynamics of everyday organizational life, management can be more easily portrayed and understood as an art form, and what successful professionals do as professional artistry. Further, it will be argued that managers can best provide leadership by doing what they do 'well'. Both management and leadership functions are inextricably intertwined and are part of the cultural dynamic of an organization. Treating them as separate sets of activities which differ in kind is an attempt to enforce an unnatural separation.

In the remainder of this chapter, a number of dimensions of leadership as a cultural activity will be explored and analysed. First, it will be argued that an essential part of leadership is the development of an *awareness* of self, of the nature of the job and its context, and of the roles of others. Second, leadership will be discussed as *reflective action*. Third, leadership will be viewed as an *interactive process* between and among individuals in an organization. Fourth, leadership will be examined as a *transformational* activity within a complex cultural setting. Fifth, consideration will be given to how the managerial and organizational structures, functions and processes *can be used to facilitate leadership* in the organization. Finally, implications will be derived for leaders and leadership within the school setting.

[. . .]

Leadership as awareness

Grob[17] extols Socrates' virtue of embracing

> . . . the *critical spirit* as the moral ground of all human endeavor. If as Socrates claims . . . 'an unexamined life is not worth living', then it is encumbent on the philosopher (leader) to subject him or herself to the practice of an endless humility: the practice of opening oneself to the limitedness of one's perspective and thus, in effect, to the finitude of one's being. (pp. 36–7)

Grob agrees with Hodgkinson[18] that the leader is, primarily, a philosopher whose first obligation is to seek answers to questions about the self. Hodgkinson concludes that, for leaders, there are certain 'knowledge imperatives or knowledge obligations', one of which is to *know oneself* (p. 211). The pursuit of this knowledge is, according to him 'an unending obligation, limited only by individual capacity'. Above all, he argues, leaders should be aware of their limitations and weaknesses.

Discovering and articulating one's beliefs and values is an important process in coming to know oneself. If, as has been argued in recent years by a number of authors [. . .] leadership is critically concerned with the beliefs and values of individuals and groups in complex organizational cultures, it is necessary for 'would-be leaders' to examine carefully their own value and belief systems, and use them as reference points in the cut and thrust of everyday organizational interactions. This does not imply that leaders should 'force' their belief systems on other organizational members, but only through an awareness of where they stand on important issues can leaders hope to engage in meaningful interaction with others. Hodgkinson[18] exhorts the leader to be particularly aware of the 'three value–actor roles which he shares with his followers: carrier, educator and judge' (p. 227). In explaining these three leader-followers roles Hodgkinson states that:

> As carrier he is the bearer and propagator of values, his own and those of the organisation; as educator he is both teacher and learner of values

. . . , and as judge he is critic and decider – the executive who visibly resolves value disputes and moves values into and out of dispute. .

(p. 227)

As part of understanding oneself, it is also necessary for leaders to be aware of, and try to appreciate, the various elements of the context in which they work. Hodgkinson identifies three other areas in which it is imperative for leaders to be knowledgeable. Leaders should *know the task, know the situation* or context of the task, and *know the group* (p. 211).

[. . .]

He argues that:

It is the highest function of the executive to develop a deep understanding of himself and his fellows . . . After all, the very stuff of the administrative fabric, the warp and woof of organisational life, is protoplasmic – human nature in all its rich diversity, complexity and frequent simplicity.

There are many obstacles to be overcome, however, for leaders to develop these skills of critical self-awareness. For learning and self-growth to occur, leaders often need to be freed from their habitual ways of thinking and acting. They need to undergo what Mazirow[26] refers to as a 'perspective transformation'. Boud, Keogh and Walker[27] argue that, for such a transformation to occur, we must become 'critically aware of how and why our assumptions about the world in which we operate have come to constrain the way we see ourselves and our relationships' (p. 23). We tend to revise our assumptions (based on our experiences) about ourselves and others 'until a stage occurs in which the assumptions become transformed'. Such transformations occur through a process of reflection on action which leads to growth and learning.

Leadership as reflective action

An important emphasis in Hodgkinson's philosophical definition of leadership is that of reflective action. Using Aristotle's concept of praxis (a combination of man's distinctive ways of knowing and modes of action), Hodgkinson suggests that philosophy-in-action combines 'consciousness or reflection on the one hand and behaviour and commitment on the other'. Praxis implies 'the conscious reflective intentional action of man' and is the bridge between theory and practice – between reflection, analysis and action. Praxis is, according to Hodgkinson, the 'quintessence' of leadership, and it is in the end what must be 'explicated because it is the true link between theory and practice' (p. 56). It is 'the bridging sector of administrative (leadership) process' that links administration (leadership) to management in the general sense. (Hodgkinson uses the terms administration and leadership synonymously.)

Through such reflection in – and on – action, leaders build up a repertoire of exemplars of practice[14,16,28]. In uncertain, unstable and unique situations (typical of modern organizational settings), leaders select from their repertoire specific strategies and techniques appropriate to the nature of the problem setting. Through such reflection-on-practice, leaders build their theories-in-action[14] to guide their new practice. Such theories are used not as prescriptions for behaviour, but to 'provide alternative frames for reinterpreting concrete experiences'[29] (p. 3). If practitioners have such a theory, they use it to guide their reflection-in-action[14] (p. 274).

It is through a process of reflective awareness of past practice that present practice can be improved. Oberg and Field[29] argue that practitioners 'who are thoughtful about the source and reasons for their actions are open to other possibilities – other actions, other reasons, other sensitivities, other understandings, other commitments and strivings' (p. 4). Leaders reflect-on-practice and on their theoretical constructions of practice in order to make sense of their organizational reality. Such 'theoretical reflectivity'[27] is essential if perspective transformation is to occur.

A major message in these writings is that, for improvement in practice to occur, leaders (indeed any practitioners) must constantly reassess their practical knowledge to ensure that their theories-in-action are effective guides for their professional conduct. Successful practitioners use such theories as frameworks for interpreting and reinterpreting actual practice with the purpose of improving it. Such reflection and reassessment is essential when mangers have to respond to new, unique, often confusing and ambiguous problem situations. Tried and true methods may work in such situations, but unless managers are constantly alert to the possibility that new conditions and situations may require new and perhaps creative remedies, they are likely to find that their management efforts may not have the desired effects. Such is the nature of professional artistry in action.

Reflection, while essential for learning, will not on its own, however, ensure that organizational purposes are achieved. Leaders usually must work through or with others in order to achieve organizational goals. The quality of this interaction is an important feature of leadership in organizations.

Leadership as interaction: A dialectic perspective

A number of authors have proposed that leadership is, at least partially, a dialectical or dialogical process [. . .]. Watkins[13] argues that 'leadership should be seen as a processual dialectical relationship which can offer insights on the production, reproduction and demise of certain organizational practices and structures' (p. 34). A basic assumption of the dialectical perspective is that leadership does not reside within any one individual, but is a product of the ongoing process of interaction and negotiation which is part of the cultural activity of an organization. Watkins argues that a dialectic view of leadership within a school 'involves the consideration of all human agents –

pupils, parents, teachers, support staff, as well as the principal' as they go about the construction and reconstruction of the reality of living together in an organizational setting. The dialectic perspective focuses on the interaction of individuals and groups as they try to come to terms with the constraining or enabling structure of the institution. This ongoing dialectical interaction between people and structures 'implies that both are continuously "becoming" in time and space, as the dialectics of practice and structure unfold' (p. 34).

In situations of uncertainty, where leaders are faced with competing values, theories and confused and/or ambiguous ends, their 'best bet' is to try to discover common ground or shared problems, what Walker[30] refers to as *touchstone*. Leaders should endeavour to 'extract common standards from overlapping accounts of shared problems' or from 'shared areas of the theoretical frameworks of participants' (p. 9). Successful leaders typically move from 'shared problems, through shared standards of enquiry and justification to, hopefully, shared solutions' (p. 15). While Watkins and Walker differ fundamentally in their theoretical perspectives, they conceive of similar processes for organizational members to negotiate new policies, structures and practices. Touchstone is achieved essentially through dialectical processes. It is a process through which leaders can make judgements in choosing between incompatible theoretical assumptions or perspectives and practical options. Walker provides a lucid description of the application of touchstone:

> Once touchstone standards have been established, the very point of open-mindedness is that people are prepared to change their minds as well and frankly defend their own views and criticise those of others. The application of touchstone tests is aimed at determining which of the competitors (theories) is the best available solution to the shared problems.
>
> (p. 17)

He argues that leaders must be prepared to judge between competing theoretical views and then assume responsibility for the practical solutions generated from touchstone. Successful 'educative' leaders should, therefore 'be aware of, and capable of responding to the changing balance of relevant considerations, in both their horizontal and vertical relationships in the educational framework' (p. 13). Through touchstone, knowledge grows and the organization's learning system is 'fine tuned'.

However, leaders are often faced with the ethical dilemma of what the right thing to do is in a problem situation. Choosing the 'best' course of action in a context of competing values is difficult. As stated earlier, leaders may have to call on their professional artistry to select morally defensible solutions from their repertoire of exemplary practices. As Schrag[31] suggests: 'The administrator's dilemma must be resolved in a decision, but there is not a single "correct solution" to be discussed.' Precise, standardised management techniques may be inadequate or irrelevant. [. . .] This is why we refer to management as an art, and it is the reason why successful managers rely on professional artistry.

Schon[14] argues that the essential feature of successful leadership is to 'keep the dialectic moving' (pp. 253–4). He admits that the term dialectic is not in common usage in business organizational cultures, but he cites a particular organization in which managers 'talk freely about dialectic, by which they mean the surfacing and working out of conflicting views among participants in the development process'.

[. . .]

As stated earlier, an important role of leadership is critically to examine and analyse not only leadership practice but the context in which the leadership takes place. Any attempt to redefine leadership must come to terms with the realities of existing organizational structures and relationships. [. . .] Grob,[17] argues that leadership is in essence 'a dialogical movement in which participants engage in that process of critique – the love of wisdom – in which their very identities as leader and the led are continually in question' (p. 42).

The focus of Grob's argument is on the act of leadership, not on the person as leader. This complements Hodgkinson's view[18] that leadership is 'an event, not an attribute of a personality' (p. 228). Again, Hodgkinson reminds us that as leadership is essentially philosophy-in-action and 'since everyone has an inalienable birthright to philosophy, anyone can lead' (p. 229).

There is an unresolved tension in this article which warrants careful consideration. It is that between defining leadership in essentially in-dividualistic and personal terms (as in those propositions relating to self-awareness and reflection) and regarding leadership as a shared or communal act (as in the proposition on leadership as a dialectical and interactive process). The tension can be partly resolved by viewing leadership as an act which engenders certain types of relationships. The leadership act emerges from this network of relationships. It is not an independent act, inasmuch as leadership cannot exist without its interpretation by others. In this sense, leadership resides in the network of relationships which are generated and sustained through the leadership act. The leadership propositions that are personal in nature (self-awareness and reflection) apply to *all* those who are involved in the leadership act. Individual self-reflection may indeed lead to a leadership act, but it may just as easily be the other way around. The development of the skills of critical self-awareness and reflection is essential for all who contribute to the leadership act, not just those who are designated as leaders.

These emphases on the praxis of leadership and on a dialectical perspec-tive are similar to the notion of 'transactional leadership' proposed by Burns[33] and Starratt[24,25]. While transactional leadership tends to focus on one person (e.g. the principal), it is concerned that the transactions between all members of an organization, including those between the administrators and others, should be raised to a high moral level 'governed by principles of honesty, fairness, responsibility and loyalty [which are] values intrinsic to maintaining human integrity'[25] (p. 5). Starratt further points out that transactional leadership involves the leader in seeing to it 'that procedures by which people enter into agreements are clear, above board', and that the rights and needs of others are carefully considered in all transactions.

However, transactional leadership is primarily concerned with organizational members pursuing their own individual objectives. As Starrat points out: 'It involves a bargaining to aid the individual interests of persons or groups going their own separate ways'. When it comes to individuals and groups working together, with common interests, seeking common goals, a different type of leadership is called for. Burns[33] and Starratt[24,25] refer to this kind of leadership as 'transformational'. This view of leadership will be discussed in the context of leadership as a cultural activity which forms the focus for the next section.

Leadership as cultural activity

Several references have already been made in this chapter to the fact that leadership is an important aspect of the cultural activity of any organization. Before examining the nature of the relationship of leadership and organizational culture, the concept of culture will first be examined.

[. . .]

Common to most definitions of culture is the notion that its fundamental ingredients are the shared values and beliefs of organizational members which are expressed through myths, rituals, stories, legends and specialized language (often termed jargon), policies, rules, regulations and a variety of organizational structures. These expressions or manifestations of the culture are continually negotiated and renegotiated in the countless interactions that occur among organizational members every day. Culture is, therefore, in a constant state of flux, responding to the dynamic interplay of an organization's life forces. Jelinek *et al.*[35] make this point rather forcefully when they argue that culture 'persists and is changed by virtue of its continual (re)creation through the interactions of organization members, their shared interpretations and the significance they attach to what occurs' (p. 336).

Culture, then, is built through the every-day interactions of organizational members. Saphier and King[7] in referring to the development of school culture, point out that 'it is the way business is handled that both forms and reflects the culture' (p. 72). In examining the role of leaders as culture builders, these authors argue that:

> Leaders with culture-building on their minds bring an ever-present awareness of . . . cultural norms to their daily interactions, decisions and plans, thus shaping the way events take place. Because of this dynamic, culture-building occurs simultaneously and through the way school people use their educational, human and technical skills in handling daily events or establishing regular practices.

Saphier and King strike the nail on the head. Earlier in this chapter technical, human and educational skills were equated with 'management' skills. In establishing the nexus between management and leadership within a cultural framework, Saphier and King advance the proposition that:

> . . . leaders show their symbolic and culture-building skills through those same activities (technical, human, educational) and not in separate activities that are exclusively symbolic or cultural.
>
> (p. 72)

Organizational culture, it can be argued then, finds its expression, at least partly, through the management structures and activities of the organization. While these structures and procedures can act as enabling forces for cultural expression, they can also act as barriers and constraints, a point that will be discussed in detail later.

Leaders, as culture builders, work through the daily management structures and routines to achieve organizational purposes or end values. Daily management transactions are not ends in themselves, but means to higher ends (although some managers often treat them as such by enshrining procedures and rules). Leadership, in this sense, is above all else, concerned with uncovering the deeper meanings of human interaction in the organization. It deals with such questions as: what are the purposes or goals for which the organization exists? What does it mean to be a member of the organization? How is the leadership act best accomplished to help achieve common goals? How can organizational members pool their energies to achieve common goals, i.e. what structures can be established for shared leadership?

The type of leadership that is concerned with such questions is referred to by Burns[33] as 'transformative'. Starratt[24] points out that transformative leadership is a type of leadership which 'calls people's attention to the basic purposes of the organisation', and is, therefore, concerned with 'end values such as freedom, equity, justice, brotherhood' (p. 6). It is the type of leadership that breathes life into the routines of every-day work experiences. It recognizes the 'drama' that is played out in the organization each day.

Starratt[36,24] also alludes to this dramaturgical role in addressing the leadership role of the school principal. He suggests that the principal should develop a 'dramatic consciousness' about the nature of people's experiences in the school. The school setting is a stage for the everyday enactment of real-life drama. Students, especially, are making life choices on a daily basis which can lead them to come to conclusions about their worth as individuals and their place in society. Some, from their daily experience of the drama, may conclude that they are worthless, while others may view themselves as vital and valuable members of their school and society. What Starratt is arguing is that there is really no such thing as dull, routine, uneventful days, and the leader (or leaders) in the school should be aware of this.

It is the leader's duty, then, to make others conscious of the drama and facilitate all organizational members in their quest for meaning and in their pursuit of the end values mentioned above. In this sense, then, transformative leadership is 'an elevating activity that lifts people beyond their routine and pragmatic concerns to a higher common purpose'[24] (p. 6). It is not, according to Starratt, a question of asking people 'to *do* more but to *be* more'.

Bennis[2] also points to this transformative power of leadership when he suggests that:

> . . . it is the ability of the leader to reach the souls of others in a fashion which raises human consciousness, builds meanings and inspires human intent that is its source of power. Within transformative leadership, therefore, it is vision, purposes, beliefs and other aspects of organizational culture that are of prime importance.

A number of writers on leadership have alluded to the importance of leaders having this sense of vision and being able, through interactive processes, to share this vision with others (e.g. Pettigrew[37], Bennis[2], Sergiovanni[4], Starratt[36,24,25], Rutherford[38] and Foster[12]). Pettigrew[37] defines organizational vision as 'not merely the stated purposes of an organization' but 'the system of beliefs and language which give the organization texture and coherence' (p. 577). Vision helps to 'create the patterns of meanings and consciousness defined as organizational culture'. Sergiovanni[4] states that 'vision refers to the capacity to create and communicate a view of a desired state of affairs that induces commitment among those working in the organization' (p. 8). Transformative leaders communicate their sense of vision by words and examples. Rutherford[38] highlights the effects of such visionary leadership when he reported from the results of effective schools' research that 'when principals had visions for the future of their schools, the teachers described these schools as good places for students and teachers' (p. 32).

One further point about leadership as a cultural activity is worthy of consideration. Duignan and Macpherson[23] have argued that, by using a cultural- and value-based paradigm, leadership can be viewed as essentially educative in nature and process. They envisage an educative leader as one who challenges others to participate in the visionary activity of identifying what is worthwhile, what is worth doing, and preferred ways of doing and acting in education. He/she encourages educators to commit themselves to administration and professional practices that are, by their nature, educative. As Evers[39] argues, an educative leader is one who creates, promotes and applies knowledge. Duignan and Macpherson[23] believe, as Fay[15] has argued, that theory can change practice through an educative process, theory can help broaden the horizons of practitioners by increasing their self-consciousness of the conditions in which they find themselves. It is an 'enlightening' process which helps people see the opportunities for change and break the bonds imposed by habitual ways of knowing and doing. An educative theory, according to Fay, helps in

> . . . the transformation of the consciousness of the actors it seeks to understand, a transformation which will increase their autonomy by

making it possible for them to determine collectively the conditions under which they will live.

(p. 105)

Foster[12] holds a similar view of leadership. He argues that leadership involves being critically educative, which 'involves the merger of analysis and practice' (p. 21). Indeed, Foster argues further that a responsibility of leadership lies in critical education. He explains that, in his view, critical education involves 'the notion of power, but not "power over" but "power to"'. He goes on to argue that:

> The leader . . . must have intellectual power-to-analyse and power-to-criticise, and dialogic power to present. *The educative use of power is realised in the empowerment of followers*, an empowerment which provides the actors themselves with insight and reflection into the conditions of their existence and into the possibilities of change.
>
> (p. 21)

The possibilities for change! This is at the heart of any cultural activity. Through critical analysis, negotiation and compromise, the dialectic of leadership, leadership praxis or leadership as philosophy-in-action, the leadership act can become 'educative', thereby making all organizational members aware of the possibilities in organizational life.

Such leadership is 'empowering' in another way as well. Starratt[24] speaks of the need for organizational members to have a sense of belonging, a feeling of being part of a community, and a feeling that they have control, at least to some degree, over important aspects of organizational life. Leadership should help everybody within an organization to be somebody. It should help reduce feelings of anonymity and impotence, and facilitate the development of the sense of the possible. It should allow organizational members 'to dream the impossible dream', to see opportunities and potential in the routine and the mundane, to cultivate the art of the possible.

However, it is easy to get carried away and forget, or ignore, the fact that leadership does not take place in a vacuum. Daily interactions are mediated through roles, rules and structures for power distribution. Starratt[25] states that 'organisational structures influence the actions and meanings of people in the organisation, and in turn, people are constantly changing, adapting, modifying organisational structures and meanings to suit both personal and task-related needs' (p. 12). Organizational learning systems may also constrain individual growth and learning and the effective operation of the 'dialectic' and 'touchstone' processes.

A discussion of how management and organizational structures and learning systems can be (re)constructed to facilitate leadership is now presented.

Management and organizational structures can and should facilitate leadership

All organizational members spend their working lives carefully negotiating their way through a forest of formal and informal organizational 'do's' and 'don'ts'. Foster[12] puts the point well when he states that 'any consideration given to leadership as a construct must incorporate an analysis of context' (p. 18). He argues that structure in an organization is closely related to power. Quoting Clegg[40], who refers to structure as 'structure-in-process', Foster argues that:

> . . . the structure of organisations becomes a dialectual process where-in basic relations of power are confirmed through sedimented rules which are absorbed through what might be considered ideological rituals in the work place. This becomes the paradigmatic reality for organisational members.
>
> (p. 17)

Power processes are key factors in the negotiation, production and reproduction of social structures[13]. Any analysis of leadership and its possibilities must be sensitive to the reality of the distribution of power in an organization. To ignore this power dimension is to be naive. The freedom to negotiate alternative structures will, necessarily, be constrained by organizational power frameworks and other historical artefacts. For, as Foster[12] points out, 'organisations restrict alternatives' and frequently 'impose a system of control on organisational members' (p. 16).

The organization's learning system – the way knowledge is generated and cumulatively built up in the organization – can also either promote or inhibit growth and development within an organization. Kolb[41] argues that 'the most effective learning systems are those that can tolerate differences in perspective' among organizational members (p. 41). Some organizations have a culture in which criticism, reflection and assessment are encouraged and cultivated. Other organizations have norms that inhibit such actions. Schon[14] sums up very well the potential positive and negative characteristics of an organizational learning system:

> . . . managers live in an organizational system which may promote or inhibit reflection-in-action. Organizational structures are more or less adaptable to new findings, more or less resistant to new tasks. The behavioral world of the organization, the characteristic pattern of interpersonal relations, is more or less open to reciprocal reflection-in-action – to the surfacing of negative information, the working out of conflicting views, and the public airing of organizational dilemmas. Insofar as organizational structure and behavioral world condition organizational inquiry, they make up what I will call the 'learning system' of the organization. The score and direction of a manager's reflection-in-action are strongly influenced, and may be severely limited, by the learning system of the organization.
>
> (p. 242)

Leaders must endeavour to 'create' organizational learning systems that encourage reflection, criticism, assessment and negotiation – dialectic and touchstone processes. They must help to create the conditions within which such processes can occur. They must become 'agents of organisational learning'[14] (p. 265). They must try to build a culture in which all organizational members can appreciate the possibilities for change and contribute their talents in bringing about desirable change.

If leaders are to cultivate the 'art-of-the-possible' so that structures can be changed to make them more enabling and liberating (in a relative sense), it is essential that they develop the critical sense referred to earlier. Because, as Grob[17] points out, without this critical faculty leaders can easily find themselves 'in the service of fixed ideas or causes, and thus agents of the use of power in their behalf' (p. 39). If this critical process is not part of the leader's central armoury of philosophical tools, then, Grob claims, 'leadership "dries up" and becomes finally, the mere wielding of power on behalf of static ideals'. He goes on to argue that, as long as 'leaders succumb to fixed notions and static ideals', creativity is stifled. He advocates an alternative leader–follower relationship which 'empowers the follower – indeed, both members of the relationship – to that creative activity in which the horizons of meaning surrounding the issues at hand are perpetually stretched' (p. 44).

Foster[12] advocates 'emancipatory leadership' as a means by which organizational members can become involved in the negotiation and reconstruction of organizational structures. He proposes that such leadership, first and foremost, 'involves the demystification (penetration) of structure' (p. 19). It is the duty of leaders to develop an enquiring and critical stance and question the way things are. Foster is optimistic that the structures and 'sedimented rules' of organizations can be penetrated.

Bolman and Deal[42] are also convinced that structures are amenable to change and that they can serve symbolic and cultural ends. They argue that:

> . . . one purpose [of structure] is to express prevailing values and myths of the society. In many organisations, goals are multiple and elusive, the technology is underdeveloped, the linkages between means and ends is poorly understood, and effectiveness is almost impossible to determine.
>
> (p. 169)

Because of this condition of uncertainty and ambiguity, organizational members are often content to maintain a stereotypical organizational facade with traditional organizational structures so as to beam 'the correct signal of the day to the appropriate audience. The signal provides reassurance, fosters belief, cultivates and maintains faith, and keeps the organisation viable' (p. 173). These authors maintain that:

> Structures may do little to co-ordinate activity or dictate relationships among organisational participants, but they do provide internal symbols that help participants to cope, find meaning, and play their roles in

the drama without reading the wrong lines, upstaging the lead actors, or responding to a tragedy when it is supposed to be a comedy.

Structures, whatever their organizational purposes, are, after all, cultural artefacts created to facilitate organizational interactions (at least most structures are created for such a purpose). They need to be regarded as 'temporary', in a process of changing to meet new needs and new challenges.

However, there is no intent here to advocate a revolutionary approach to leadership wherein the organization's pillars and structures are brought tumbling down. Far from it! Starratt[25] points out that such leadership 'can be seen not as some explosive phenomenon that is anti-institutional, but rather one that requires an institutional framework for its fullest expression' (p. 18). Change takes time and leaders have to be sensitive to this fact.

If, as has been suggested earlier, structure is seen as 'structure-in-process', which is both a characteristic of the interaction of organizational members and a product of those interactions, then the development of alternative structures and forms is essentially a cultural activity. As leadership is also a cultural activity, it must be sensitive to its own framework or context which often finds expression in organizational structures. It is in the interplay of action and structure (action often facilitated or constrained by the concrete expressions of structures in terms of rules and regulations) that leadership and management find themselves inextricably intertwined.

The question still remains: 'Should the educational administrator be *either* manager *or* leader?' To put the dilemma more accurately: 'Does an educational administrator have to become less of a manager in order to become more of a leader?' How helpful is it to examine and analyse this question in such dichotomous terms as 'management vs. leadership', 'bureaucratic vs. cultural', 'strategic vs. tactical', and so on? If we regard leadership as the prerogative or property of an individual, or individuals, then perhaps this distinction is meaningful. However, if we regard leadership as an act, an event, and a cultural act or event at that, then thinking in such 'either–or' terms is not very helpful.

It is through the organizational structures, and the management processes and procedures, that the leadership act finds concrete expression. Individuals, even those in positions of authority who are expected to lead, when pooling their energies and efforts in the pursuit of common goals, work through such structures, roles and rules. If such structures are stifling and constraining, they must be critically appraised, and, if necessary, reconstructed to become facilitating and enabling forces within which educative leadership can occur as a true cultural activity. People and structures must, together, be in a constant state of becoming.

By using a critical, reflective, educative approach to leadership, structures, rules and management practice can become vehicles for the transformative action referred to by Burns.[33] In the interest and pursuit of the *end values* of freedom, equity, justice, brotherhood,[24] temporal structures and arrangements can be renegotiated and reconstructed. Otherwise, as suggested earlier, leadership will dry up and become the slave of static ideas.

For those who are saying 'pie in the sky', consider this. Even within the framework of the present organizational metavalues of efficiency and effectiveness,[18] and what these entail in terms of structures and power relationships, there is much room to manoeuvre, to negotiate, given the will, and the good will, to do so. We have many examples from the corporate and educational world from which to take heart. Such negotiation, reinterpretation, and reconstruction of structures and relationships have already taken place within what we would regard as traditional (and some would say oppressive and dehumanizing) organizations.

A number of implications for school leadership will now be addressed.

Leadership as a cultural activity: Implications for leadership in schools

First, leadership in schools should be regarded as an act. It should therefore be a shared experience, a communal act. The wisdom and skills related to the leadership act are not necessarily the monopoly of any one individual, nor are they, necessarily, hierarchically distributed in an organization. Teachers, students, parents, as well as those designated as administrators, all have a right to play their part in the leadership drama.

Second, structures, rules and regulations should be regarded as means to higher ends, and not ends in themselves. Structures and rules, where they are restrictive and dehumanizing, need to be negotiated, reinterpreted and changed to become facilitating factors in schools. Where they do not already exist, there is an urgent need for enabling and empowering structures to be negotiated – e.g. participative structures for teachers, students and parents.

Third, leadership *and* management must be viewed as a critical and reflective activity – philosophy in action. All who participate in school life must become more aware of self, of the task, and of the context in which they work.

Fourth, leadership in an educational institution must become educative. Teachers, students, parents, administrators must all have a desire to learn, to be taught. This is similar to Grob's notion[17] of the Socratic leaders who 'teaches no doctrine, no fixed body of knowledge: what he or she teaches is the desire to be taught' (p. 41). Through such critical enquiry, school members become aware of the opportunities, the possibilities. Leadership, then, becomes the 'art of the possible'.

Fifth, the school principal can play a key role in the leadership act. Initiatives must be taken, resources must be garnered, examples must be given. Who better to play the catalyst than the principal? He/she is ideally placed to appreciate the school in its fullness and, in terms of available time and access to the system, to act as facilitator in the transformation process that is an essential part of leadership as a cultural activity.

Sixth, just as leadership is a cultural activity, so, too, is management. These constructs are not at opposite ends of a continuum or, indeed, on two separate continua. They are inextricably intertwined within the school's culture. Management practice and procedures are vehicles for the leadership act when both activities are viewed as cultural action. Management done well is leadership in disguise. Peters and Waterman,[1] in their bestseller, really came to the same conclusion without actually stating it. Time and again they conclude that it is 'the 1,001 things done well' that distinguish excellent leaders from the others. There is no need for us to enquire as to the nature of these 1,001 things. Suffice it to say that they are what busy managers do every day.

One can therefore take issue with Bennis[2] when he states: 'Managers do things right. Leaders do the right thing.' Perhaps it should read: 'Leaders do the right thing and do it right!'

References

1   Peters, T. J. and Waterman, R. H., *In Search of Excellence: Lessons from America's Best-Run Companies*, Harper and Row, New York, 1982.
2   Bennis, W., 'Transformative Power and Leadership', in Sergiovanni, T. J., and Corbally, J. E., (Eds.), *Leadership and Organizational Culture: New Perspectives on Administrative Theory and Practice*, University of Illinois Press, Urbana, Illinois, 1984.
[. . .]
4   Sergiovanni, T., 'Leadership and Excellence in Schooling', *Educational Leadership*, Vol. 41, 1984, pp. 4–13.
[. . .]
7   Saphier, J. and King, M., 'Good seeds grow in strong cultures', *Educational Leadership*, Vol. 42, No. 6, 1985, pp. 67–74.
[. . .]
9   O'Dempsey, K., 'Time Analysis of Activities, Work Patterns and Roles of High School Principals', unpublished MEd Admin thesis, University of Queensland, 1976.
10 Willis, Q., 'The Work Activity of School Principals: An Observational Study', *Journal of Educational Administration*, Vol. 18, No. 1, 1980.
11 Thomas, A. R. and Phillipps, D., in Simpkins, W. S., Thomas, A. R. and Thomas, E. B. (Eds.), *Principal and Task*, University of New England Press, Armidale, 1982.
12 Foster, W., *The Reconstruction of Leadership*, Deakin University Press, Geelong, 1986.
13 Watkins, P., *A Critical Review of Leadership Concepts and Research: The Implications for Educational Administration*, Deakin University Press, Geelong, 1986.
14 Schon, D., *The Reflective Practitioner: How Professionals Think in Action*, Basic Books, New York, 1983.
15 Fay, B., *Social Theory and Political Practice*, Allen and Unwin, London, 1975.
16 Schon, D., *Educating the Reflective Practitioner*, Jossey-Bass, London, 1987.
17 Grob, L., 'Leadership: The Socratic Model', in Kellerman, B. (Ed.)., *Leadership:*

Multidisciplinary Perspectives, Prentice-Hall, Englewood Cliffs, New Jersey, 1984.

18   Hodgkinson, C., *The Philosophy of Leadership*, Basil Blackwell, Oxford, 1983.

[. . .]

23   Duignan, P. and Macpherson, R. J. S., 'The Educative Leadership Project', *Educational Management and Administration*, Vol. 15, No. 1, 1987, pp. 49–52.

24   Starratt, R. J., 'Human Resource Management: Learning our Lessons by Learning to Learn', paper presented to the Annual Conference of the Australian College of Education, Adelaide, September 1986.

25   Starratt, R. J., 'Excellence in Education and Quality of Leadership', Occasional Paper No. 11, Institute of Educational Administration, Geelong, 1986.

26   Mazirow, J., 'A Critical Theory of Adult Learning and Education', *Adult Education*, Vol. 32, No. 1, 1981, pp. 3–24.

27   Boud, D., Keogh, R. and Walker, D. (Eds.), *Reflections: Turning Experience into Learning*, Kogan Page, London, 1985.

28   Sergiovanni, T., *The Principalship: A Reflective Practice Perspective*, Allyn and Bacon, Boston, 1987.

29   Oberg, A. and Field, R., 'Teacher Development through Reflections on Practice', *Australian Administrator*, Vol. 8, No. 1, 1987, pp. 1–4.

30   Walker, J., 'Educative Leadership for Curriculum Development: A Pragmatic and Holistic Approach', in Walker, J. (Ed.), *Educative Leadership for Curriculum Development*, Educative Leadership Monograph Series No. 2, ACT Schools Authority, Canberra, 1987.

31   Schrag, F., 'The Principal as a Moral Actor,' in Erickson, D. A. and Reller, T. L. (Eds.), *The Principal Metropolitan Schools*, McCutchan, Berkeley, 1978, pp. 208–32.

[. . .]

33   Burns, J. M., *Leadership*, Harper and Row, New York, 1978.

34   Smircich, L., 'Concepts of Culture and Organizational Analysis', *Administrative Science Quarterly*, Vol. 28, 1983, pp. 339–58.

35   Jelinek, M., Smircich, L. and Hirch, P., 'Introduction: A Code of Many Colors', *Administrative Science Quarterly*, Vol. 28, 1983, pp. 331–8.

36   Starratt, R., 'Educational Leadership', presentation to a seminar for school principals at Catholic College Sydney, August 1984.

37   Pettigrew, A. M., 'On Studying Organizational Cultures', *Administrative Science Quarterly*, Vol. 24, No. 4, 1979, pp. 570–81.

38   Rutherford, W. L., 'School Principals as Effective Leaders', *Phi Delta Kappa*, Spring 1985.

39   Evers, C., 'Ethics and Ethical Theory in Educative Leadership: A Pragmatic and Holistic Approach', in Evers, C. (Ed.), *Moral Theory for Educative Leadership*, Educative Leadership Monograph Series No. 3, Victorian Ministry of Education, Melbourne, 1987.

40   Clegg, S., 'Organization and Control', *Administrative Science Quarterly*, Vol. 26, No. 4, 1981, pp. 545–62.

41   Kolb, D. A., 'Learning and Problem Solving', in Kolb, D. A., Rubin I. A. and McIntyre, J. M. (Eds.), *Organisational Psychology*, 2nd ed., Prentice-Hall, Hemel Hempstead, 1974.

42   Bolman, L. G. and Deal, T. E., *Modern Approaches to Understanding and Managing Organisations*, Jossey-Bass, London, 1985.

9
Leadership and the effective school

Steve Murgatroyd and H. L. Gray

[. . .]

In this chapter we seek to define the effective school in terms of the quality of interpersonal relationships which exist within it and to examine the role leadership plays in the development of such an institution. In addition, we describe an in-service training activity offered at Huddersfield Polytechnic designed to facilitate leadership in educational organizations. However, it needs to be made clear at the outset that the notion of an 'effective school' is grossly problematic. Reynolds *et al.* (1980) seek an operational definition in terms of the outputs of the school – attendance rates, reported rates for delinquency and academic achievement. Whilst focussing upon 'products' is a conventional way of viewing organizational effectiveness, in educational institutions such a focus is not adequate. There needs to be a process focus too. A school can be good at producing O and A-level performers, have a high level of attendance and low rates of delinquency and be an oppressive environment in which to work. An understanding of the 'effective school', if such an organization exists, will involve an appreciation of staff:staff relationships, staff:pupil relationships and school:other relationships. In addition, the degree of acceptance a person within the organization feels and the willingness to admit failure and embrace change all appear crucial to organizational effectiveness.

The place of the person in the effective school

In studies of effective helping relationships four qualities are regarded as essential. These are: (1) *empathy* – the ability to see another person's problem as if it were one's own without losing that 'as if' quality; (2) *warmth* – the vitality of sharing; (3) *genuineness* – the acceptance of another person's right to their attitudes, values, beliefs and assumptions and to be honest and accepting in transactions with others; and (4) *concreteness* – the ability to focus upon present issues rather than constantly looking back or to the future. Whilst different researchers use different terms for these qualities, these are both necessary and sufficient qualities for helping others (Rogers, 1957; Carkhuff, 1967; Lieberman *et al.*, 1973).

Schools set themselves up as helping institutions. Teachers and other school personnel speak of the school's role in 'helping students learn'. Networks are created within school to help the person make subject choices, to help them make career-relevant decisions, to help them cope with family disturbance or illness. Both the 'academic network' and the 'pastoral network' aim at helping pupils learn; helping them realize their potential; helping them cope. What is more, the helping role extends beyond helping pupils cope with present demands. The school also aims to help pupils prepare for future roles in the community. Helping is very much a currency-word in the language of the school.

Yet schools are rarely evaluated in terms of the necessary and sufficient conditions outlined above. What is more, these conditions are often regarded by teachers and managers in schools as potential disruptors, as recipes for revolution; as a beginning manifesto for pupil-power. One headmaster, in reviewing the research associated with these constructs, wrote 'whilst they may be of value in every other helping context they are not valid in the context of school: no pupil can learn whilst his teachers are trying to understand him from his point of view, trying to be warm and trying to be genuine. It's not in the nature of the school.' Another, following a similar review, wrote 'schools are not person-centred they are subject-centred', despite the voiced concern to educate the 'whole-person'.

There is a view amongst some who look at schools from the outside that they are primarily concerned with encouraging pupils to learn cognitive skills. The emphasis on academic achievement gives rise to schools not treating their pupils or their staff as whole-persons. Pupils are rewarded for imaginative compliance to the regime of the school rather than for being warm, genuine, empathic persons. Whatever the merits of this view, those who advance it view the position of the 'person' within the school as marginal to its purposes. One problem with this view of the school is that it assumes that the school is able to determine its own purposes and that it is desirable for personal development to be regarded as the key to these purposes. Schools serve many functions on behalf of constituencies not represented by those who occupy the schools' rooms. They act as regulators for the daytime behaviour of young people. They act as gatekeepers of knowledge on behalf of those who develop and sustain that knowledge. They are expected to promote employability even at times of high unemployment. Finally, they are expected to care for their pupils as would a careful parent. So many purposes and so many potential conflicts between them. Yet the point being made by these outsiders – people like Carl Rogers (1980), Reinhard Tausch (1978) and others (Aspy, 1972; White, 1974) – is that learning about a subject, like chemistry, French, poetry or maths, need not, and indeed cannot, be divorced from learning about one's self (Murgatroyd, 1976). The question that needs to be addressed, therefore, is the extent to which people in school are enabled to learn about themselves as well as the subjects they are studying. Another way of expressing this is to ask how much of what happens in the process of schooling is due to the people who participate in this process. There is considerable evidence that the achievement of pupils in a subject is a function of: (1) the quality of their interpersonal relationships with their teachers (Aspy, 1969; Dickenson *et al.*, 1970; Moon, 1966); (2) the quality of interpersonal relations with peers (Hargreaves, 1967); (3) the strength of their positive self-concept (Brookover *et al.*, 1967); and (4) the strength of their internal focus of control (Barr-Tell *et al.*, 1980). Whilst other features of the situation – resources, social support, level of intellectual ability – are also important, the features described above seem critical. What is interesting about these features is that they are intensely personal qualities: they are about people *not* about skills. What is more, these characteristics are best enabled by the use of the necessary and sufficient conditions mentioned above: empathy, warmth, genuineness and concreteness. Finally, they can be stimulated by leadership in the classroom.

Classroom and organizational leadership

There would appear to be a strong relationship between the style of leadership and type of negotiation within the classroom and that which exists in the organization at large. The classroom acts as a mirror for the relationships which exist in the school organization. Classrooms are not islands, they are very much sections of a larger community. Whilst some teachers are able to run their classrooms as if they were islands within the school, the pupils arriving in these classes bring with them the ethos of the school and their experience of its regime. Teachers seeking to run their classes in ways radically different from the way the organization operates thus have a great deal to do. One teacher working in a school run very much as a 'top-down' institution with a 'tells' style of management ran a class along the lines of a teacher-initiated negotiation group only to be constantly interrupted by colleagues saying things like 'I came in to quell a riot, I didn't realise that this is what you call teaching!' When the same teacher tried to run a participative assembly he was advised by the deputy head to 'stick to the well established formula of two hymns, a prayer and a bollocking!' In subtle but significant ways these and related incidents brought strong pressure to bear on the teacher to conform to the normative classroom behaviour expected of teachers within the school.

Reynolds (1976) has argued that schools may be viewed as arenas of potential conflict. Reynolds suggests that for many pupils in a school the aims of the teachers and their own aims are not compatible. As Waller (1932, pp. 195–6) observed:

> The teacher represents the established social order in the school, and his interest is in maintaining that order, whereas pupils only have a

negative interest in that feudal superstructure. . . . Pupils are the material in which teachers are supposed to produce results. Pupils are human beings striving to realize themselves in their own spontaneous manner, striving to produce their own results in their own way. Each of these hostile parties stand in the way of the other, in so far as the aim of either are realized, it is at the sacrifice of the other.

What is important to note, according to Reynolds, is that this underlying conflict rarely shows itself. He explains this in terms of the idea of 'the truce'. The truce is between teachers and pupils. Essentially it implies that 'the teachers will go easy on the pupils and the pupils will go easy on the teachers' (Reynolds, 1976, p. 133). The teachers will not try to exercise authority in relation to the non-pedagogic, expressive or character moulding goals of the school and in return pupils are cooperative in their classroom behaviour, showing most respect for those teachers who facilitate learning which is personally significant to them. Where such a truce does not exist – and Reynolds provides illustrations of such schools (Reynolds, 1976, pp. 134–7) – delinquency, truancy, academic failure, pupil violence and disruption are high. Whilst the form of the truce is similar between institutions, it clearly takes different forms in different schools. In some, it takes the form of having rules about smoking, uniform and chewing gum in class (for example) but rarely enforcing them. In others, it takes the form of project-based teaching which maximizes pupil involvement and their powers of negotiating what is to be studied and how it is to be studied. In others it takes the form of a large variety of extra-mural activities in which teachers stop playing the role of authority-expert and become more of themselves. This notion of truce highlights again the relationship between the nature of the school as an institution and the work of the teacher in the classroom. For when the truce is broken and, to use Reynolds's phrase, a school 'goes to war' against its pupils and seeks to enforce its control over the non-pedagogic, expressive and character moulding behaviours of its pupils, the effects of this campaign are felt in the classroom.

Just as a decision to 'break' the truce taken by a group or an individual within the school at large can affect the experience of the classroom, so a decision to change the experience of the classroom can affect the school. Teachers who initiate new curriculum materials and create a new atmosphere in their classrooms can act as a focus for change or for increased pressure towards conformity: teachers seen to be 'deviant' can be incorporated and made to conform or can be used as models for development. In the latter case they often develop a leadership-initiation role. Leadership can thus be a description of the relationship between the teacher's role in the classroom *and* her role as a classroom teacher within the organization of the school. Leadership in these respects concerns acting as an examplar and in so doing encouraging followership. The effective school permits the individual to experiment in her classroom, enables the dissemination of classroom experiences and encourages, in an accepting climate, the evaluation of classroom

processes. In short, it facilitates rather than hinders personal staff development. It is an organization willing to learn from the experience of any one of
its members, irrespective of their status.

Ineffective leadership

These views of leadership derive as much from observations of schools that
are clearly failing as from schools having effective interpersonal relationships. To illustrate some key points about the nature of interpersonal
effectiveness and the role of leadership in its promotion this section describes
some of the findings of an LEA advisory team's study of a school about which
there had been much local concern. We shall call the school Leasehold
Comprehensive.

There were local concerns about the school which precipitated the
decision to investigate thoroughly. These included: (1) the number of parents
opting to send their children to Leasehold as opposed to a nearby comprehensive was declining rapidly; (2) the failure of the school to attract an academic
sixth form; (3) a high incidence of internal vandalism; (4) a high level of pupil
truancy and staff absences; (5) an unusually high use of pupil suspension as a
sanction – sixty-four pupils were suspended in one term, twenty-eight of
them for a period in excess of five days; (6) the use of corporal punishment
was also high and had recently featured in the local press; and (7) the low level
of pupil achievement in the school.

In their investigation, the local advisory team talked with staff and
pupils and explored as fully as possible a variety of issues. They issued a very
full report (23 pages) and gave it a wide circulation. We are not able here to
examine the report in full. What it possible is a review of their findings as they
relate to leadership and the interpersonal qualities of the school. The following points are made in the report:

1 A feature of effective leadership is visibility. Leaders need to be seen.
   Ineffective leaders generally hide or remain unobserved. The advisors
   comment on senior staff at Leasehold that 'there is insufficient recognition
   of the fact that the observable presence, involvement and interest in the
   work of the school by those with ascribed status is of considerable
   importance in the generation of a corporate spirit and in the maintenance of
   a high level of morale'. They also note that 'the majority of teachers
   consider that the headteacher is too remote' and lacks empathy.
2 Leaders, to be effective, need to be able to communicate thoughts and
   feelings and describe behaviours to others. Ineffective leaders usually have
   poor communications skills. This was noted at Leasehold. The advisors
   say 'the quality of communication, whether written or oral, often leaves
   much to be desired . . . most of the communication is downwards only
   and the appropriate machinery for effective dissemination has not been
   established. The result is that many members of staff feel ill-informed and
   isolated and there is a widespread sense of frustration with, and suspicion

of, the leadership.' Having reviewed the written communications within
the school, they conclude that 'the style of presentation does not encourage
reading . . . it is frequently turgid, dictatorial and patronizing' and it
concludes that the leadership fail to 'recognize the teaching staff as pro-
fessionally trained people'. Turning their attention to meetings held within
the school, the advisors say 'instead of meetings enhancing the quality of
communication, they tend to generate tension, frustration, suspicion and
animosity' and they note that meetings chaired by the head are conducted
in an atmosphere described as 'less than cordial'.

3 Leaders need to accept others, not reject them. At Leasehold meetings are
held in a 'less than cordial' atmosphere since 'any points raised tend to be
dealt with in a patronizing manner which tends to discourage further
participation' and reduce feelings of mutuality.

4 One feature of acceptance displayed by effective leaders is openness and
genuineness. Ineffective leaders tend to be secretive and not genuine. At
Leasehold the advisors report 'an unwarranted degree of secrecy' about
matters which all staff have a right to know about. In addition they note
that the head 'presents a facade of democracy but frequently acts in an
autocratic manner'.

5 To be able to follow a leader others need to know why it is they are
following. Ineffective leaders rarely declare their intentions. At Leasehold
the advisors found that 'the headteacher had not presented nor explained
his educational beliefs' and that major changes in school policy were
implemented without staff being informed of the motives for the change or
their rationale. This led to staff feeling 'abandoned to face the problems on
their own' which has led some to 'walk away from problems' preferring to
'pass by on the other side'.

6 Ineffective leaders do not face problems but seek to avoid them. Effective
leaders face problems, share them and seek to learn from them. The
advisors at Leasehold note that 'major issues tend to be discussed at far
too late a stage because monitoring procedures in the school are either
inadequate or non-existent'.

7 Ineffective leaders resolve difficulties in a punitive fashion, effective leaders
seek appropriate responses to particular circumstances. At Leasehold
punitive responses are most commonly applied to pupils, as the figures
concerning suspension provided earlier show. As the advisors observe,
'the school's use of the power to exclude from school is symptomatic of the
school's general approach to the application of sanctions . . . positive,
constructive use of counselling is not undertaken as frequently as it could
be, whereas resort to the application of more serious sanctions is too readily
taken'.

Leasehold Comprehensive School seems to lack leadership and to be a failure
in terms of many different measures of school effectiveness. At the core of its
problems, according to those who have studied the school, is the lack of
mutual respect, warmth, empathy and genuineness. It is a depersonalized,

punitive institution. The failures of Leasehold are not the failures of a bold experiment with new curriculum or the weaknesses of a particular teaching method; rather, its failure is intensely personal. There are few personally significant relationships between working colleagues and real and effective blocks to the development of these relationships.

Training and support for leadership

Leadership, according to the analysis offered here, revolves around two key features: (1) the degree of followership a leader can generate by means of the personal qualities of empathy, warmth and genuineness; (2) the concrete nature of the action the leader and her followers wish to take. Whilst additional qualities have been examined briefly here, these two remain the necessary and sufficient conditions for effective leadership in the school. Our experience of educational organizations suggests that where these qualities are present the organization is more likely to be effective in achieving its aims and objectives. We have documented in the case study of Leasehold Comprehensive the consequences of ineffective leadership. They are that the educational institution not only fails to achieve its educational objectives but also fails to provide satisfactory environments for the development of personally significant learning or personal relationships.

Given the importance attached in this paper to effective leadership for the achievement of educational objectives in schools, it is necessary to examine two questions. First, can the skills associated with leadership be developed through training? Secondly, what support do leaders require to enable them to maintain leadership in the school? Before it is possible to examine these two questions four essential points need to be made.

First, the analysis of leadership provided here does not relate to role. Leadership is a term used to describe a particular combination of personal qualities ('ways of being') which both encourage and enable others to follow. The idea of a person having a leadership role implies that leadership is a set of skills which can be learned and developed. Leadership is not about skills, rules or procedures but about the person and the quality of their relationships with others. Leadership training and support need therefore to focus upon the person and her relationship with others.

Secondly, leadership as described in this paper is not about power. Rather, leadership is here defined in the context of openness, acceptance, sharing and exchange. Yet notions like 'power' and 'authority' are often equated with leadership. Leaders who see themselves as organizer, decision-maker, arbiter or supreme authority will experience difficulty as leaders since they will both create dependency and find themselves increasingly isolated and the subject of criticism. Our experience of leaders who see themselves as reformers and agents of radical change in their schools is that they unduly intrude upon the natural development of the school, disturb carefully built relationships which are more likely to lead to change if they are allowed full expression, work too hard and have difficulty coping with the responsibilities they seize for themselves. A reforming leader who drops dead in her study will be replaced within twenty-four hours by another person who will undo some if not all of her work. Leadership training needs therefore to avoid normative prescriptions about how to achieve reform, how to administer staff, how to write job descriptions. Instead, it needs to maximize the individual talents and personal qualities of those who see themselves as leaders.

Thirdly, leaders may occupy any position in the school. Whilst many expect the head and her senior colleagues to display leadership, there is a sense in which leadership is an issue for those who teach and a possibility that leadership may, at a given time, come from any point in the school. Indeed, there are many schools which have innovated in their curriculum as a result of the curriculum ideas and practices of young, 'novice' teachers.

Finally, training for leadership cannot be normative, prescriptive, skill-based or problem-centred. Instead, it needs to focus upon the personal and interpersonal qualities of the person. It needs to develop and sustain openness, empathy and warmth and to encourage exchange, acceptance and exploration. Though the aims may be pursued by means of studying specific problems or issues or by exploring key concepts and research, such training needs to be person-centred.

[. . .]

Conclusion

This paper has: (1) described the nature of leadership in educational organizations, (2) shown the importance of leadership to educational organizations in terms both of classroom activities and of the school as an organization, and (3) briefly described a programme aimed at facilitating leadership through training and support. One underlying assumption has been that effective organizations depend upon effective leadership.

Preston and Post (1973) describe three stages of management development which they refer to as the 'three managerial revolutions'. The first management revolution was the appearance within a hierarchical organization of management itself. In schools, the period of comprehensivization saw the emergence of a variety of management roles (head, deputy head (academic), deputy head (pastoral), year tutors) which were recognized as such. The second management revolution is described as 'professionalization'. The development of comprehensive education in the 1970s saw an increased emphasis on the professional skills of managers, especially in the pastoral care and guidance sector. The third management revolution is described by Preston and Post as 'participation', which they define as 'the inclusion of persons and groups involved and concerned with the diverse outcomes of managerial activity as participants in the managerial process'. The concept of leadership and the programme of leadership education described here falls very much into the participative frame. Given the demands upon schools and their need to embrace change and development, the participatory nature of management activity and the importance of leadership in the development of participation will increasingly be realized. Schools, to be effective both in terms of managing change and enhancing the quality of interpersonal relationships, need leadership.

References

Aspy, D. N. (1969) 'The effect of teacher offered conditions of empathy, positive regard and congruence upon student achievement', *Florida Journal of Educational Research*, 11, 1, pp. 39–48.

Aspy, D. N. (1972) *Towards a Technology of Humanizing Education*, Illinois, Research Press.

[. . .]

Barr-Tell, S. *et al.* (1980) 'Relationship of locus of control, achievement, anxiety and level of aspiration', *British Journal of Educational Psychology*, 50, pp. 53–60.

Brookover, W. B. *et al.* (1967) *Self-Concept and Ability and School Achievement*, Final Report of the Co-operative Research Project No. 2831, Michigan State University Press.

Carkhuff, R. R. (Ed.) (1967) *The Counselor's Contribution to Facilitative Processes*, Urbana, Ill., Parkinson.

[. . .]

Dickenson, W. A. *et al.* (1970) 'A humanistic programme for change in a large inner-city school system', *Journal of Humanistic Psychology*, 10, 2.

[. . .]

Hargreaves, D. (1967) *Social Relations in a Secondary School*, London, Routledge and Kegan Paul.

Lieberman, M. *et al.* (1973) *Encounter Groups – First Facts*, New York, Basic Books.

Moon, S. F. (1966) 'Teaching the self', *Improving College and University Teaching*, 14, pp. 213–29.

Murgatroyd, S. (1976) 'Counselling and continuing education', *Teaching at a Distance*, 6, pp. 40–5.

Preston, L. E. and Post, J. E. (1973) 'The third managerial revolution', *Academy of Management Journal*, 3, 17, pp. 476–86.

Reynolds, D. (1976) 'When pupils and teachers refuse a truce: The secondary school and the creation of delinquency', in Mungham, G. and Pearson, G. (Eds.) *Working Class Youth Culture*, London, Routledge and Kegan Paul.

Reynolds, D. *et al.* (1980) 'School factors and truancy', in Hersov, L. and Berg, I. (Eds.) *Out of School*, London, John Wiley.

Rogers, C. R. (1957) 'The necessary and sufficient conditions of therapeutic personality change', *Journal of Consulting Psychology*, 21, pp. 95–103.

Rogers, C. R. (1980) *A Way of Being*, Boston, Houghton-Mifflin.

[. . .]

Styles of Leadership (1962) 16 mm. Film (3 reels), California, Round-Table Productions.

Tausch, R. (1978) 'Facilitative dimensions of inter-personal relations', *College Student Journal*, 12, 1, pp. 2–11.

Waller, W. (1932) *The Sociology of Teaching*, New York, John Wiley.

White, A. M. (1974) 'Humanistic mathematics', *Education (USA)*, 95, 2, pp. 128–33.

Section III

Communication and negotiation

10

Communication: process and problems

William W. Savage

The school administrator devotes virtually all of his time to dealing with people as individuals or in groups. Therefore, communication with others consumes virtually all of his time. Van Miller recognized this fact when he said: 'Administration is first and foremost communication'.[1] And Jack A. Culbertson, Paul B. Jacobson, and Theodore L. Reller declared that 'in the broad sense, administrative behavior is communicative behavior'.[2]

The administrator's task can be viewed as that of coordinating human efforts designed to provide adequate programs of education for the pupils enrolled in a school or school system. The role of communication in this task was emphasized by S. I. Hayakawa who declared that 'coordination of effort necessary for the functioning of society is *of necessity achieved by language or else it is not achieved at all*'.[3] Although language may not be involved in all communication, it is a major ingredient in much of it, and the ability to communicate is essential when more than one person participates in any endeavor. [. . .] Today school personnel, including administrators, often 'confound' their own language by failing to communicate adequately and effectively or by communicating unintentionally in a manner that is detrimental to them and the schools with which they are associated.

Definitions

There is a variety of definitions of communication found in professional literature in the fields of human relations, education, and communication. Most of the definitions are given within the context of some specific type of communication and must be accepted cautiously in any examination of the school administrator's total responsibility as a communicator.

Wilbur Schramm stated that through communication a person is trying to share an idea, information, or an attitude.[5] Leland Brown said that communication is 'the transmission and interchange of facts, ideas, feelings, courses of action'.[6] [. . .] Communication [. . .] is both intentional and unintentional. When an administrator writes a letter or talks with a citizen, he is using intentional communication. When his appearance or that of his office conveys an unfavorable attitude to a citizen, unintentional communication is involved. Communication, therefore, is an exceedingly complex process in which people, behavior, and objects transmit information, ideas, and attitudes.

The process

In any form of communication there are a sender, a message, and a receiver. Furthermore, there are a means by which and a medium through which the message is transmitted. For example, a superintendent of schools (the sender) tells a community organization (the receiver) that its request to meet in a school building has been denied by the school board (the message). He transmits this information by sending a letter (the channel or medium) to the group. Seemingly, this process is quite clear and simple. Nevertheless, as Schramm's well-known diagram (Figure 10.1) indicates, actually it is a complex procedure replete with possible pitfalls.

Assume that the circle on the left represents the superintendent, and the one on the right represents the group that is denied permission to use the school building. As the diagram indicates, the superintendent must encode his message in words typed on a sheet of paper (the letter). He must decide

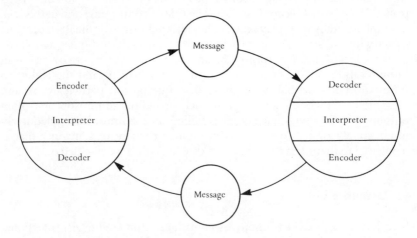

Figure 10.1   The process of communication

From Wilbur Schramm, 'How Communication Works', *The Process and Effects of Mass Communication*, ed. Wilbur Schramm (Urbana, Ill.: University of Illinois Press, 1960), p. 8. Reprinted by permission of the publisher.

what words arranged in what manner will convey the decision of the school board and the reasons for it to the group in the clearest and most constructive manner possible. He must deal with questions such as the following: What words should I use? How can I arrange them most effectively in conveying not only the board's decision but also an attitude or feeling that will cause the least amount of disappointment, frustration, and antagonism on the part of the group? Once he answers these questions, he completes the encoding process. The result is a letter which he has chosen as the medium or channel of communication through which the message is conveyed.

When the letter reaches the group, a decoding process begins. The words used by the superintendent are read. The readers may assign the same definitions to them that the superintendent had in mind; or they may use other definitions. They may grasp the attitudes and feelings that the superintendent attempted to express; or they may 'receive' quite different attitudes. In any event, when they have decoded the message, they place an interpretation on it; they react to what the superintendent has said. They may accept the reasons for the denial of their request, understand them, and conclude that the board had no alternative to the action that it took. As a result, they place a favorable interpretation on the action and actually feel a sense of appreciation for the serious consideration given the request by the board and superintendent. On the other hand, the readers may interpret the message in an unfavorable manner. They may view the board's action as discriminatory, unfair, or even a declaration of war between them and the board. Instead of interpreting the superintendent's words as reasonable and fair, they view them as arrogant and unreasonable.

The interpretation that follows the decoding process will determine the receiver's response to a message and the channel or medium used in conveying it. The response may be in the form of antagonistic feelings encoded in words that are arranged in some manner and placed in a letter which is sent to the superintendent and/or board. Of course, the response may not be sent directly to either the superintendent or board. It may be one encoded in words that become a strong letter of condemnation of the school system that is sent to the local newspaper for publication in its letters-to-the-editor column. Or it may not be a letter; instead, it may be in the form of behavior on the part of the organization's members. They may oppose school policy generally, attempt to exert political or economic pressure on the superintendent or board, condemn the schools orally in meetings or groups, or initiate destructive rumors. Regardless of their behavior, it constitutes a message that is a response to the superintendent's message. When it is received by the superintendent and board, they must decode it, place an interpretation on it that includes a decision with respect to the response (if any) that they will make, and encode their response in words, behavior, or some other means of communication.

Communication can be between two persons talking in an office or on a street corner. It can be through the exchange of letters, through a speech delivered before a group, through behavior rather than words, through perception of a place or object, and through media such as newspaper articles or other forms of mass communication. Regardless of its form, however, the process is essentially the same. And it is a two-way process. There are a sender and a receiver, but they exchange roles. As the process evolves, the sender becomes the receiver and again the sender; interaction takes place. Some writers declare that there is no communication occurring unless a receiver responds, but such a statement must be interpreted cautiously. A lack of any visible response on the part of a receiver, of course, may indicate that no communication has taken place because he did not receive a letter addressed to him, did not see some other form of a message, or did not hear what was said. On the other hand, his apathy may be a very clear response to a message. It may say, in effect, that he is not interested, that he is not concerned, or that he refuses to cooperate. Refusal to respond may be a truly belligerent response in some situations; communication is occurring regardless of whether or not the sender grasps the fact.

In some situations communication cannot be a two-way process in the manner in which generally it is described. For example, the appearance of an administrator's office communicates something to people who see it. The interpretation placed on what is seen causes a favorable or unfavorable reaction on the part of the viewer. Nevertheless, he does not respond to the office; his reaction is directed to the administrator who occupies the space. Therefore, in this situation the office is a means of communication through which the administrator, perhaps unintentionally, is transmitting a message. In this sense, communication remains a two-way process because the administrator sends a message, someone receives it and reacts to it, and the administrator responds in some manner to the reaction.

Means

People utilize many means of communication. A truly exhaustive list of them is not necessary in this discussion, but the following enumeration will illustrate the wide range that exists:

1 Words, oral and written (or printed).
2 Pictures.
3 Diagrams, drawings.
4 Symbols, such as arrows, shapes of highway signs, the pointing finger, punctuation marks, etc.
5 Colors, such as red to indicate danger or yellow to denote the need for caution.
6 Sounds other than words. A groan may be utilized to indicate pain or displeasure. Laughter often is used to denote pleasure, although it may result from embarrassment. [. . .] Inflection, emphasis, volume, and speed in speech often communicate more clearly than the words a speaker uses; in other instances, they are used to assign specific meanings to words being spoken.

7 Facial expression. Persons communicate feelings of anger, happiness, fear, love, disapproval, approval, contentment, etc., through facial expression.
8 Appearance. An individual's grooming and clothes convey messages. They may indicate wealth and success or poverty and failure. The appearance of a home, place of business, office, automobile, or school intentionally or unintentionally 'tells' people something about it, despite the fact that the accuracy of its message may be questioned. [. . .]
9 Behavior. Intentionally or unintentionally, a person communicates with other people through his behavior. He tells them of his fear by cringing or retreating. His posture declares that he is bored or weary. He communicates his happiness or exhuberance by jumping, dancing, etc. He demonstrates his distaste for someone by deliberately avoiding him, and he yawns when he is bored or sleepy. [. . .]
10 Regalia and insignia. The style, colors, and appurtenances on an academic robe may say: 'The wearer holds a doctoral degree in education from the University of —'. [. . .]

Media

Some of the means of communication, such as words and pictures, are utilized in the common media of communication. Although it is not exhaustive, the following list of media includes those utilized most frequently by administrators and other school personnel:

1 Face-to-face conversation.
2 Speeches (before groups).
3 Telephone conversations.
4 Speeches and discussions transmitted by radio or television.
5 Letters, memoranda, and telegrams.
6 Bulletins, brochures, pamphlets, and periodical publications (newsletters, journals, etc.).
7 Newspapers (news items, feature stories, advertisements, and letters to the editor).
8 Motion pictures, film strips, slides, and tape recordings.

Media, of course, generally are associated with intentional communication. Nevertheless, as the following discussion will illustrate, even a letter may be a medium of both intentional and unintentional communication.

Types of communication

Intentional communication

[. . .] This refers to the type generally considered in discussions of the communication process. When an administrator writes a letter, interviews a parent or teacher, speaks to a group, confers with a school board member, releases a news story to a newspaper, sends a notice to parents, or writes an article for an educational journal, he is engaged in intentional communication. He is attempting deliberately to transmit information, ideas, or attitudes. [. . .]

Unintentional communication

[. . .] This is when there is no conscious effort on the part of an individual or group to transmit anything; it is unintentional. Every administrator should be aware of this process. He should realize that at all times he is communicating intentionally and/or unintentionally with all people with whom he has contact. And he should realize that he never understands fully what he is communicating. As Edward T. Hall said, 'We must never assume that we are fully aware of what we communicate to someone else.'[9]

The means and media of intentional communication are those of unintentional communication. For example, an administrator may write a letter designed to transmit some type of information, an idea, or an attitude to someone else. In preparing the letter he is engaged in the process of intentional communication. Nevertheless, the recipient of the letter may see not only the message that the administrator has encoded in words but also a poorly printed letterhead, an inferior quality of paper, a misspelled word, incorrect sentence structure, or something else in the letter that conveys the idea that the administrator is ignorant, careless, or associated with a poorly operated, backward school or school system. As a result, the recipient may lose confidence in or disregard what the administrator has attempted to say. Thus, the letter has become a medium through which both intentional and unintentional communication has taken place. Unfortunately, of course, the unintentional communication frequently is harmful to the intentional.

Often there is unintentional communication in face-to-face communication. As an administrator talks to a person, his personal appearance may be transmitting ideas and attitudes to the individual that are quite foreign to the conversation. [. . .]

Perceived personality communicates. As a matter of fact, it is not one personality of an individual that communicates something to another person or group. Orrin D. Wardle, for example, referred to Oliver Wendell Holmes's idea that when two people converse there are six personalities involved.[10] In the case of each individual, there is the person as he actually is, the person as he believes himself to be, and the person as perceived by the other individual participating in the conversation. Frequently, there are significant differences among these three personalities. [. . .]

The importance of a problem of personality perception should be emphasized in any discussion of communication. For example, if a principal conducts a faculty meeting involving twenty-nine teachers and himself, each individual's real personality may be different from what he believes it to be and may be perceived differently by every other individual. The meeting of the group of thirty people, therefore, may involve 930 personalities![11] To find them communicating as well as they do is perhaps amazing.

Behavior is such an important aspect of unintentional communication that its influence should be emphasized even further. Perhaps the best known comment with respect to communication and behavior is the following one made by Ralph Waldo Emerson: 'What you *are* stands over you the while, and thunders so that I cannot hear what you say to the contrary.'[12] In other words, a person generally reacts to another individual's behavior more than he reacts to what he says. Andrew W. Halpin used the term 'muted language' in stressing the communicative power of behavior. He defined it as the 'language of eyes and hands, of gesture, of time and status symbols, of unconscious slips which betray the very words we use'.[13] He emphasized that 'man communicates to his fellow man with his entire body and with all his behavior'.[14]

The messages conveyed by a person's behavior are not necessarily detrimental. A school administrator's demonstrated concern for the welfare of his staff and the pupils enrolled in a school will communicate his beliefs far more eloquently than any written or oral statement that he may provide concerning his belief in the dignity and worth of the individual. As a matter of fact, many persons express the conviction that effective human relationships improve communication far more than communication improves the relationships.[15] [. . .]

Behavior, of course, may convey a truly correct message despite the fact that an administrator would prefer to avoid transmitting it. The story has been told often of a nationally known superintendent of schools who voiced undying loyalty to the principles of democratic administration in speeches that he made locally and nationally. His behavior in his own school system, however, expressed loyalty to arrogant and authoritarian administration. Perhaps the most disagreeable experience confronted by principals and teachers in the school system he administered was that of having to listen to him periodically as he extolled the virtues of harmonious and cooperative staff relationships.

[. . .]

Judgment and concealment

Much of each person's communication is evaluative in nature. He tends to convey his judgments rather than factual information. A teacher will note that 'Mary is an atypical child' rather than describe Mary's behavior and permit another person to interpret it. A superintendent who describes a person as an 'effective principal' does not say that such a description is his evaluation based on his perception of the person's behavior in a school with certain characteristics. [. . .] In fact, the hypothesis has been advanced that the greatest barrier to communication is the 'natural tendency' of people to evaluate.[28] Persons seem to feel that they must approve or disapprove anything that is said by an individual or group, regardless of whether or not anyone is seeking their evaluation. Therefore, 'I agree', 'I disagree', 'that's stupid', 'that's smart', 'that's right', 'that's wrong', 'that's true', or 'that's untrue' are characteristic responses in communication between or among individuals and groups. At times, words or phrases are used to conceal information or to direct attention away from significant facts. [. . .]

Similarly, phrases and statements at times are used to direct attention away from a more importantant fact. [. . .]

Omission of facts also avoids emphasis on important aspects of a situation. [. . .]

Upward and downward communication

In any organization such as a school or school system there is communication downward from the chief administrative officer, through subordinate positions, and to persons holding positions at all levels in the organizational structure. All communication downward, of course, may not originate at the same level or may not travel from the top to the bottom of the organization. A superintendent may address a letter or speak only to principals with respect to some matter. On the other hand, he may communicate certain information or instructions to an assistant superintendent who confers with the principals concerning it; in turn, the principals discuss it with the teachers in the schools where they are the administrative heads. Finally, of course, the downward communication may originate with a principal and be directed to the teachers. Regardless of the level of its origin, it involves communication flowing almost exclusively in one direction despite the emphasis on the two-way characteristic of the process.

Communication becomes truly a two-way process only when there is an upward as well as a downward flow of information, ideas, and attitudes. Every administrator seems able to inaugurate and stimulate the downward flow through staff meetings, memoranda, directives, letters, and even publications with such titles as 'From the Superintendent's Desk'. Upward flow, on the other hand, often is inadequate in quantity and quality because (1) frequently no conscious effort is made by administrators to encourage it, (2) administrative behavior indicates that ideas, reactions, and criticisms are not welcome, and (3) communication is affected often by a 'filtering' process. Any alert administrator can rectify his failure to encourage upward communication by (1) urging his subordinates to talk with him, (2) participating in social affairs that bring him in contact with subordinates, (3) welcoming even more formal communication such as letters and memoranda from persons below him in the administrative hierarchy, and (4) demonstrating that he really means what he says with respect to needing and wanting the ideas, reactions, and criticisms of staff members. The point should be emphasized, however, that unless ideas are considered seriously by an administrator, their source 'dries up'. And when constructive criticism is treated as a personal affront, it is discussed in the informal organization but no longer finds its way into the upward communication channels of the formal organization.

The problems created by the 'filtering' process – the elimination or deletion of relevant and important information – are perhaps more difficult to solve. Communication of accomplishments and personal successes flows upward far more fully and rapidly than do reports of problems and failures. Many subordinates view such reports as admissions of personal inadequacies or incompetence. [. . .] A teacher who has blundered badly filters out as much as possible the information that seems personally damaging when he reports the matter to the principal. Recalling that he urged the appointment of the teacher, the principal is likely to filter out any details of the report that seem to place him in a personally awkward position before he submits the information to the superintendent's office. And even the superintendent may filter out part of the report if it involves a matter to be presented to the school board. He cannot overlook completely the fact that he recommended the appointment of both the principal and the teacher! The teacher's blunder and the apparent failure of the principal to provide the leadership that might have prevented it may be viewed by the board members as evidence of the superintendent's incompetence. Therefore, as communication moves upward in such a case it tends to be rather thoroughly filtered. The 'full story' may not reach its destination.

In addition to the protective nature of the 'filtering' process, there is another use made of it at times by antagonistic and unethical persons. If a report moving upward can be filtered to de-emphasize mistakes, weaknesses, and blunders, it can be filtered also to distort the facts and depict a person's actions in a manner that exaggerates his weaknesses or mistakes. A prejudiced principal can so filter a report to the superintendent that a teacher's career in that particular school system can be ruined. A superintendent reporting to a board can so filter a report of some incident involving a principal that the principal either loses his position or has no opportunity for further advancement.

The only adequate solution to the problems of the 'filtering' process is the employment of ethical, moral, competent, and personally secure personnel who work in an environment where (1) admission of failure, mistakes, and problems is viewed as a mark of a truly professional person rather than a proclamation of inadequacy and (2) unethical and prejudiced conduct at any level is not condoned or tolerated by the school board. Perhaps few school systems can achieve this environment. In any event, only school boards and administrative staffs can develop the attitudes and constructive, ethical working relationships that result in such an environment. And they should realize that proclamations to the effect that the environment exists do not make it a reality. As indicated previously, words must be accompanied by actions that support them before the words are believed.

Despite the emphasis on downward and upward communication, there are situations in which downward communication can be so harmful to someone that it must be avoided. Staff members should be made aware of the fact that these situations arise from time to time. The problem should be discussed with them before an incident occurs, however. Otherwise, the mere discussion of it adds to rumors and speculation.

[. . .]

Rumor

A rumor is a report of some incident, situation, decision, action, or plan which has no known foundation. It is an unverified account of something; frequently, it is communicated with great speed. In fact, some persons have termed it 'the most rapid form of communication'. At times, it is accurate advance information of some decision or event that will be communicated officially at a later time. In these instances, often someone who is supposed to remain silent fails to do so. And, of course, some rumors are 'educated guesses' based on bits of available information pieced together by a perceptive person.

There are other rumors that have no foundation. Perhaps they result from wishful thinking. There is the likelihood, for example, that a disgruntled teacher may express the hope that the contract of the superintendent of schools will be terminated by the school board. Another person hearing him make the statement may repeat it to someone else but omit the important fact that what he heard was merely something that was expressed as a hope. Thus, 'I hope that the school board fires him' becomes 'I hear that the school board plans to fire him'. Certainly such a statement as 'I'll wager that they consolidate the two schools' often becomes 'They plan to consolidate the two schools'. And statements such as 'If somebody doesn't stop the move, I predict that they'll bus half of our children all the way across the city to integrate those schools' become positive statements of a policy already adopted by a school board.

When rumors spread

Rumors develop and are circulated in many situations, but they are more frequent and are transmitted more rapidly when the following conditions exist:

1 When people are afraid or feel threatened in some way.
2 When people do not know the facts and/or not know whether or not they are being given the full and actual facts.[30] Bass emphasized this condition when he said: 'When formal communications in an organization are infrequent, slow to be transmitted, or given less than complete credibility, rumors are transmitted instead'.[31]

[. . .]

The dynamics of rumors

Gordon Allport and Leo Postman pointed out that studies have indicated rather clearly the dynamics of rumors. Hence three important characteristics of the process should be understood by the school administrator. They are enumerated below.[32]

1 As a rumor spreads, it becomes more concise. In other words, fewer details are given. It becomes easier to repeat and easier to grasp.
2 A rumor tends to focus attention on some detail that remains after it has been shortened (made more concise). Different persons may emphasize different details.
3 When a person hears a rumor, the details that he assimilates will depend on his habits, interests, and sentiments. Therefore, when he repeats it to someone else, he fills in any gaps that are evident in what he attempts to tell. He fuses ideas to fit his memory of what he was told. Furthermore, what he repeats will fit his prejudices and interests, his expectations, and the feelings aroused in him by stereotype words used when the rumor was told to him.

   [. . .]

Dealing with rumor

Inevitably, most school administrators must deal with rumors and the effects of them. Therefore, every principal and superintendent should consider their responsibilities relevant to the problem. Specifically, the following recommendations merit their consideration:[33]

1 Develop a plan of communication whereby school personnel and the public remain informed of what is happening in the schools, what is planned and why, what the schools' problems and achievements are, what changes are being made, and why the changes have been inaugurated. Whenever possible the people who are concerned with and affected by the changes should be involved when decisions are being made with respect to them. Informed and involved people are not as susceptible to rumor as are the uninformed.
2 Develop skill in analyzing rumors. What do they mean? Often, of course, they are symptoms of unrest, fear, hostility, anxiety, and even hopes or aspirations. Once the causes are identified, take the necessary action to fulfill the needs that rumors indicate are unfulfilled and rectify problems that are emphasized by the existence of the rumors.
3 When unfounded rumors start that are harmful to school personnel or programs, provide accurate information quickly that will demonstrate the inaccuracy of the statements that are being made.
4 Provide leadership that results in an effective program of interpersonal and group relations. Such a program causes school personnel and the public to have confidence in the administration and programs of a school system.

And when such confidence exists, persons are far less inclined to believe rumors or be affected by them. In fact, the most effective contradiction of a rumor is one made by a person not involved in or affected by the statements being made. For example, when a respected newspaper editor or reporter states that he has heard a rumor, enumerates the details of it, and declares unequivocally that it is false, his statements are usually far more effective than denials issued by persons who are involved in some way.

5 Remember that the effects of a rumor rarely can be eliminated entirely regardless of its inaccuracy. Always there will be persons who want to believe it and who refuse to believe contradictory facts. And there are always people who hear or read the rumor but actually fail to hear or read the correct information. Therefore, never overlook the dangers inherent in any laxity that develops in communicating with staff members and the public. The more constant the flow of important and needed information, the less likelihood there is of rumors.

A school's business is children. Children are important not only to their parents but also to American culture. Therefore, there are few areas of human activity that are more involved in the values, attitudes, hopes, and ambitions of American citizens. Furthermore, there are few areas that can equal schools as potential sources of conflict and differences of opinion. As a result, they are fertile fields for the growth of rumors. School administrators must be cognizant of the potential of rumors and competent in dealing with them.

Mass communication

The term 'mass communication' usually brings to mind the utilization of mass media such as newspapers, magazines, books, television, radio, motion pictures, billboards, and widely distributed publications such as brochures, pamphlets, and bulletins. From the standpoint of the school administrator, the following should be added to the list: (1) annual printed reports; (2) form letters, memoranda, and notices sent to parents; (3) speeches or talks made before groups; and (4) any other media utilized to communicate with the public generally.

[. . .]

Through the use of at least some of the media of mass communication, a school administrator attempts to communicate regularly with the public. He provides information, he transmits ideas, and he seeks to communicate attitudes. On a certain day, he may confine his communication to a letter distributed to all pupils with instructions to give the copies to their parents. On another day, he may address the membership of the largest civic organization in the community, or he may work with the school system's director of public relations or a reporter in the preparation of a feature news article to be published by a local newspaper. At the same time, if he is a superintendent, he may be working closely with members of his staff in the preparation of the school system's annual report which is to be distributed widely in the community in the form of an illustrated bulletin. Furthermore, if he is a superintendent, he may be meeting regularly with a subcommittee of the school board to complete the tentative plans for an appeal to the public to support a referendum vote that will permit the issuance of additional school bonds.

School administrators are involved in mass communication. They utilize it to gain support that is based on knowledge and understanding. They utilize it to inform parents and the public generally about the regulations, activities, accomplishments, and needs of the schools. They use it to contradict rumors, to combat unfavorable attitudes, and to create favorable sentiment toward schools and their programs. These tasks are difficult, demanding, and exceedingly complex. There is no simple set of instructions that will assure success in the use of mass communication. On the other hand, some understanding of generalizations derived primarily from research in communication can give every administrator a better sense of direction in his efforts and an awareness of some of the pitfalls that he should seek to avoid. Virtually all of the generalizations enumerated below are supported at least in part by research findings.

1 *Citizens tend to know less about their public schools than many administrators believe that they know.* [. . .]

2 *Despite the avowed interest of school personnel in communicating with the citizens of their communities, there is considerable evidence that parents and other citizens gain most of their knowledge of schools from sources other than school personnel.* [. . .]

3 *The acquisition or possession of information does not necessarily assure or create favorable attitudes.* [. . .]

As emphasized earlier in this chapter, communication involves the transmission of information, ideas, and attitudes. In most instances, the school administrator's communication tasks must involve much more than information. A principal or superintendent provides what is termed 'leadership' when he is successful in conveying not only information but also ideas with respect to stronger, more effective educational programs and, through his communication, creating favorable attitudes toward the ideas. Communicating information is a relatively easy task as compared with conveying ideas and attitudes. Every administrator needs an understanding of the generalizations that follow. [. . .]

4 *When a school administrator attempts to communicate with individuals or with groups, he must compete for their attention.* [. . .]

5 *The administrator's success in communicating will depend to a considerable extent on whether or not his message is concerned with the needs of the receivers and is in accord with their values and loyalties.* First, of course, his message must be relevant to the needs that are felt by the people to whom it is directed; otherwise, they will have no interest in it. A businessman who is childless is not likely to become enthusiastic about a discussion of the school lunch program, but he will be interested in what effect education has on the amount of money people spend for the goods or services that he has to sell. [. . .]

A discussion of 'messages relevant to the needs and concerns of people' is related closely to the daily problems of school administrators. As a matter of fact, every advertisement an administrator reads in newspapers and magazines is attempting to appeal to the needs and concerns of people. Persons buy merchandise and services because they believe that they will fulfill some of their needs. For example, some advertisements promise that the use of a certain soap, oral antiseptic, or hair preparation will fulfill an individual's needs for affection, achievement, and belongingness by leading to romance and universal acceptance in groups. Although such results may never be realized, the study of advertisements can help administrators to gain a better understanding of the necessity of using messages relevant to the needs of the receivers. Of course, no administrator should seek to mislead the receivers of his messages. His communication must be based on a much higher ethical level than that permitted in commercial advertising.

[. . .]

This discussion has been concerned with heeding or listening to messages that convey ideas, attitudes, or information contrary to a person's or group's values or loyalties. As a matter of fact, people tend to read or listen only to messages that are in accord with what they already believe, to messages that are favorable to 'their side'. An individual strongly opposed to any increase in taxes for the operation of schools is not likely to read a brochure or newspaper article advocating the increase. A faithful member of one political party is not likely to tune in a half-hour telecast sponsored by another party. And a person who believes that teachers already are well paid usually will not take the time to read a newspaper editorial urging increases in salaries for teachers. If, for some reason, a person does hear or read a message contrary to his beliefs, values, and/or loyalties, generally he reinterprets what he hears or reads rather than change his attitudes.[41] [. . .]

6 *Even when an administrator is communicating with groups likely to have a favorable attitude toward the ideas, attitudes, or information that he is attempting to transmit, the message must be understood by the receivers.* [. . .] National Teacher Examinations scores, or standardized testing generally can be meaningless to a group of parents who have never written a standardized test or dealt with an institutional budget. [. . .]

7 *Generally, an administrator should present both sides of an argument when communicating with a group, particularly if the persons are initially opposed to his position or if they will be exposed to both sides of the argument later.*[43] Usually, a presentation of this nature is more effective. It will be less effective, of course, if the receivers agree with the administrator's position or will not be exposed to the other side. Because of the widespread use of media of communication, however, there are few instances in which people are not exposed to both sides of any argument.

[. . .]

8 *The administrator should be cautious about the use of any message that calls upon the receivers to draw their own conclusions with respect to what is said, particularly if the message deals with a complex matter.*[44] An administrator is quite

effective when he can communicate certain facts in a manner that motivates the receivers to reach the conclusion that is desirable. Nevertheless, when issues are complex, when the receivers are not experts in the field in which the issues exist, or when the intelligence of the receivers is average or below, the administrator should state explicitly the conclusions justified by the facts in the case. [. . .]

9 *The use of fear appeals may do no more than create tension; or they may cause receivers of messages to ignore a situation because facing it is so disagreeable.*[45] [. . .]

10 *The amount of confidence that readers and listeners have in an administrator affects the extent to which they believe the information that he provides and the extent to which what he says affects their opinions. Nevertheless, the effect of credibility may be temporary.*[46] Even persons who hold different points of view may be influenced by a message communicated by a high-credibility person such as a school administrator who is recognized as an honest, objective, and competent professional man or woman. [. . .]

11 *Although school administrators should be persuasive, generally they are righly opposed to the highly persuasive communication used by some individuals and groups. Nevertheless, they should understand the effect of persuasive communication on persons with low self-esteem.* At times, administrators seem puzzled by the ability of so-called 'rabble rousers' and 'extremists' to incite discord and conflict in communities. They should recognize, however, that those persons who have such influence generally are using persuasive communication among people who have low self-esteem. And, as Hovland, Janis, and Kelley said, people with 'low self-esteem are predisposed to be highly influenced by persuasive communication'.[49]

[. . .]

12 *School administrators should understand and appreciate the typical skepticism of mass news media rather than be antagonistic toward it.* [. . .]

13 *School administrators should be conscious of the critical importance of timing in mass communication.* The term 'timing', of course, refers to when public support of an idea or plan is sought. [. . .] Communication should be timed to reach the public when personal needs are not so involved that a reasonably objective assessment of a plan or idea is too difficult for most people to achieve.[52] And, where possible, it should be timed to be reinforced by current events. The fact that current events can be detrimental has been emphasized, but they can be helpful also. An appeal for public support of a plan to replace school equipment or buildings generally is viewed more favorably if a child has been injured recently because of defective school facilities. An outbreak of juvenile delinquency can increase support for after-school recreational programs. And an announcement that an important industry has decided not to locate in a community because the educational system did not have the programs and quality that the industry desired provides an opportune time to seek public acceptance of a long-sought plan for educational improvement.

14 *Communication must be repeated and reinforced.* Every school administrator should realize that stating a fact or making some type of appeal once does not mean that the public will know the fact or be aware of the appeal.

Relatively few persons may read a particular article in a newspaper, glance at a brochure or notice sent to their homes, or remember something said in a public meeting. If a major business firm has a message it wishes to convey to the public, it repeats it so often in so many forms and ways that eventually it is widely known. If a school administrator wishes to be effective in mass communication, he must repeat the schools' message frequently, stating it in different ways and using various forms of communication that not only serve the objective of repetition but also that of reinforcement. For example, as Schramm pointed out, a 'suggestion carried by mass media plus face-to-face reinforcement is more likely to be accepted than a suggestion carried by either alone, other things being equal'.[53]

    15 *Every school administrator needs an understanding of the actual operation of newspapers, radio stations, and television stations; their purposes, problems, and policies; the procedures involved in gaining and retaining their cooperation in interpreting school programs; and some of the knowledge that they have about the public's reading and listening habits and skills.* [. . .]

School administration already is an exceedingly complex responsibility. Its complexity will increase. Therefore, what is the solution to the school administrator's need for technical knowledge with respect to communication through newspapers, radio, and television? The answer, of course, lies in the employment of full-time or part-time public relations staff members who work closely with a school system's board and administrators in the development of news stories, feature stories, and special columns focused on the work, the achievements, and the needs of the schools. They can provide also the technical know-how in the preparation of brochures for widespread public distribution, handbooks for parents or faculty members, etc. The administrative and supervisory staffs of the school system, of course, should retain control over the content of any news story or publication.

    [. . .]

Notes

[O. This chapter is written in a US context and some of its terms have different connotations from those in the UK.]

1 Van Miller, *The Public Administration of American School Systems* (New York: The Macmillan Company, 1965), p. 475.

2 Jack. A. Culbertson, Paul B. Jacobson, and Theodore L. Reller, *Administrative Relationships: A Casebook* (Englewood Cliffs, N.J.: Prentice-Hall, Inc., 1960), p. 380.

3 S. I. Hayakawa, *Language in Thought and Action* (New York: Harcourt, Brace, 1949), p. 18.

[. . .]

5 Wilbur Schramm, 'How Communication Works', *The Process and Effects of Mass Communication*, ed. Wilbur Schramm (Urbana, Ill.: University of Illinois Press, 1954), p. 3.

6 Leland Brown, *Communicating Facts and Ideas in Business* (Englewood Cliffs, N.J.: Prentice-Hall, Inc., 1961), p. 2.

[. . .]
9 Edward T. Hall, *The Silent Language* (Garden City, N.Y.: Doubleday & Company, Inc., 1959), p. 52.
10 Orrin D. Wardle, 'Forgive Me – You Didn't Understand', *Educational Administration and Supervision*, XLIV (November 1958), 357–365.
11 *Ibid.*
12 Ralph Waldo Emerson, 'Social Aims', *Letters and Social Aims* (Boston: Houghton Mifflin).
13 Andrew W. Halpin, 'Muted Language', *School Review*, LXVIII (Spring 1960), 85.
14 *Ibid.*
15 See, for example, Douglas R. Bunker, 'Communicating Person to Person', *National Elementary Principal*, XLI (May 1962), 16–20.
[. . .]
28 Carl R. Rogers and F. J. Roethlisberger, 'Barriers and Gateways to Communication', *Human Relations in Management*, ed. I. L. Heckman, Jr., and S. G. Huneryager (Cincinnati: South-Western Publishing Co., 1960), p. 298.
[. . .]
30 Gordon Allport and Leo Postman, 'The Basic Psychology of Rumor', *The Process and Effects of Mass Communication*, ed. Wilbur Schramm (Urbana, Ill.: University of Illinois Press, 1954), pp. 141–155.
31 Bernard M. Bass, *Organizational Psychology* (Boston: Allyn and Bacon Inc., 1965), p. 311.
32 Allport and Postman, *op. cit.*, pp. 146, 148, 150.
33 These recommendations are based in part on those enumerated by Culbertson, Jacobson, and Reller, *op. cit.*, pp. 399–405.
[. . .]
41 *Staff Relations in School Administration*, Thirty-third Yearbook (Washington, D.C.: American Association of School Administrators, 1955), p. 170.
[. . .]
43 See [Carl T. Hovland, Irving L. Janis, and Harold H. Kelley, *Communication and Persuasion* (New Haven, Conn.: Yale University Press, 1953], chapter 4, for a discussion of this point.
44 Ibid.
45 Ibid, chapter 3.
46 Ibid., chapter 2, and Carl I. Hovland and Walter Weiss, 'The Influence of Source Credibility on Communication Effectiveness', *The Process and Effects of Mass Communication*, ed. Wilbur Schramm (Urbana, Ill.: University of Illinois Press, 1954), pp. 275–288.
[. . .]
49 [Hovland, Janis, and Kelley, op. cit.], p. 277.
[. . .]
52 Gordon McCloskey, *Education and Public Understanding*, 2nd ed. (New York: Harper and Row, Publishers, 1967), chapter 3.
53 Wilbur Schramm, 'The Nature and Behavior of Attitudes', *The Process and Effects of Mass Communication* (Urbana, Ill.: University of Illinois Press, 1954), p. 213.
[. . .]

11

Negotiation skills

T. J. Lowe and I. W. Pollard

Negotiation is part of the everyday experience of any professional. It is a way of reconciling interests and reducing conflict in situations where people have to interact but where no side is powerful enough to impose its will. All human relationships have an element of co-operation and competition, and negotiation is a lubrication between these two tendencies. Negotiation is therefore an integral aspect of the network of human interactions within and between organizations. This chapter will devote itself largely to negotiating skills but it will be useful first to consider briefly the broad context within which negotiation takes place.

Mastenbroek (1987) identifies power and dependency relationships as the crucial element of interaction within organizations. Power can be defined as the capacity to determine or influence the behaviour of others whilst dependency is the reciprocal: dependency means one is uncertain, dispensable, or peripheral within a situation. Handy (1976) points out that there are various sources of power that can be drawn on, and that can to some extent accumulate or substitute for each other. Control of resources, and position power, or the right to organize the environment and the flow of tasks and of information, are the two sources most obviously conferred by the organization. Personal power, or charisma, is developed by individuals, and is perhaps reflected in personal image or reputation, and in the ways that others approach or respond to that individual. Similarly, expert power, which can attach to individuals or to a specialist group, is conferred by the way that others react, and depends on their perception of their need for the individual. Finally, everybody has negative power, or the capacity to throw a spanner in the works. Individuals and groups devote a considerable amount of time and energy developing these sources of power, either deliberately or haphazardly. This is sometimes referred to as 'networking', which Morley (1986) defines as 'building relationships based on information, resources and support, the basic commodities or organizational power'.

The power of an individual or group is generally built up over a longer rather than a shorter period of time. It depends on the gradual establishing of personal reputations, the forging of friendships, establishing of precedents and habits, and the gaining control of resources. It follows from this that any individual negotiation, whilst depending on the state of power relations, is unlikely on its own to alter the balance of power. Consequently, it is rarely worth winning a particular negotiation at the expense of an important relationship. Experienced negotiators will work to insulate the bargaining situation from the rest of their relationship or, if comparative strangers, will build up counterbalancing positive relationships or interactions. Ultimately the most skilful networker is the one whose strategy is long term and who can distinguish between negotiations which must be won and those which can or should be lost.

The model of negotiating that is described in this chapter is based not only on a reading of the results of empirical research, but also on the ideas that people in training situations have been most able to use.

We would suggest that the negotiator's effectiveness is based on factors on at least three different levels:

1 The frame of mind that the negotiator adopts;
2 The procedures adopted;
3 The process of interpersonal communication.

I Frame of mind

A detailed description of two alternative approaches to negotiation – positional bargaining and principled negotiation – is provided by Fisher and Ury (1981). They support the latter, describing the dangers of viewing negotiation as a win–lose competition, which fosters besting, points-scoring and conflict. They suggest that it is much more helpful to view negotiation as a joint exploration of the situation in which potential adversaries find themselves, and as a joint attempt to find mutually satisfactory solutions. The paradigm is of negotiators as joint problem-solvers, on the same side of the fence, and mounting an attack on 'the problem'. They go on to identify a number of principles which we believe define a frame of mind conducive to conflict resolution. Some of the most important of these are:

(a) Separate the people from the problem: be soft on the people and hard on the problem. The unskilled negotiator is liable to confuse the people with the problem, and to direct his own feelings of frustration or anger at his protagonists. He may indeed label the other people *as* the problem. On the other hand, he does not think through problems and issues, or focus on the soft spots where there may be some possibility of change. The unskilled negotiator is hard on the people and soft on the problem. The antidote is to credit your protagonist with humanity, to assume his motivation is honourable, to treat him well, and together to undertake a probing intellectual analysis of the circumstances and problem.

(b) Go for a wise outcome reached efficiently and amicably. This recognizes that people usually have to go on living with their protagonist, and a short-term personal victory may merely set the scene for a future conflict.

(c) Proceed independently of trust. Even whilst assuming that people are trustworthy, it is important to recognize that there may be continuing tensions or conflicts of interest that will lead to misunderstanding. With the best will in the world, people usually place more emphasis and effort into those aspects of an agreement that accord with their own views and interests. It is therefore important to aim for agreements that can be monitored objectively, and can be clearly observed to be succeeding or failing. 'Verifiability' is the term used to describe this feature in the context of nuclear weapons negotiations.

(d) Insist on objective criteria. This follows from the previous point. It is also the way to resolve the genuine conflicts of interest that will emerge in most negotiations. Your department wants a larger slice of the budget and so does the other department. A common way out of this impasse is a contest of wills or power politics, perhaps with a dash of horse-trading. The more satisfactory and long-term solution is to work at the objective criteria: just how unsatisfactory are those textbooks you want to change, and how important is the new equipment wanted by the other department? One needs ideally to apply objective standards, although these can be difficult to identify in many aspects of education. At minimum, objective criteria need to be independent of each side's will, perhaps depending on an outsider's judgement.

(e) Reason and be open to reason: yield to principle, not to pressure. Reasoning is the way to solve problems, and it is constantly necessary to appeal to the power of good ideas rather than to the power of personalities or of precedent. Sometimes indeed the protagonist will take a stand 'on principle'. However, such a stand conveys a hidden message that (a) the other side has no principles, and (b) their position has no validity or legitimacy. The starting point must be that everybody has principles: the problem is to explore the range of application of the principles, or to find superordinate principles to which you can both subscribe. The mechanism for doing this is reason, and that implies you come to the negotiation with an open mind.

(f) Don't get sucked into a push–pull battle. It may be that the protagonist is a less skilled negotiator than you are, and slips into, or even starts, by viewing the negotiation as a contest. He may engage in personal attacks either explicitly or by innuendo, or play the game of power politics. He may even try to engage in blackmail, whether moral or otherwise. No matter what dirty tricks are used, however, the long-term advantage to all sides will be in adopting principled negotiation.

(g) Stay cool. No matter how much you try, you will find that some negotiations push you to the limits of your skill, making you feel inadequate, frustrated and angry. It can be helpful to acknowledge the emotion being generated: 'I think we are both finding this frustrating and difficult – I know I certainly am' or 'You must know that some of my colleagues are pretty upset about the situation'. But naked emotion is rarely advantageous except in the short term, because, even if effective, it will leave the protagonist uncommitted to the agreement.

2　The procedures

The right frame of mind only carries a negotiator so far, however. It is important also to establish within the negotiation a feeling of optimism and progress; without this, anger and frustration can easily take over. Establishing progress depends on having a procedure at your fingertips – a chart of the territory to carry you forward and give you the right things to say at the right time.

Preparation

Wherever possible, sound preparation should be undertaken, and this will go a long way toward providing a chart of the relevant territory. It will be necessary to give thought to:

(a) The problems or issues. Your problems, certainly, but also the problems faced by the protagonists. Identifying who faces what problems will give a good indication of motivation for change.

(b) The facts and technical details. Most people are well aware of the difference to their personal effectiveness in a meeting when they have taken the opportunity to brief themselves beforehand. This is particularly apparent when other people do not, but is equally important when dealing with a well-informed protagonist.

(c) The interests of all parties. Negotiators will normally state a position which they believe best meets their interests. If, however, you are able to suggest alternative positions which serve their interests as well or almost as well, you may stimulate some movement.

(d) Multiple solutions. There is a tendency to stop thinking as soon as a desirable outcome is identified. It pays to generate a variety of possible solutions which can be considered in the light of the emerging analysis of the problem.

(e) The best possible BATNA, which stands for 'Best Alternative to a Negotiated Agreement'. Fisher and Ury suggest it is better to have identified what you will do if the negotiation fails, as this can be used as reference point against which to compare any proposal. The better your BATNA, the stronger your negotiating position. For instance, if you are negotiating to produce a joint scheme which will attract funds, you are in a much stronger negotiating position if you have an alternative source of funding up your sleeve. By contrast, having a negotiating 'bottom line' is much more inflexible, preventing you from responding genuinely to new proposals that are made.

The agenda for negotiation

Having charted the issues thoroughly, the agenda will furnish you with guidance on the timing of what you say in the meeting. Timing is clearly a crucial factor in the successful resolution of problems, and indeed the most intractable industrial problems only seem capable of resolution at the point of crisis. Even in more local or even mundane negotiations, there is a clearly desirable sequence, the violation of which is liable to lead to slower progress:

(a) Common problems. In preparation, you have looked at the *range* of problems, but now you need to focus on the *common* problems so as to create the feeling of a joint approach. It may indeed take some creativity to reconceptualize problems in a form where they can be seen as common. A headteacher who sees the amount of special needs teaching support as 'the problem' may need to be exposed to a number of issues before he can share the Education Officer's problem of 'how to share out the limited special needs resources across an area', and move to the common problem of 'how to use special needs support effectively in the school'. But a shared understanding of common problems is an essential step if conflict is to be fully resolved.

(b) Common needs/interests. Moving on from problems, it is helpful to describe in general terms the situation that you both would like to see. If such a situation is out of reach, it may be possible to identify some important steps towards it.

(c) Options for mutual gain. As in preparation, a focus on multiple options is more likely to keep the negotiation moving forward than a premature emphasis on a single option.

(d) A way forward. This is the point at which a preferred option is selected, including if possible agreed action. It is important not to think of this as having to be a full solution of the problem. In most cases, there will not be a solution that satisfies all the needs of all the parties, and everybody will need time to adjust to this reality. The most that can usually be hoped for in a single meeting is to find a way forward. In some circumstances the best way forward will be to agree specific ways to investigate and observe the problems that are being considered. However, where there is a strong clash of interests both sides may wish to explore other avenues such as recourse to higher authority. They may wish to break off the negotiation temporarily.

(e) Review date. Setting a review conveys the message that you are seriously interested in progress, and are not merely stalling for time. It should be scheduled far enough ahead for evidence to be apparent on whether the agreed way forward is yielding any results.

3 The process

At an even more specific level, there are ways of talking and behaving that can help the negotiation along, or sabotage it. The main elements are setting the scene, listening to understand, and stating your views:

Setting the scene

Establishing rapport, and ensuring that all participants come to a meeting with the same expectations, are important preliminary steps. This will involve greeting people appropriately, breaking the ice, ensuring that people are physically looked after, and then checking that everybody agrees the nature and purpose of the meeting, and what can be realistically achieved.

Listening to understand

Listening is the cheapest concession that you can make. Listening, as part of an active attempt to understand what is said, and seeing the situation through the other person's viewpoint, is an important and rare skill. There are a number of sub-skills to active listening, the most important of which is 'learning to keep your trap shut'. Two others are:

(a) Questioning. The art of asking the right question is an important communication skill. Question. can be used to obtain information, but are also a means of conveying interest, encouraging reflection and enlightenment, and maintaining attention. Three aspects of questioning should be borne in mind:
   - (i) Open questions v. closed questions. Open questions can be answered in many different ways, and hence encourage your negotiating partner to state his views. Open questions encourage self-disclosure and a prolonged reply. Closed questions have very specific answers, and close down a conversation.
   - (ii) Avoidance of leading questions which prejudge the other side's motives, position and values. These very quickly raise hackles and serve little useful purpose.
   - (iii) Probes. These are essential follow-up questions, which can help to clarify ('how do you mean?'), establish relevance ('how does that help us in this case?'), or seek an illustration ('can you give me an example of that?'). These can convey interest and sustain the conversation or they can be used to challenge people's statements.

(b) Summarizing. This involves putting back into the conversation something that the other person has just said. It is a most powerful technique for checking that you have understood, and more importantly, demonstrating that you have understood. The other person will then be able to correct you, and may be encouraged to elaborate, but will certainly be most gratified that somebody has understood their message.

Stating your own views

If you have demonstrated that you have understood and respected the other person's views he will be in more of a frame of mind to hear you out. When explaining your views, do so if possible in the manner of sharing a problem. It can be helpful to:

(a) Create some time. In some meetings it can be difficult to get a word in edgeways. You have kept quiet and listened carefully, so warn people they will need to do the same: 'I think I have understood your view . . . Now I have some views that we should also take into account, so let me make a number of points. Firstly . . .'

(b) State your points briefly. Make clear specific points that cover the most essential part of the message. Ideally, your views should have been thought through in advance, so that they can be delivered in clear, fluent, jargon-free language, avoiding unnecessary repetition and vagueness.

Negotiating skills in education

Negotiating skills are most obviously relevant to the relationships in large organizations, whether they be schools, or looser networks such as LEAs. They will be particularly important where there is an ambiguous or balanced power structure, such as between officers and sections of the education department, between the education department, headteachers and governing bodies, and between professionals and parents. However, they are equally apposite in the context of team leadership, both in supporting colleagues, and in negotiating arrangements or resources.

The power of applying negotiating principles might be illustrated by an example where these principles were applied only belatedly. The education department had approached the governing body of a school for children with emotional and behavioural difficulties with a view to advertising for a headteacher who would establish a behavioural management approach. The governing body insisted that the officers first consult the teaching staff, and this was arranged for a fortnight later. The subsequent meeting, which would normally have been the staff meeting chaired by the headteacher, was half handed over to the Education Officer, who outlined the situation faced by the school. During the remainder of the meeting, a succession of teachers attacked both the proposal, and the idea that the Education Officer should seek to influence them. Essentially the staff did not have time within the meeting to digest and address the information that was presented at the beginning and were voicing the position they had developed over the preceding fortnight.

The situation was partly recovered when one of the other officers circulated, through the headteacher, a document presenting 'The Facts' faced by the school, and 'The Issues' for decision by the staff. At a second staff meeting, chaired constructively by the outgoing headteacher, the staff and the officer together discussed the facts which had by now been well digested by the staff and made productive decisions. It was only by easing the teachers out of a Them/Us battle, and helping them to focus on the problems faced by the school, that they were able to decide to work together to support whichever headteacher was to be appointed.

References

Fisher, R. and Ury, W. (1981). *Getting to Yes*. London, Hutchinson.
Handy, C. B. (1976). *Understanding Organisations*. London, Penguin.
Mastenbroek, W. G. (1987). *Conflict Management and Organizational Development*. Chichester, Wiley.
Morley, I. (1986). Negotiating and bargaining. In O. Hargie (ed.) *A Handbook of Communication Skills*. London, Croom Helm.

12
What the teachers say: an evaluation report of progress in Beacon LEA TVEI pilot project

Colin Morgan and Glyn Morris

Foreword

What follows is an edited version of a report we produced as 'local evaluators' of the progress of a Technical and Vocational Education Initiative (TVEI) pilot project in 1988. Its inclusion in this book is primarily intended to offer some interesting evidence on the relationship between the leadership of, and communication with teaching staff and the achievement of agreed specific educational aims. It is presented here, therefore, more for its bearing on human resource management than on TVEI *per se*. It is important that the reader appreciate the contractual context under which this report was written, also for whom it was written, and most importantly the ethics position that governed the gathering of the data from the teachers involved in the project. We have given the pseudonym 'Beacon' to the actual LEA involved.

Our brief as evaluators was to furnish evidence of the extent to which the curriculum innovation aims of the local 'managers and owners' of the pilot project in Beacon LEA were being achieved. We worked to an evaluation agenda set by them, and to the policy in the contract agreed between Beacon and the then Manpower Services TVEI division. We did not interpose our own assumptions of what the aims should be, nor did we see our role as necessarily implying any assent for the 'TVEI cause'. In addition to the evaluation role however, our contract called on us to be *formative*, to adopt to some extent an advisory posture in the writing-up of our findings so as to signal the directions which could assist policy development. The format of the report is therefore different from that which we would have used in preparing a research paper from the same findings.

The report was written for two audiences. Primarily it was addressed to the management panel of the TVEI consortium. TVEI pilot projects and the

TVEI extension projects which are following them as we write, are run on a consortium basis. An explicit understanding for all the contracting parties is that a *consortium* of schools and colleges rather than the LEA owns, delivers, and is accountable for the innovation. The heads of all the institutions involved therefore form a board or management panel to plan the innovation and be corporately responsible for what happens in the constituent institutions. Our report was primarily addressed to this panel, and only secondly to the LEA. Even then it was written with the LEA's professional officers as the audience in mind rather than the members.

Finally two further matters by way of context. All the interviewees on whose responses '*What the Teachers Say*' was based, were given a written statement of the ethics governing the evaluation transactions at first meeting; in these it was stressed that no individual or institution would be identified in any report material, hence the allocation of a random letter to the institutions referred to in the report. There are also references in this account of teachers' perceptions of TVEI progress in Beacon to 'our findings elsewhere'. This is to be explained by the fact that prior to Beacon we had carried out similar evaluations in two other LEAs.

Introduction

It can be claimed that the major constituents of any school curriculum innovation are: (a) the new plans, organizational arrangements, materials and technology; (b) the pupils who are to receive it; and (c) the teachers who are to deliver it.

So far in our reports to the Beacon TVEI consortium we have said a good deal about the first two but virtually nothing about teachers' perspectives. We thought it important therefore, whilst making our visits to the TVEI institutions during the 1987–8 academic year in order to gain an early view of the progress of Post-16 TVEI, to assess how teachers have been reacting and feeling about the implementation of TVEI in their schools. We have interviewed the headteachers and 88 members of staff in the five TVEI schools.

The teacher interview sample

Table 1 indicates that about two-thirds of the teachers we interviewed in the five Beacon TVEI schools were directly involved in delivering TVEI. We thought it important to also obtain where we could the views of some teachers who, though not involved, had observed the development of TVEI. We knew from our experience elsewhere that teachers are not neutral about what happens generally in their schools, for they can have some decided views about matters in which they themselves are not taking a direct part. In fact there were some teachers in this category who have asked to see us in order to express some strongly held views about TVEI.

Table 1   Teacher interview sample by school, gender and TVEI role

School	Male	Female	Total	TVEI role	No TVEI role
A*	12	7	19 (22)	12	7
B	8	8	16 (18)	7	9
C	14	3	17 (19)	12	5
D	6	14	20 (23)	14	6
E	12	4	16 (18)	12	4
Totals	52 (59)†	36 (41)	88 (100)	57 (65)	31 (35)

*There is no correspondence between the letter designation and the actual name of the school.
† The figures in parentheses are percentages of the total interviews.

We used a standard approach in all our interviews which was only ever varied where the teacher's time was insufficient to complete the schedule. In the main we used a checklist of questions which was designed to find out: how our respondents initially came to be involved in TVEI; their perceptions of the start-up and development of TVEI in their schools; the nature of their TVEI roles; the extent of their knowledge about the various components of TVEI; and what they perceived to be the achievements and deficiencies of TVEI so far.

We did not choose the teachers we wished to interview as timetable constraints did not allow this. We asked the schools to arrange for us a timetable of interviews when teachers were not teaching and to give us a selection of teachers in TVEI and some who were not. We made it clear that we would welcome criticisms. A consequence of arranging interviews on this basis is that there is no guarantee that the sample of teachers interviewed is fully representative of the range of views and experience of TVEI as a whole, or that it is balanced in that a similar profile of interviewees is drawn from each school. This limitation is inevitable and cannot be avoided. Nevertheless, we feel sure that the views of 88 teachers give a good picture of the teachers' perspective of TVEI in Beacon.

As Table 1 shows we interviewed more or less the same overall total in each of the schools though the proportions of the two categories of staff were different between schools.

Overwhelmingly those involved in TVEI were teaching officially designated TVEI courses rather than as part of senior management or because they were, for example, heads of year involved in option choices and hence having a role explaining TVEI to pupils (see Table 2).

In terms of the job category we have divided our interviewees (Table 3) into senior management (other than headteachers), heads of department of whatever grade, and other teachers without departmental responsibility who could be scales 1–4. Our reason for defining heads of department by status rather than scale, is that it can be argued that anyone with the overall responsibility for teaching a subject throughout the school (of whatever scale, even if they are the only teacher of that subject) would need to be more

Table 2 Type of role

Category	%
Teaching TVEI courses	91
As part of senior management duties	5
Other TVEI involvement	4
Total	100

aware of a major policy initiative such as TVEI than teachers without a curriculum leadership responsibility.

We collected data on the age range of our interviewees; though we do not have any base data for comparison, it is our clear impression that the distribution shown in Table 3 would be representative of the teaching body as a whole in these five schools. We followed a standard list of questions in all our interviews and in as many as possible we also asked our respondents to answer a set of self-completion questions and two exercises. The first of these was designed to measure on a true/false basis the extent to which interviewees knew which were the national TVEI criteria. The second sought to record on the basis of the teacher's perceptions what had happened at the start-up of TVEI in their school and the extent to which TVEI had now 'penetrated' the school.

TVEI start-up, development and penetration within the pilot schools

From our interviewees we wanted to know first how they perceived the start-up of TVEI and its development from the initial presentation or decision; also, how they themselves became involved in their TVEI roles if indeed they were. We have found from our evaluation work elsewhere that patterns of project start-up and staff involvement can have significant results on the outcomes or levels of TVEI achievement over time. The patterns of TVEI start-up are composed of sets of discrete management activities which

Table 3 Interview sample by staff category and age group

Staff category	Interviewees	Age category (years)	% interviewees
Senior management	5 (6)	22–30	12
Head of department	53 (60)	31–40	44
Other teachers	30 (34)	41–50	31
		50-plus	13
Totals	88 (100)		100

Table 4   How staff became involved in the project

Category	%
Was persuaded by head, HOD, coordinator, etc.	50
Because taught an appropriate subject	31
Asked a key person if they could participate	19
Total	100

reflect the differing approaches of heads and their senior staff. Hence we wished to ask of our Beacon teacher interviewees a series of questions, and we set them some self-completion tasks which would shed some light on these issues.

How staff became involved in TVEI

From what the teachers said (Tables 4 and 5), then, the overall picture is clear – the vast majority of staff were 'invited'/drafted into TVEI rather than themselves positively seeking a TVEI role having considered the issues. Indeed for most teachers it all came about very quickly and there is a widespread belief that 'we were in whether we liked it or not because the Head had decided we must get the money'.

It is clear from our conversations with the teachers that in reality the meanings behind being *invited* or *persuaded*, could be either one of being nominated or drafted, or sometimes really having a choice to refuse:

> I had a scheme of work plonked in front of me by the headmaster and invited to join the TVEI working party . . . I was annoyed I wasn't consulted earlier.
>
> Head of department

> I was told I was teaching TVEI

> I received a timetable with TVEI sessions on it . . . I didn't realize that I would be involved in TVEI

> I was put down on the timetable to do it

> Not invited to be part of TVEI at the beginning, but last year we were told we were to be part of the enhancement of TVEI

Table 5   How staff perceived their departments became involved in TVEI

Category	%
The head 'nominated'/'invited' appropriate departments	81
There was a general invitation to bid, and the department responded	19
Total	100

At start-up the overall picture then was one of staff being drafted rather than negotiated into TVEI though there were some important inter-school differences as we shall see below.

Regarding the enlistment of the department as distinct from the individual, Table 5 shows that the predominant approach was for a department to be sponsored into TVEI by the headteacher rather than to respond to an invitation to put up a proposal. This has, we know, been the main initial strategy across many TVEI pilot projects, and probably for the reason that the other more 'whole school' and 'open to bid' approach is clearly much more managerially demanding. Nevertheless, as we shall see, at least one of the Beacon TVEI schools clearly adopted this more demanding approach and with results that repay handsomely the management difficulties involved.

Start-up and development patterns

We have found from eliciting data on perceptions of TVEI start-up and penetration in our evaluation work elsewhere that there are three types of strategy which school heads have used in implementing the TVEI pilot project in their schools: the enclave, sponsored rolling, and whole school approaches. We would define the three strategies as follows:

1 Enclave strategy – where the intention is to initiate TVEI within a minority of departments which are seen to be the relevant subjects; only a minority of heads of department are invited to make bids; TVEI is perceived to have a low profile within the school and externally; no real attempt is being made to break out from the enclave approach as development proceeds.
2 Sponsored rolling strategy – a non-enclave rolling approach intended to phase the bringing in of departments; the most appropriate, energetic, or sympathetic departments are sponsored to come in first, other departments are not denied access to the overall criteria and policy; though a restricted number of departments participate at first, knowledge of TVEI is widely and effectively disseminated both inside and outside the school.
3 Whole school strategy – where there is an invitation to all departments to bid for TVEI resources and encouragement for wide participation made to the whole school from the beginning; this is sometimes accompanied by a vote of all staff; 'up-front' presentation of the expectations and criteria of TVEI is made to all. Wide dissemination of what TVEI is all about to staff, pupils and parents.

In order to discern the Beacon patterns we asked our respondents in the five schools to complete a checklist of a range of activities which might have taken place in the start-up of TVEI; we also recorded any comments they made about this early stage of TVEI. From these two sources our judgement is that only one project school used a whole school strategy and one a sponsored rolling approach. The others were, and still are, very much enclave in their management of TVEI.

Based on the checklist which our interviewees completed, Table 6 gives a summary of the range of activities adopted in the start-up and early development of TVEI across the schools involved. We do not present this as a complete picture of everything that happened in each of the schools, for as we have already made clear, it was not possible to ensure that our interviews trapped the full range of staff experience. Also, of course, there can be some conflict between categories of perception on a topic; where this occurs we have made a judgement based on the totality of the evidence available.

Nevertheless we believe Table 6 gives a fair approximation of what happened and, more importantly, shows a range of options available to schools in introducing a scheme such as this.

Table 6   Patterns of start-up and development in Beacon TVEI schools – based on staff perceptions

			School		
Start-up elements	*A*	*B*	*C*	*D*	*E*
Presentation to full staff meeting	Yes	Yes	Yes	Yes	Yes
Vote taken among staff about adoption of TVEI	Yes	No	No	No	No
Staff were widely consulted about starting TVEI	Yes	No	No	No	No
TVEI development committee set up	★	No	No	No	Yes
Open to most/all departments to bid/ propose course	Yes	No	No	No	No
TVEI discussed at departmental meetings called for the purpose	Yes	No	No	Yes	No
Information about TVEI was on staffroom noticeboard	Yes	Yes	No	Yes	Yes
Policy documents about TVEI were circulated	Yes	Yes	★	Yes	Yes
TVEI coordinator gave staff information	Yes	Yes	Yes	Yes	Yes
A great deal of discussion about TVEI took place at the time	Yes	Yes	Yes	Yes	Yes
Judgement on strategy used based on above and other data	Whole school	Enclave	Enclave	Enclave	Rolling

★ The evidence as to whether this happened in this school is ambiguous.

School A in Table 6 is the only one we have designated 'whole school' in its start-up management approach. This is because the staff were widely consulted and, more crucially, there was a general invitation for all to participate. In fact, our interviewees from this school recorded that there had been a formal vote about participating in TVEI. School E we have designated as having used a 'rolling' start-up strategy, that is, a sort of halfway between the 'whole' and 'enclave' approaches. This is on the basis of evidence not wholly categorized in Table 6. We found that the head had invited bids from a wider range of departments than the more obvious ones who would be taking part anyway (a feature of the 'enclave' schools); he had prepared an explicit and polished policy statement about TVEI which was widely circulated, and a development committee had been set up. Moreover, there was clear evidence that the head, the deputies, and the coordinator concerted and communicated a clear policy throughout the school even if some staff disagreed or were sceptical about TVEI. This is also true where staff felt they had not been consulted adequately despite the evidence of Table 6.

Table 6 shows that only school A had been perceived to use wide consultation in the start-up of TVEI. We were interested to assess this whole aspect of consultation in more detail in order to discover how essential is 'wide consultation' to the achievement of TVEI aims. We therefore asked our interviewees to circle a position on a ten-point scale in answer to the question on the self-completion sheet: 'In your opinion to what extent were staff consulted about the start-up of TVEI?' 1 represented a minimum and 10 a maximum of consultation.

Overall, our interviewees were saying that there was only a modest amount of consultation. The scores in Table 7 for consultation at TVEI start-up fall within a close range for four of the participating schools, and to our mind indicate an unsatisfactory level of consultation to have been the norm. The score for school A, however, clearly sets it apart so that the finding on this test confirms other categories of data for that school.

TVEI penetration within the schools

We also asked our interviewees to record on a distance scale their perceptions of the extent to which individual teachers in their school had been influenced/affected by TVEI; and also their view of how many departments in their school had been influenced/affected by TVEI. The answers were to be made

Table 7 Perceived degrees of consultation in start-up of TVEI

School	Mean score
A	6.9
B	3.5
C	4.0
D	4.5
E	3.7

on a scale presenting five options: The Majority; More than Half; About a Half; Less than Half; and A Minority. We acknowledge that this is a crude measure and especially having regard to what we have said earlier about our sample, but we made it because we have found in the past that a reasonably close relationship can exist between whichever of the three start-up strategies had been adopted and the extent to which TVEI is either seen to be an enclave or minority activity within the school, or has moved significantly or wholly towards incorporation into the whole school culture.

Table 8 compares the overall positions to come out of our question on penetration with our earlier findings on start-up strategy and consultation. We find here, as we have found elsewhere, a broad match between the management approach used in the start-up of TVEI and its perceived degree of penetration two and a half years later. Those project schools which we earlier characterized as enclave are the ones perceived to have the least penetration of TVEI ideas across staff or departments.

There are three points we would wish to make arising from our presentation of this data. The first is that in the rapid start-up of a radical innovation such as TVEI, the response by staff is likely to be proportional to the stimulus or degree of expectation for actions that comes from senior management. An enclave approach will produce an enclave result. That is, a softly-softly approach is likely to evoke a softly-softly response, an ambivalent approach a mixed result, a divided approach among top management a divided perception among staff and so on. Some writers refer to this aspect as the management *vision* and *scope* which is being communicated. 'Vision' means getting across an accurate image of the changes required and 'scope'

Table 8   Summary of start-up strategies, degree of consultation and penetration of TVEI

Pilot school	A	B	C	D	E
Start-up strategy	W	E	E	E	R
Degree of consultation	High	Low	Low	Moderate	Low
Perceived degree of penetration: Majority					
More than half	T				T
Half	D				D
Less than half		T D	T D	D	
A minority				T	

Key:
Start-up strategies: W = whole school approach; R = sponsored rolling approach; E = enclave approach.
Penetration:
T = TVEI influence on teachers in the school; D = TVEI influence on departments in the school.

means the decision about, and accurate communication of, who is to be involved in the desired changes. For effective management of change both must be communicated.

Second, there is the matter of *consultation*. Our evaluation findings from the Beacon TVEI pilot schools are consonant with other researches dealing with consultation in educational management. They show that wide consultation is not an absolute requirement for the start-up and development of a major innovation, but that where it happens it buys a greater degree of *consent* with enhanced results, as we shall demonstrate later.

Third and most important of all, the different approaches or start-up strategies are really all about *communication* – managing the knowledge base of participants and audiences; an enclave of communication produces an enclave result! From across the consortium our evidence from what the teachers say shows that there is still more that can be done to communicate more fully to many teachers what TVEI is all about. The link between communication and knowledge is obvious; that between knowledge and outcomes less so, yet as we shall see below, it is a very real one.

Teachers' knowledge of TVEI

The main purpose of our staff survey was to find out how teachers saw the world of TVEI in its general shape or in detail, whether directly involved in the delivery of the Beacon pilot project or not. Furthermore, we assumed that this type of survey might expose any obstacles to the full flowering of TVEI in the pilot project and might potentially offer useful lessons for the extension of TVEI policies elsewhere in the LEA. Such an assumption is based on the proposition that any complex innovation such as TVEI only achieves its optimum success through its adoption into teachers' work practices. Teachers, like any other professionals, do not receive new policies and recommendations as a homogeneous mass. Their perceptions and reactions will vary with their professional circumstances, and this needs to be recognized by those responsible for management. Given such differences, it is likely to be the case that the early stages of major experimentation reveal some strategies which work better than others, and which given indicators of how some aims might be even more successfully achieved. What staff know about TVEI is a measure of what has been communicated to them from formal and informal sources. We therefore began by asking our teacher interviewees what they understood TVEI to be all about – that is, to give us their perceptions of the prime aims of TVEI (see Table 9).

On the basis of this evidence the teachers see TVEI to be more about the vocational and technical than the *educational* process changes, but not overwhelmingly so. In the early days it is inevitable that the 'V' and 'T' of TVEI are the more emphasized; however, it is now relevant to give extra momentum to the 'E', and especially with regard to the prominence of the process aspects of more pupil autonomy and new methods of assessment.

Table 9   The teachers' view of what are the aims of TVEI ($N = 105$)

Category of comment	%
Giving pupils a technical training	32
Relating school and work	26
Encouraging new methods of teaching	24
Making the curriculum more relevant	10
Providing school with more equipment	5
Giving pupils more choice of subjects	2
Stimulate new methods of assessment	1
Total	100

Accuracy of teachers' knowledge of TVEI national criteria

We also sought evidence of what staff do and do not know about TVEI aims from their responses to a true/false exercise which 88% of our interviewees completed. This consisted of twelve statements about TVEI, each requiring the respondent to enter T in the appropriate box if they believed the statement to be true or F if false. Of those completing the T/F exercise, 39% were not directly involved in TVEI work in the schools so we were able to test the data to see if TVEI knowledge is directly related to having an active TVEI role or not. At the end of each assertion in Table 10 we have indicated its truth or falsehood by a (T) or (F) as the case may be.

What follows in this section comes from our subsequent analysis of the answers to the twelve statements. Each of the twelve statements contained an assertion about TVEI intended to assess awareness of its published national criteria. First, Table 11 shows overall that there is a sound knowledge of the main aims of TVEI. There are no glaring deficits of knowledge, but there are some weaker areas of awareness about TVEI aims which can be addressed.

The weakest area of TVEI knowledge revealed by this questionnaire was that concerned with the curriculum scope of TVEI, as the answers to questions 3, 7 and 10 reveal. A large number of teachers believe that TVEI does not concern those subjects in the school curriculum probably usually described as the 'traditional'. Even the minority of teachers in this category anxious to participate did not always receive the response they expected: 'I was positively discouraged not to take part in TVEI' (HOD, History). It is of course officially not the case that the traditional subjects are ineligible; it is a fact that all traditional subjects have received TVEI status in some or other TVEI pilot project.

Table 10 also shows the diminution of sex stereotyping in the curriculum (Q.9), and the need for more pupil autonomy (Q.10) to be other TVEI aims insufficiently known (in our view) by teachers in the pilot schools. We see the summary position of strengths and relative weaknesses of teachers' knowledge of TVEI to be those shown in Table 12.

As we have said, Tables 10 and 11 show a sound knowledge of the main TVEI aims as a whole but that there are some gaps to be rectified as Table 12

Table 10 Aims of TVEI questionnaire – % correct by item

Assertion	% obtaining correct answer
1 TVEI is concerned only with new subjects appearing in school curriculum (F)	78.4
2 TVEI intends there to be changes in methods of teaching and learning (T)	94.3
3 TVEI does not concern itself with the older established subjects (F)	74.3
4 TVEI courses are only for pupils of modest or lower ability (F)	92.4
5 TVEI insists that participating schools must work together in consortium (T)	88.08
6 TVEI insists on the adoption of assessment by pupil profiles (Records of Achievement) (T)	97.75
7 TVEI requires work experience for all pupils (T)	88.67
8 TVEI does not cater for the good A level candidate (F)	77.78
9 TVEI requires a breakdown of sex stereotyping in the curriculum (T)	87.59
10 Under TVEI pupils should have more say in their learning (T)	87.88
11 TVEI concerns only the scientific and technical subjects (F)	61.52
12 Experiential teaching methods are required as a means of delivering the TVEI curriculum (T)	94.52

suggests. To what extent, though, are these knowledge 'gaps' associated with those not directly involved in TVEI delivery?

Table 13 shows that there is no significant difference between the scores on the T/F questionnare between teachers who have a direct role in TVEI and those teachers who do not. What this finding means (and we have found this to be the case in the other LEAs where we have run this test) is that *teachers' knowledge of TVEI, whether involved or not, is a function of the overall communication effectiveness of school management.* If, as we have suggested earlier, the *vision*

Table 11 Overall level of TVEI knowledge as revealed by true/false test

Knowledge category	% achieving
Interviewees obtaining all correct	12
Interviewees scoring over 90% correct	30
Interviewees scoring over 60% correct	55
Interviewees scoring less than 50% correct	6

Table 12   Aims of TVEI best and least known

Best known		Least known	
TVEI criterion	% correct answers	TVEI criterion	% incorrect answers
Pupil profiles	98	TVEI can be across the curriculum	38
Change to experiential teaching methods	94	To break down sex stereotyping	13
		To promote pupil participation/autonomy	13

and *scope* of the innovation are communicated effectively, then a greater number of teachers have a sound knowledge, independent of whether involved or not.

Staff category and awareness of TVEI aims

Only one of our sample from senior management staff completed the T/F questionnaire, so we were only able to obtain a comparison on levels of awareness of TVEI aims between heads of department and other teachers (Table 14). The teachers obtained higher scores than their heads of department.

Two schools, A and E, stand out in Table 15 as having a significantly better performance on the T/F questionnaire than the others, all of whose scores are within a similar range. These are the very schools which from other data we judged to have used a non-enclave management approach to the development of TVEI. Also they are the same schools for which all of the evidence suggests the communication to have been particularly good in terms of the vision and scope of the innovation presented to teachers. Quality management leads to greater knowledge and greater knowledge leads to better quality outcomes as we shall see.

Teachers' knowledge of TVEI – a summary

Taking together all of our evidence about teachers' knowledge of TVEI, what we think it is saying is that given the time-span which has elapsed since the commencement of the experiment, the level of awareness is sound but not yet optimal. There are some criteria, particularly those connected with

Table 13   Average overall scores for TVEI and non-TVEI staff

Category	Average total % score correct
TVEI staff ($N = 55$)	78.3
Non-TVEI staff ($N = 22$)	75.0

Table 14   Staff category and average correct answers obtained
(TVEI participants only)

Staff category	Average number of correct answers
Heads of departments	9.6
Teachers	10.5

development across traditional subjects, sex-stereotyping and, importantly, more pupil autonomy for which the time is probably now opportune to make a specific push in communication. TVEI is a complex innovation for which it should not be expected that all of its ramifications can be ingested quickly or easily, and especially bearing in mind that teachers have busy timetables.

Whilst we know that some headteachers and coordinators have made special efforts to set the aims of TVEI down on paper, we wonder how a teacher not involved, or new to the school, would come to understand what, for example, *experiential methods* or *negotiation* means in practice in the classroom situation. Is there perhaps a means of putting into audio and video form samples of the current best practices of Beacon TVEI so the teachers can appreciate the full meaning of the TVEI criteria away from the pressures of their timetables?

Overview of findings on TVEI start-up, development and awareness of its criteria

We do feel that what we have reported above has important implications for management strategies. Earlier we drew attention to the elements of effective communication (and perhaps especially to vision). There are three other crucial elements in the management of complex curriculum innovations and we wish to draw attention to these in conclusion to this section of our report.

There has been in other occupational contexts some stimulating research which demonstrates the management strategies needed for major innovations such as TVEI. Major innovations are seen to be distinctive and different in degree (if not in kind), in their managerial needs from the

Table 15   TVEI awareness – differences between schools

School	Mean % incorrect on T/F questionnaire
A	7.82
B	22.0
C	15.62
D	18.4
E	9.9

non-development situation. Four elements or words have been used to summarize the required management emphases in the innovation start-up situation:

Vision – A strong image of what is to be achieved

Expertise – The perception to bring together the expertise necessary for achieving the innovation goals

Team – Creating a team of key influencers to sell the innovation in the institution

Support enlistment – Attracting the support of key groups: staff, governors, parents

The need for expertise is self-evident and we have discussed vision earlier. Regarding 'team', our evidence shows that this is not everywhere achieved in the project institutions. Also, there is evidence of considerable variability in the extent that the project schools have set about enlisting the support of that most key group – the staff! Those schools achieving the best outcomes have in our view enacted the above four elements.

Staff perceptions of TVEI's extended classroom

The TVEI pilot project has a number of features which we characterize as *the extended classroom*. We are referring to those mechanisms or provisions – residential experience, work placements, diary keeping, etc. – intended to secure a growth in pupil autonomy, resourcefulness, and realistic self-image, in terms of competence development for the real world. We therefore wish to know how Beacon pilot project teachers looked upon these since they can be seen to present radical changes to traditional practice.

Residential experience

There was high teacher support (Table 16) for the residential component of the pupils' TVEI course, and all the staff who had been involved praised the benefits even if their approval of aspects of organization was not so forthcoming. The small percentage who disapproved did so on the grounds

Table 16   Staff involvement and approval of TVEI residential experience

Category	%
Had involvement	15
Approve value	79
Disapprove	8
Unsure	13

Table 17   Staff involvement and approval of profiling

Category	%
Had involvement	77
Approve value	67
Disapprove	20
Unsure	13

that residential experience was not something seriously concerned with education, which was about getting good examination results.

Profiling

It will be recalled that profiling was the TVEI criterion best known by Beacon teachers, and our data showed that of all the 'extended classroom' activities it was in profiling where the largest number of our interviewees had an involvement. It is this element, however, which has the lowest level of approval by teachers (Table 17).

At the present time the level of approval of Beacon teachers is moderate; a significant number disapprove and, when those who are unsure are added, the overall picture is one in which a third have yet to be convinced of the purpose of profiles. It is clear why this is so:

> It is difficult to categorize a child into the bank of comments

> The problem with profiles is time . . . without sufficient time the idea doesn't get a fair start

> Profiling is a good idea but I don't agree with the comment banks . . . it needs to be open

> profiling very confusing . . . I shouldn't think anyone makes head or tail of it

> I don't believe it is legitimate to assess a child's social skills

> Not happy with bank of statements . . . you can't pigeon-hole pupils

> must be a better way of doing these profiles

Whilst a clear majority of our interviewees believe that 'Profiles are more fair to the child', it is clear that the organization and methods have yet to be worked out to the approval of teachers as a whole.

We are conscious that the development of records of achievement was an activity particularly badly hit by the teachers' disputes in the early years of TVEI and that, given these and other constraints, the provision was often rushed in order to get the profiling show on the road. We know from our studies elsewhere that where profiling is working well (and here we pre-eminently mean its formative component) the payoffs are seen to be enormous by staff and pupils alike. Given that profiling is an absolute TVEI requirement, a clear policy on profiling – especially its formative aspects – needs in our view to be sorted out by the consortium.

Table 18　Staff involvement and approval of work experience

Category	%
Had involvement	44
Approve value	97
Disapprove	3
Unsure	0

Work experience

The work experience results (Table 18) depict the highest level of teacher involvement in, and approval for work experience which we have recorded in our survey work in Wales.

> I've had so much follow on from it . . . I've had companies contact me and ask have I a suitable pupil to go and work there.

This teacher's view is representative of plenty of others. When seen alongside what we reported last year regarding pupils' appreciation of work experience – what we said about the very high quality of its organization in Beacon – these further findings mean that work experience really is the major success story of Beacon TVEI so far. Where teachers have any reservation about it, it only concerns the scheduling of work experience and not its purpose: 'Great idea as long as it doesn't break into their ordinary work'.

TVEI and staff development

Of our Beacon interviewees, 46% said that they had received specific INSET in respect of TVEI development and we sought to categorize this with respect to the three main strands of TVEI aims. The pattern shown in Table 19 is similar to our findings elsewhere, save that there are fewer reporting INSET specifically in teaching methods. It is clear from the discussions with our interviewees that the training courses they had been on, had been crucial to the launch and development of TVEI in Beacon!

We also asked our interviewees whether they felt they had In-Service Education Training (INSET) needs which they would like to have met, and 47% said that they had. In fact there seemed to us to be some heartfelt needs, and we could not help setting them in the context that the Beacon teachers we spoke with reflected a picture of long tenure and low mobility from post to post. This has many advantages to a teaching service but it also implies the need for very careful assessment of staff development needs, especially to ensure that those who have held the same post for a long period receive opportunity for professional renewal or retraining. This is not specifically a TVEI problem and we assume that under the LEA's GRIST (Grant Related In-Service Training) -based staff development policy the needs assessments are taking place. However, it did become clear in our interviews, that TVEI has exposed the need for this issue to be addressed on a systematic basis.

Table 19 What teachers had to learn to fulfil their TVEI role

Category	% response
Subject content – completely new subject/addition to existing	78
Teaching methods – interactive processes	18
Counselling skills	2
Total	100

As we have found elsewhere there is after the initial stage of TVEI a great awareness of need for categories of INSET other than that which is directly subject-content related (see Table 20). While further extension of subject content was still the most common response, its relative frequency had declined, and expressed needs for training in various aspects of the delivery of the curriculum had come into prominence. Also there was in our view a significant level of need expressed for periods of experience away from education. The latter category obviously reflects the industrial 'awareness raising' aspects of TVEI, as well as the prominence it gives to process and management.

The following are typical statements of the felt INSET needs:

I need practical training in XYZ . . . haven't been asked about my needs

I need training in Electronics

I need training in how to use APIL

I want help in assignment writing

I would like INSET in computer-assisted learning

School administration

I would like more on methodology, a change from talk and chalk with pupils

I need INSET on computing in general

A course on evaluation of staff

Would like training in project work and profiling

Really need an industrial secondment

Table 20 Categories of future INSET need declared by Beacon teachers

Category	% response
Subject content courses	51
Teaching methods	23
Counselling methods	2
Industrial experience	7
Other INSET, management especially	17

There were of course many who felt equipped as they were and some who felt they had had a surfeit of training:

> I feel I'm trained up to the hilt . . . been out more than most

Teachers' perceptions of TVEI outcomes and achievements so far

We also wanted to evaluate what the teachers saw were the gains and losses of TVEI so far, and more specifically whether TVEI had changed the way they teach or their relationships with pupils.

Table 21   Teachers' perceptions of the gains arising from TVEI

Category of comment	%
There is more and new equipment	47
Improved teaching methods and new impetus to teaching	26
Curriculum enriched by new subjects	17
Improved performance by pupils	5
Pupils have more autonomy	3
Pupils are more highly motivated	2
Total	100

Perceived gains of TVEI

To begin with we asked our interviewees the open-ended question 'What do you see the gains of TVEI to be?' and categorized their answers as shown in Table 21. Allowing for the perhaps very obvious visible benefit of the equipment deriving from TVEI, the table does suggest significant gains for new teaching methods:

> Definitely a lot of benefit to the children . . . we cannot do without the TVEI approach from now on as life is going more technical

> There is a far more personal level of contact – an inevitable consequence of experiential learning – and certainly a beneficial trend for both teacher and pupil

> Overall, pupils are more highly motivated . . . assessment has changed very much . . . children now expect career advice

> Allows more individual work from children . . . opens up their individual and group awareness

> More assessment during lessons . . . more practical work with less loss of time due to smaller classes

In the eyes of the teachers in the pilot schools, then, some of the key process aims of TVEI are being fulfilled. We saw earlier that the need for experiential teaching methods was one of the two best-known TVEI criteria, so a strong link is suggested between knowledge of a particular aim and the strength of its outcome. There is little perception by these teachers of increased pupil autonomy and this matches what we earlier saw to be their lower level of knowledge of this TVEI aim.

Perceived losses of TVEI

We similarly asked teachers if they perceived there to be any losses brought about by TVEI. A very much smaller number of losses than gains was mentioned by our interviewees (Table 22). The demands of TVEI-related INSET have been a burden in respect of teacher cover in all of the TVEI pilot projects with which we have had contact. We think it can be fairly argued that these are inevitable consequences of the start-up of any major innovation and that this main category of perceived loss should be discounted. The other categories of comment should quite clearly merit management attention:

Traditional subjects lose out

We feel the poor relations because the traditional subjects were left out at the beginning

We were alarmed by what we saw as the erosion of the academic tradition of the school

I gave the head my comments on ILEA's open learning materials . . . he said he wasn't including my subject – a *fait accompli* . . . Then I heard it was happening in other TVEI schools

We had an INSET day for staff at the school to learn about TVEI and there was a suggestion that humanities would come in but nothing has come of it

The TVEI core

Fifth years don't take the core seriously . . . lot of absenteeism on core days . . . it is not projected as a worthwhile subject

No losses to TVEI but mini-modules are tough going . . . it's all talk and chalk really, they don't get much practical work . . . can only do

Table 22 Teachers' perceived losses arising from TVEI

Category	% comments
Disruption to school because of TVEI-related INSET	39
Traditional subjects lose out	18
The TVEI core is a waste of time	15
Technological imbalance in curriculum	12
Curriculum decisions taken outside school	12
Other, e.g. lower ability lose out	4
Total	100

demonstration really because there is such a lot to cover . . . children
don't seem to enjoy it . . . say they are bored

Curriculum decisions taken outside the school

All the important curriculum decisions are taken at the TVE Centre

We thought it an imposition of curriculum by government

Lower ability children lose out

In making way for TVEI we had to lose subjects of value to the lower
ability children

Some subjects which were useful to the lower ability have disappeared.
I'm concerned about the lower ability range of choice

TVEI has helped higher ability more than lower ability . . . bit
disappointed in this

The four issues displayed above by some of the comments we received,
deserve comment. The first concerns the traditional subjects. We heard a lot
about how teachers of these feel they have lost out (more in some schools than
others) and about promises made to them which have not come to fruition.
There are scars and they need healing. We think it is time to win back the
dispossessed by some judicious management, and there is time to do this
within the second half of the resourcing of the pilot project.

Secondly, we did not meet any teacher who had received feedback on
the progress of TVEI nor even a deputy head who had read the evaluation
reports. We know from our own part, let alone the work which others have
done, that there is substantial feedback about the progress of the core. There
is much negative opinion about the TVEI core, and particularly so in
one school. It is our view that if the arguments for the core were more
widely known and if the evaluation detail was similarly known, then
teachers would have a more balanced view of whether the core is a *loss* or
not.

Thirdly, the Beacon TVEI Centre is perceived more in some places
than in others to be a negative, even satanic, influence. It is high time that this
issue of the balance of individual school autonomy and a central curriculum
policy model with consortium control is finally resolved, for there is a great
deal of wasted energy over the issue in our view. The root of the problem
where it exists is that the nature of consortium working has not been
communicated to the teachers in general. It is not realized that the decisions
flow from a management panel composed of the institutions themselves. It is
clear from what we heard that the Beacon TVEI Centre is presented in some
places as a convenient scapegoat for passing on decisions thought to be
unpalatable to those receiving the news.

Also, we found that in one school there was a widespread view, and in
another some view, that the lower ability children had lost out as a consequence of TVEI. We are frankly amazed about this, for elsewhere the
evidence is that TVEI has meant a better deal for the lower ability.

Table 23 Effect of TVEI on teaching and pupil relationships (teachers directly involved in TVEI)

Category	% answering 'Yes'
Affected way teach	77
Affected relationships with pupils	38

Teachers' view of the effect of TVEI on teaching methods and pupil relationships

We asked the interviewees to complete in writing several questions dealing with whether they had altered their teaching methods or relations with pupils as a result of TVEI (Table 23). We feel that this is a further significant piece of evidence indicating success in this aspect of process innovation in the Beacon pilot project. Once again though, there is some interesting variation between schools (Table 24), which correlates with the earlier measures of TVEI awareness we discussed.

We asked our interviewees to write down how their teaching methods or pupil relations have been changed by TVEI, and we received very substantial evidence of the existence of experiential teaching:

More use of computers and work sheets

Has made me less prescriptive and more questioning of received wisdom . . . there is more oral work . . . more pupil orientation

It [TVEI] has involved me in a new type of practically based teaching

Less talk and chalk; more experiential and practical

I now circulate far more among the pupils when teaching

More hands on for pupils

There is now CAL and supported self-study in my A level teaching

Pupils are learning by doing . . . individual teaching is possible . . . and there is far more group work

Made the approach more practical . . . essentially through individualism and relevance

Table 24a TVEI changed teaching methods by school

School	% yes
A	92
B	57
C	75
D	71
E	75

b TVEI changed pupil relations by school

School	% yes
A	50
B	14
C	16
D	35
E	50

work is done through work sheets and pupils have to find out for themselves

More investigation

Brought enterprise in . . . and teach more through computer software

Of course some teachers were quick to point out to us that 'it is difficult to differentiate the effect of TVEI and GCSE'. Nevertheless, the significance of the type of comments we have illustrated above is that teachers can describe in their own words how they have changed in the classroom so that 'experiential' is not just a piece of official jargon in policy documents or an abstraction but a reality.

Teachers' written comments on the effect of TVEI on pupil relationships:

Much more personal and individual contact with pupils

Improved relationships through negotiation of content and direction

Better communication . . . they ask questions more freely

More discussion with pupils

It leads naturally to more discussion . . . learning through experience nurtures closer relationships

Interrelationships far greater

Many of our interviewees interpreted the question to mean whether the quality rather than the format of their relationships with pupils had changed, and answered 'no' on that basis. A significant number did, however, declare that the format or pattern of their relationships with pupils had been affected by TVEI and described these changes in the way illustrated above. What these comments are saying in our opinion is that consequent on the adoption of more experiential methods there is significantly more interaction with pupils on an individual rather than group basis.

Communicating TVEI – the challenge

We said earlier that there is still much scope to communicate more widely to teachers about TVEI. The following are examples of the sort of comments we received which to our mind raise issues of communication in addition to those indicated already by inter-school differences in outcomes, or by relative shortfalls in the level of awareness of certain official aims of TVEI:

Fifth years don't take the core seriously . . . lot of absenteeism on core days . . . it is not projected as a worthwhile subject

It [i.e. core in sixth form] takes time from the academic

TVEI encourages new methods of teaching but there has been an information gap for people who aren't involved

ILPAC – Pupils don't like working independently

ABAL – pupils have lost confidence to some extent

I believe that modern ideas and concepts have become ends in themselves . . . In reality pupils do not enjoy modular courses lasting a matter of weeks

Why haven't we seen the evaluation reports you have been writing

Nothing really lost by TVEI but pupils are bored stiff by it

I don't know anything about TVEI really, haven't been at the school long but I would like to get to know about it and be involved

The children are saying that they have filled in questionnaires etc. and haven't had any feedback. Will there be feedback of this?

The general comment we would wish to make on the basis of the above statements is that we do not feel that many of them would have been made if the full purposes of a particular TVEI policy had been effectively communicated, or if systematic feedback about the progress of TVEI had been given to teachers. In the absence of detailed knowledge there is always a tendency to label the whole on the basis of simple anecdote or hearsay. Take, for example, the comments on the TVEI core and TVEI generally. They are just not true regarding pupils as a whole, for we know this from pupils' own verbal and written statements in evaluation, yet such views are, in the absence of hard knowledge, being transmitted as the received wisdom. School management has the facts to rectify these knowledge deficits on the part of teachers. Similarly with regard to profiling or the use of open learning materials – have the purposes of these been fully explained in relation to existing practices?

The staff survey – overall conclusions

We see some very encouraging messages indeed coming out of the findings of this staff survey; also, some issues for development action on the part of the consortium. Of most importance is that the teachers see TVEI to have overwhelmingly brought gains to schools and pupils. There is clear evidence from the teachers' own words that the intended innovations in teaching methods are being achieved and interpreted as a spur to professional satisfaction and pupil benefit.

Whilst there is generally a good awareness of the aims of TVEI among many participating staff and others, a first issue for development action is that teachers do not all yet understand what these mean in terms of the totality of changed practice desired. Here we have in mind the issues of profiling, more pupil autonomy, access for the traditional subjects, and issues of sex stereotyping. Moreover, the teachers have not received feedback on the achievements of TVEI to date. Teachers, even deputy heads, are carrying around with them judgements on TVEI formed from their own partial experiences (or prejudices) and their views are informing actions which in some places are self-defeating to the very aims desired. It is crucial that staff as a whole should be resourced by systematic evaluation data on the progress of TVEI.

Secondly, the nature of the TVEI development strategy used in a school looks to be a crucial factor in the rate of diffusion of TVEI awareness and practice. In those schools where TVEI is perceived by teachers to have penetrated most, this greater success is correlated with a management strategy that deliberately intended it for the whole school or to roll it increasingly through the departments, and with evidence of very systematic and clear communication from the top. In the two schools where this has happened most, we see from hard evidence greater progress in TVEI awareness and practice. In all of this the degree of commitment and vision of top management is the crucial factor, even though it may be expressed in outwardly different styles. There are therefore some important disparities in the level of TVEI achievement between institutions, and these need to be eroded. Leadership, communication and consultation are the keys to the more even achievement of TVEI aims.

Thirdly, and without detracting from the very definite success of Beacon TVEI so far in making significant content and teaching methods innovations (in the eyes of pupils and teachers), there is still the issue of some balance between content and process achievement to be addressed, and here we are referring to those process mechanisms requiring more autonomous and active pupil roles.

Selection, appraisal and development

from Colin Riches and Colin Morgan, eds. _Human Resource Management in Education_. Philadelphia: Open University Press, 1989.

13

The spirit of performance

P. F. Drucker

The purpose of an organization is to enable ordinary human beings to do extraordinary things.

No organization can depend on genius; the supply is always scarce and unreliable. It is the test of an organization to make ordinary people perform better than they seem capable of, to bring out whatever strength there is in its members, and to use each person's strength to help all the other members perform. It is the task of organization at the same time to neutralize the individual weaknesses of its members. The test of an organization is the spirit of performance.

The spirit of performance requires that there be full scope for individual excellence. The focus must be on the strengths – on what people can do rather than on what they cannot do.

'Morale' in an organization does not mean that 'people get along together'. The test is performance. Human relations that are not grounded in the satisfaction of good performance in work are actually poor human relations. There is no greater indictment of an organization than that the strength and ability of the outstanding individual threatens the group and that his or her performance becomes a source of difficulty, frustration and discouragement for the others.

Spirit of performance in a human organization means that its energy output is larger than the sum of the efforts put in. It means the creation of energy. This cannot be accomplished by mechanical means. A machine cannot deliver more energy than is put into it. To get out more than is being put in is possible only in the moral sphere.

By morality I do not mean preachments. Morality, to have any meaning at all, must be a principle of action. It must not be speeches, sermons or good intentions. *It must be practices.* Specifically:

1 The focus of the organization must be on *performance*. The first requirement of the spirit of performance is high performance standards, for the group as well as for each individual. The organization must cultivate in itself the habit of achievement.

2 The focus of the organization must be on *opportunities* rather than on problems.

3 The *decisions that affect people* – their placement and their pay, promotion, demotion and severance – must express the values and beliefs of the organization. They are the true controls of an organization.

4 Finally, in its people decisions, management must demonstrate that it realizes that *integrity* is one absolute requirement of managers, the one quality that they must bring with them and cannot be expected to acquire later on. And management must demonstrate that it requires the same integrity of itself.

The danger of safe mediocrity

The constant temptation of every organization is safe mediocrity. The first requirement of organizational health is a high demand on performance. Indeed, one of the major reasons for demanding that management be by objectives and that it focus on the objective requirements of the task is the need to have managers set high standards of performance for themselves.

This requires that performance be understood properly. Performance is not hitting the bull's-eye with every shot – that is a circus act that can be maintained only over a few minutes. Performance is rather the consistent ability to produce results over prolonged periods of time and in a variety of assignments. A performance record must include mistakes. It must include failures. It must reveal a person's limitations as well as strengths. And there are as many different kinds of performance as there are different human beings. One person will consistently do well, rarely falling far below a respectable standard, but also rarely excel through brilliance or virtuosity. Another will perform only adequately under normal circumstances but will rise to the demands of a crisis or a major challenge and then perform like a true 'star'. Both are 'performers'. Both need to be recognized. But their performances will look quite different.

The one to distrust, however, is the person who never makes a mistake, never commits a blunder, never fails in what he tries to do. Either he is a phony, or he stays with the safe, the tried and the trivial.

A management which does not define performance as a balance of success and failure over a period of time is a management that mistakes conformity for achievement, and absence of weaknesses for strengths. It is a management that discourages its organization. The better a person is, the more mistakes he will make – for the more new things he will try.

The person who consistently renders poor or mediocre performance should be removed from the job for his or her own good. People who find themselves in a job that exceeds their capacities are frustrated, harassed, anxiety-ridden people. One does not do people a service by leaving them in a job they are not equal to. Not to face up to failure in a job is cowardice rather than compassion.

One also owes it to the manager's subordinates not to tolerate poor performance in their boss. They have a right to be managed with competence, dedication and achievement. Subordinates have a right to a boss who performs, for otherwise they themselves cannot perform.

One owes it finally to all the people in the organization not to put up with a manager who fails to perform. The entire organization is diminished by the manager or career professional who performs poorly or not at all. It is enriched by the one who performs superbly.

At first sight the Japanese seem to violate this rule. For few, if any, people are ever fired for nonperformance in the Japanese organization. Actually the Japanese organization may be as demanding and even as competitive as any in the West. The poor or mediocre performer is not fired. He is quickly side-tracked and assigned to activities that are in effect 'made work'. And both he and the organization know it. Moreover, while everyone advances in pay and title according to seniority, there is a day of reckoning at or around age forty-five when the very few who will become top management are chosen from the many others who will, ten years later, retire as section managers or department directors.

The only thing that is proven by a person's not performing in a given assignment is that management has made a mistake in giving him or her that assignment. It is a mistake that managers cannot avoid, no matter how carefully they work on the placement of people. 'Failure' in such a case may mean only that a first-rate career professional has been miscast as a manager. It may mean that someone excellent at running an existing operation has been miscast as an innovator and entrepreneur. Or it may mean the opposite: that a person whose strength lies in doing new and different things has been miscast to head a continuing, well-established and highly routinized operation.

Failure to perform on the part of an individual who has a record of proven performance is a signal to think hard about the person and the job. And sometimes, of course [. . .] it is the job rather than the person that is at fault.

George C. Marshall, Chief of Staff of the US Army in World War II, was an uncompromising and exacting boss who refused to tolerate mediocrity, let alone failure. 'I have a duty to the soldiers, their parents, and the country, to remove immediately any commander who does not satisfy the highest performance demands', Marshall said again and again. But he always asserted, 'It was my mistake to have put this or that man in a command that was not the right command for him. It is therefore *my* job to think through where he belongs.' Many of the men who emerged in World War II as highly successful commanders in the US Army were once in the course of their careers removed by Marshall from an early assignment. But then Marshall thought through the mistake *he* had made – and tried to figure out where that man belonged. And this explains, in large measure, why the American Army, which had gone into World War II without a single one of its future general officers yet in a command position, produced an outstanding group of leaders in a few short years.

'Conscience' decisions

The toughest cases, but also the most important ones, are those of people who have given long and loyal service to the company but who have outlived their capacity to contribute.

There is, for instance, the bookkeeper who started when the company was in its infancy and grew with it until, at age fifty or so, she finds herself controller of a large company and totally out of her depth. The woman has not changed – the demands of the job have. She has given faithful service. And where loyalty has been received, loyalty is due. But still, she must not be allowed to remain as controller. Not only does her inability to perform endanger the company, her inadequacy demoralizes the entire management group and discredits management altogether.

Such cases – fortunately not too numerous – challenge the conscience of an organization. To keep the controller in her job would be betrayal of the enterprise and of all its people. But to fire a person who has given thirty years of faithful service is also betraying a trust. And to say, 'We should have taken care of this twenty-five years ago', while true, is not much help.

The decision in such cases must be objective, that is, focused on the good of the company: the person must be removed from the job. Yet the decision is also a human decision which requires utmost consideration, true compassion, and an acceptance of obligations. That Henry Ford II could revive the moribund Ford Motor Company after World War II was in large measure the result of his understanding the crucial importance of these 'conscience cases'.

At that time, none of the nine management people in one key division was found to be competent to take on the new jobs created in the course of reorganization. Not one was appointed to these new jobs. Yet, for these nine men, jobs as technicians and experts were found within the organization. It would have been easy to fire them. Their incompetence as managers was undisputed. But they had also served loyally through very trying years. Henry Ford II took the line that no one should be allowed to hold a job without giving superior performance, but he also held that no one should be penalized for the mistakes of the previous management. The company owes its rapid revival largely to the strict observance of this rule.

The frequent excuse in a conscience case, 'We can't move him; he has been here too long to be fired', is bad logic and rarely more than a weak-kneed alibi. It harms the performance of management people, their spirit and their respect for the company.

But to fire such a manager is equally bad. It violates the organization's sense of justice and decency. It shakes its faith in the integrity of management.

'There, but for the grace of God, go I', is what everybody will say – even though he or she would be the first to criticize if management left an incompetent in a position of importance.

A management that is concerned with the spirit of the organization therefore takes these cases exceedingly seriously. They are not too common, as a rule – or at least, they should not be. But they have impact on the spirit of the organization way beyond their numbers. How they are handled tells the organization both whether management takes itself and its job seriously, and whether it takes the human being seriously.

Focus on opportunity

An organization will have a high spirit of performance if it is consistently directed towards opportunity rather than towards problems. It will have the thrill of excitement, the sense of challenge, and the satisfaction of achievement if its energies are put where the results are, and that means on the opportunities.

Of course, problems cannot be neglected. But the problem-focused organization is an organization on the defensive. It is an organization that feels that it has performed well if things do not get worse.

A management that wants to create and maintain the spirit of achievement therefore stresses opportunity. But it will also demand that opportunities be converted into results.

A management that wants to makes its organization focus on opportunity demands that opportunity be given pride of place in the objectives and goals of each manager and career professional. 'What are the opportunities which, if realized, will have the greatest impact on performance and results of the company and of my unit?' should be the first topic to which managers and career professionals should address themselves in their performance and work plan.
[. . .]

Integrity, the touchstone

The final proof of the sincerity and seriousness of a management is uncompromising emphasis on integrity of character. This, above all, has to be symbolized in management's 'people' decisions. For it is character through which leadership is exercised; it is character that sets the example and is imitated. Character is not something managers can acquire; if they do not bring it to the job they will never have it. It is not something one can fool people about. A person's co-workers, especially the subordinates, know in a few weeks whether he or she has integrity or not. They may forgive a great deal; incompetence, ignorance, insecurity or bad manners. But they will not forgive a lack of integrity. Nor will they forgive higher management for choosing such a person.

Integrity may be difficult to define, but what constitutes lack of integrity of such seriousness as to disqualify a person for a managerial position is not. Someone whose vision focuses on people's weaknesses rather than on their strengths should never be appointed to a managerial position. The manager who always knows exactly what people cannot do, but never sees anything they can do, will undermine the spirit of the organization. Of course, a manager would have a clear grasp of the limitations of subordinates, but should see these as limitations on what they can do, and as challenges to them to do better. A manager should be a realist; and no one is less realistic than the cynic.

A person should not be appointed if he or she is more interested in the question 'Who is right?' than in the question 'What is right?' To put personality above the requirements of the work is corruption and corrupts. To ask 'Who is right?' encourages one's subordinates to play safe, if not to play politics.

Management should not appoint anyone who considers intelligence more important than integrity. This is immaturity – and usually incurable. It should never promote a person who has shown that he or she is afraid of strong subordinates. This is weakness. It should never put into a management job a person who does not set high standards for his own work. For that breeds contempt for the work and for management's competence.

A man might himself know too little, perform poorly, lack judgement and ability, and yet not do too much damage as a manager. But if he lacks in character and integrity – no matter how knowledgeable, how brilliant, how successful – he destroys. He destroys people, the most valuable resource of the enterprise. He destroys spirit. And he destroys performance.

This is particularly true of the people at the head of an enterprise. For the spirit of an organization is created from the top. If an organization is great in spirit, it is because the spirit of its top people is great. If it decays, it does so because the top rots; as the proverb has it, 'Trees die from the top'. No one should ever be appointed to a senior position unless top management is willing to have his character serve as the model for his subordinates.

This chapter has talked of 'practices'. It has not talked of 'leadership'. This was intentional. There is no substitute for leadership. But management cannot create leaders. It can only create the conditions under which potential leadership qualities become effective; or it can stifle potential leadership. The supply of leadership is much too uncertain to be depended upon for creating the spirit that the enterprise needs to be productive and to hold together.

Practices, though seemingly humdrum, can always be practised whatever a person's aptitudes, personality or attitudes. Practices require no genius – only application. They are things to do rather than to talk about.

And the right practices should go a long way towards bringing out whatever potential for leadership there is in the management group. They should also lay the foundation for the right kind of leadership. For leadership is not magnetic personality – that can just as well be a glib tongue. It is not 'making friends and influencing people' – that is flattery. Leadership is lifting

...on to higher sights, the raising of a person's performance to a
...the building of a personality beyond its normal limitations.
...repares the ground for such leadership than a spirit of
...t confirms in the day-to-day practices of the organization
...ies of conduct and responsibility, high standards of perform-
...respect for individuals and their work.

Summary

The purpose of organization is to enable ordinary human beings to do extraordinary things. The test of an organization is therefore the spirit of performance. This requires specific practices rather than preachment. It requires above all realization that integrity is the one absolute requirement of managers.

14

Inside the interview 'black box': the tenuous status of job-related evidence in LEA selection panel decisions

Colin Morgan

Background

Between 1980 and 1984 a team from the Open University under the direction of the author investigated the appointment of secondary school headteachers in England and Wales (the POST Project). The team, compared the LEAs' selection practices with other occupational contexts, and made over fifty recommendations for the improvement of headship selection generally to the then Secretary of State for Education. Much of what was reported to the government has already been published in two books;[1] so this paper discusses from a mass of data which the project collected over three years, the results of a previously unpublished special survey of three interview panels known at the time as the 'black box' survey.[2] The findings of this survey, which were integrated with the other data sources on which our overall critique of LEA staff selection practices was based, illustrate in their own right many of the key generic issues which apply to the selection function within human resource management whether it be in education or elsewhere. These are: What is job selection really all about? What is the connection between the criteria selectors use and performance in the job? What can and what cannot be predicted from previous experience?

Survey of three LEA secondary headteacher selection panel members

During secondary headship panel interviews in two LEAs in England and one in Wales, each lay panel member was given a short questionnaire immediately the last candidate had left the room, and before any discussion of candidates could take place. The POST team had in any case been observing all stages of these three headship appointments and making notes as part of our extensive ethnographic survey of the LEA appointment procedures. This had included over two dozen LEAs chosen as representative of the authorities as a whole in England and Wales. In the three LEAs under discussion we had been fortunate to develop a position of sufficient acceptance over time that the chairpersons of the panels allowed us to carry out a special survey at a key stage during the actual interviews. Our survey objectives were explained before the interviews started, indicating that we would be administering and collecting in the results of a questionnaire before the final discussion and decision stage of the appointment.

In order not to hold up the process of selecting the successful candidate we had to prepare the most economic of questionnaires. This meant cutting some corners and grouping together some items we might otherwise have kept separate had there not been the need to administer it quickly and with the minimum of fuss. The six items set down on the questionnaire were:

Appearance, presence, voice
Quality of question answers
Experience
Qualifications
Knowledge of local culture
Personality

These had been suggested by our earlier observations of appointment committees where we had written down all statements used by selectors which appeared to be either recommending or rejecting a candidate, that is, all statements which contained a positive or negative selection criterion in the mind of the user. These statements had been sorted into ten categories so that we could assess their relative weight of usage at various stages of the whole selection process. This ethnographic evidence was used to suggest the most potent categories for a shortened list in this quick 'black box' survey as well as to test out some further thoughts.

For example, from its observation and recording the POST team had derived an important selection criterion category, which it had labelled 'Personality/personal qualities'. This category brought together selectors' references to candidates' physical features, social impact attributes, as well as more holistic personality labels, which were conveyed in statements such as: 'Tall and physically distinguished'; 'Hail fellow well met type'; 'Very Welsh, goes on and on and on' etc. Sometimes these types of 'Personality' attributes or deficits were separately referred to, and at other times they were linked together in the same statement.

It had seemed that many selectors used constructs of 'personality' which differentiated between notions of external personality such as appearance, presence etc. and the more holistic or hidden aspects, all of which in their assumptions told them something about the fitness of the candidate for the job being filled. Hence, when we came to decide upon our 'black box' list of items we distinguished between 'Appearance/presence/voice', and 'Personality' as discrete items in the six proffered the selectors on the questionnaire.

Alongside each item on the questionnaire sheet was a box, and below the boxes were several write-in spaces with the rubric: 'other (please specify)', to record the other criteria the panel selectors were invited to write in. By this fairly crude and simple instrument it was intended to obtain evidence on the types and priorities of criteria each selector said they had been using to choose the person for whom they would vote or argue for in the decision stage that was to follow as soon as the questionnaire had been collected in.

The questionnaire simply asked the panel members:

> we are interested in the qualities which you took into account in making your choice of candidate. Please show the importance you attach to each of these by inserting a number in the appropriate box. For example, if you feel 'qualifications' are the most important factor for you, put a 1 in the box by qualifications, and so on. Leave the box blank for those qualities which you did not regard as important in making your choice. If you took into account qualities not listed, please add them in the space provided on the bottom.

The questionnaire was directed at the lay selectors only, for they alone have a vote in any appointment decision. The lay selectors, that is, the LEA members and school governors, varied in number between the three panels, though nowhere were they less than seven. In total, 28 usable questionnaires were completed, each carrying a selector's rank order. Eleven of the respondents had written in addition to their rank orders one or more additional criteria; these were: previous work performance; what the references had said; future needs of school; possess a liberal outlook; possess a community concern; educational philosophy; be pro governors; leadership; liveliness; and, outside interests. In the event we were therefore able to derive a ranking for sixteen criteria, i.e. the six set down and the ten which had been written in.

What the black box revealed

The term 'black box' has been used in the title to this paper to convey the image which best describes the traditional procedures in LEA headteacher selection; namely that the criteria the selectors use have not been explicitly agreed. They are hidden and exist in the dark or the 'black box' of the selectors' minds. In none of the three LEAs of this survey, nor any of the many others where we had observed headship appointment procedures, were selectors given any explicit guidance about the criteria they should take into account. They were also not asked to record evidence about candidates against criteria which could be called upon later.

Furthermore, and regarding the main currency of the whole interview transaction, the questions, only in a very small minority of cases did selectors prepare any questions beforehand and then this is usually left to officers. The 'resource' which each selector has available therefore on which to make a decision on his preferred candidate is basically twofold: the answers made by candidates to whatever questions they happen to be asked on the day; plus, what inferences they can make from the candidates' application forms, or summaries of these, with which they are invariably provided. Only in a minority of cases are there additional sources of information available to some selectors and then more by accident than by design: selectors may have seen candidates at previous interviews, know of them in their existing posts because they are governors of the school where they currently work, or know them in some extramural setting. Such fortuitous previous knowledge can give inputs to their selection decision in the current appointment procedure, inputs which can strike the observer as bizarre, for example: by a county councillor at an appointment in a large city: 'two weeks ago I saw him in shorts and banjo doing a music-hall act. That is why I am pushing him [for headship] now.'

Additionally, only the barest information about the job being filled or procedural direction about the conduct of the interviews is given to LEA selectors beforehand, so that overall a 'play it by ear' and 'what everybody knows' mode characterizes the whole operation. Given this context, then, what did these selectors say they took into account in their appointments of headteachers to these three large secondary schools?

Table 1 records using PW (proportional weighting[3]) scores the first ten ranks for the criteria used by the 28 lay selectors in these three appointment committees. The scores for the lowest six ranks have not been included

Table 1 Criteria declared by selectors in three LEA secondary headship appointments ($N = 28$)

Criterion	'n'	PW score (3)	Rank
Personality	28	2166	1
Experience	25	1836	2
Answers to questions	27	1679	3
Qualifications	26	1577	4
Appearance/voice/presence	27	1379	5
Local culture knowledge	18	500	6
Educational philosophy	2	159	7
Liberal outlook	2	138	8
Previous performance	2	114	9
Community concern	2	89	10

'n' = number of selectors ranking that criterion

in the table as they are so low that we can effectively ignore them from the discussion in that they reflect the minority or excentric interest of one selector only in each case. The PW score is a device to take account of the fact that individual respondents rated different individual criteria and a different number of items overall. Hence account has to be taken of the fact that the weight of influence of any one position in a selector's rank order, is relative to the total number of rankings declared as having been used in the total decision.

The table shows five criterion constructs to have dominated the selectors' choices of candidates: personality; experience; question answers; qualifications; and appearance/voice/presence. These 'black box' findings are in line with those which we had obtained ethnographically from observing a much larger number of selectors where at the final interview stage (as well as all others) the category of 'Personality/personal qualities' was a clear first.[4]

In this survey the criteria in ranks 1 and 5, i.e. 'Personality' and 'Appearance etc.', equate with the single 'personality/personal qualities' category of the ethnographic survey where it accounted for 39% of all criteria used at the final interview stage of secondary headship appointments. Interestingly, if we compute and combine the weight of usage of criteria 1 and 5 in this black box survey their weight of usage is virtually the same (38%). What these selectors said counted most in their appointment choice decisions – judgements on personality variously defined – therefore matches what we had recorded them to use. What happens in the 'black box' of selectors' minds finds parallel expression then in selectors verbal statements.

These rankings as well as the additional comments made on the questionnaires also confirmed our assumptions that some selectors find they can make a clear distinction between what we earlier labelled as internal and external constructs of personality. Those who do not when presented with such a distinction express their confusion by comments such as, 'what is the difference?' or write alongside 'Appearance/presence/voice', remarks such as 'same thing as personality'.

Discussion

The findings presented here raise, as did those of the wider POST project, several far-reaching questions for the human resource manager. First, the dominant criterion category of Personality raises perhaps more than for any other category the need for some precision in answer to the question: 'what is job selection really all about?' Should the selection process really be about the search for 'the right personality' as this and many other studies show it often to be?[5] The answer to this key question turns on whether the overriding concern of the selection process is to be a test of *social acceptability* to the selectors at the time – which in large measure is mediated through individual views of personality – or whether the concern is to be clearly focused on *future job performance.* A prime concern to predict future job performance would mean assessing the competencies associated with it.

A management perspective, concerned as it is with the achievement of performance on explicit objectives is unequivocal in its answer to this question. It must view job selection as a procedure concerned with predicting future job performance and ensuring that the criteria the selection procedure uses have predictive validity. By predictive validity is meant that the evidence used in the selection decisions does in fact predict performance in the real job situation. This latter test is central to the managerial approach. Where then does this test leave the five criterion categories revealed by this 'black box' survey to play such a significant part in headship appointment decisions?

To begin with personality, there clearly can be no predictive connection between 'Personality' or 'Appearance/presence/voice' as colloquially defined in the interview situation and performance on the job;[6] but what about *Experience, Qualifications,* or *Question Answers?* Where do these stand with regard to the test of predictive validity? Are they, as criterion categories, job related to the extent that they can reasonably be held to predict future performance as a secondary school headteacher?

Taking *Answers to Questions* first of all. Ostensibly this is what the interview is all about – a test of knowledge related to the job, which is revealed in the answers made by the candidates. Assuming the questions to be job related (which observation shows to be a problematic matter[7]), the 'black box' survey shows them not to have primacy, but to occupy a lower position in importance than that which candidates think they hold. Candidates who do not succed at interview usually attribute their failure to not having understood, or not to have answered some question correctly, rather than ascribe their 'failure' to how their personality was perceived on the day. They believe that the interview is about getting the question answers right, as we found out from another survey we did with unsuccessful candidates.

Had Answers to Questions been the top ranked criterion category, though, would the knowledge they furnished (even assuming them to have been about the job) have been a sufficient predictor for appointment? This question raises the whole issue of how we are to classify job-related competencies. A useful formulation is to see the predictive categories of evidence as attributable to Knowledge, Skill, or Attitudes, which are demonstrably job related. Of these three categories it is the skills category – what people can do and be observed to do – which the research shows to have the greatest validity. With the exception of oral communication, and possibly sensitivity to some extent, the interview as a selection method cannot measure skills. Only job simulations can test skills associated with top management posts such as headship, skills such as: organizing ability, leadership, communication, problem analysis, judgement and so on in the situation. The interview does not therefore provide evidence on the most pertinent competency category for future performance, and it is not even an efficient mechanism for testing knowledge.

What about the predictive force of the criterion category of Experience, though? Does this not carry with it the evidence needed on skills? It is a truism of occupational selection that past performance is the best predictor of future performance; that is, past performance has predictive validity. So far so good, but is the category of Experience as understood by the selectors in this 'black box' survey, the same as past performance? The answer is a clear 'no', for there are at present no mechanisms in LEA appointment practices which provide at the point of the panel interview past performance data on candidates. What *is* available under Experience for selectors to consider is in fact information on the appointments candidates have held over time. If selectors have any information on previous performance as distinct from experience then, it must be fortuitously rather than systematically derived as not even the references give performance information on any explicit basis; they serve in the main as bland seals of approval or, more frequently by innuendo, disapproval.

However, let us suppose in the three headship appointments which are the subject of this study, that instead of data on experience drawn from application forms or their summaries, there had in fact been hard data on the candidates' performance as deputy heads, which they all were. Does this lead us out of the wood? Would there then be a sufficient predictive evidential base in terms of future job performance because it would be known from that evidence how they had performed as deputies? Unfortunately not, for this past performance is related to a particular type of job profile and previously demonstrated 'developed abilities'. It does not tell us how a candidate will respond to job demands which were not part of previous performance; that is, it still does not give us information in terms of 'latent abilities'. Translated into the headship context, what this means is that excellent performance as a deputy head is only predictive of performance in those skills which carry over into the job of headship. The whole range of 'new' skills required in headship and which are not called for in deputy headship, are left untested by any evidence on previous performance, and could only be tested ahead of time by job simulations.

The remaining category of the five most prominent in the 'black box' survey – *Qualifications* – need not detain us in discussion; the predictive ability of qualifications is in proportion to their relevance to the behaviours of the future job. The dubious link between academic qualifications obtained many years previously and the managerial skills needed in top management now is obvious. All in all then, what the 'black box' survey evidences is the tenuous link between the selection system and job-related factors. The headship selection system described by this evidence does not satisfy the management perspective which must see selection as an intentional activity to secure future performance. In summary, therefore, this survey is yet more evidence to insist that the human resource manager secure answers to the key questions:

What is the connection between the criteria selectors use and performance in the job?

How are 'latent abilities' to be assessed?

Conclusion

Finally, it is important to indicate how the answers to such questions have elsewhere resulted in more sophisticated selection procedures to tackle the central issue of predictive validity regarding headship selection. The National Association of Secondary School Principals (NASSP) in the USA has responded to the inadequacies of the traditional interview methods with its present emphasis on image factors by pioneering the *assessment centre* approach.

This approach concentrates heavily on the specific skill dimensions of headship, and aims to assess them by a battery of analogous tests, otherwise known as job samples or simulations, as well as structured interviews. Twelve skill dimensions are assessed, which were derived by a job study that covered the tasks and responsibilities set out in the job descriptions and performance appraisal instruments used by the school districts, and as described in interviews with people who had a thorough knowledge of the job.[8] The NASSP assessment centre approach has been the subject of a validation study which found that the skill dimensions and tasks set were relevant to headship; that is, it had content validity; also it predicted performance in the job.[9] The significance of the NASSP methods is that, like the British Civil Service, and some industrial and commercial corporations in the UK, they apply rigorous definitions of the job competencies required, job simulation tests, and in-depth structured interviews, which are assessed by trained assessors.

What the 'black box' evidence, when set against the needs of the managerial perspective, therefore challenges for the world of education in the UK is how to accommodate requirements which can appear conflicting: the management need for impartial technical assessment methods to gather evidence on candidate fitness for headship; and the need to satisfy the demand for a visible democratic accountability and social legitimation by the local community. The application of the management perspective to selection in other public services has resolved this 'conflict' by ensuring that only those candidates who have satisfied the most rigorous technical assessment and found to be capable of doing the job to a satisfactory minimum level of performance are offered to the 'democratic controllers' for appointment decision.

Notes

1 Morgan, C., Hall, V., and Mackay, H. (1984) *The Selection of Secondary School Headteachers*, Open University Press, Milton Keynes; and Morgan, C., Hall, V. and Mackay, H. *A Handbook on Selecting Senior Staff for Schools*, Open University Press, Milton Keynes.
2 The 'black box' survey instrument was administered in one of the LEAs by Stella Fisher and the other two by Colin Morgan who alone is responsible for the analysis.

3 Proportional weighting of any ranked item was determined thus:

$$PW = \frac{100(N + 1 - r)}{\Sigma N}$$

where N = number of attributes ranked by the respondent,
   r = rank number given by respondent.

4 The top three ranked categories, based on selectors' verbal comments in a range of final interviews were: Personality/personal qualities 39%; Interview Performance 17%; and, Fitness for this School 13%. For a fuller account see: 'The selection and appointment of heads' by Colin Morgan, in *World Year Book of Education* (Hoyle, A. and McMahon, A. Eds) (1987), Longman, London.

5 Unknown to the POST project at the time, a parallel American study found that localistic notions of fit or image were central in secondary school headteacher appointments. See: Baltsell, C. D. and Dentler, R. A. (1983), *Selecting American School Principals: a Research Report*, Abt Associates, Cambridge, Mass.

6 The basis of this statement is the fact that the predictive validity as a whole is low, at best about 0.1, and for untrained panel interviewers generally taken to be no better than chance.

7 The basis of this statement is that the POST project carried out a content analysis of all the questions asked candidates in a range of final interviews and found for example that of all LEA members questions 27% could only be classified as personal.

8 Hersey, P. (1980) 'NASSP's Assessment Center: practitioners speak out', *National Association of Secondary Schools Bulletin*, 64, 439, 87–117.

9 Schmitt, N. *et al.* (1982), 'Criterion related and content validity of the NASSP Assessment Center Research Report', Department of Psychology, Michigan State University, East Lansing.

15

Assessment centers in the public sector: a practical approach[1]

Dennis A. Joiner

[. . .]

The use of assessment center technology has been evolving and accelerating since its first use in the USA by the Office of Strategic Services (a war time agency set up by the President and Congress) which assessed 5,391 persons in the United States between December 1943 and August 1945 (Murray and MacKinnon, 1946; MacKinnon, 1977; OSS Assessment Staff, 1948). The first major documented use of assessment center procedures in American industry was a monumental study, the Management Progress Study, conducted at AT&T beginning in 1956 (Bray, 1964; Bray and Grant, 1966; Bray, Campbell and Grant, 1974). The study involved 422 recently hired men who have been followed to determine their professional growth and characteristics which lead to success in management. The results of the initial eight year predictive validity study were quite positive. Eighty-five percent of the individuals who achieved the middle management level had been correctly identified by the assessment process (Bray and Grant, 1966; Thornton and Byham, 1982).

The success of the Management Progress Study at AT&T served to intensify efforts there as well as the efforts of others which in many cases were already underway. Additional accounts of assessment center programs and validity research began to appear from AT&T, (Campbell and Bray, 1967; Bray and Campbell, 1968); General Electric (Meyer, 1970); IBM (Hinrichs, 1969; Wollowick and McNamara, 1969; Kruat and Scott, 1972); Sears and Roebuck (Bentz, 1969); and Standard Oil of Ohio (Finkle and Jones, 1970 [. . .]).

In 1970 an article by William C. Byham appeared in the Harvard Business Review (Byham, 1970). The article based on Byham's experiences implementing the process for J. C. Penney, as well as the work of others cited above, captured and communicated to the general business community the excitement of the evolving assessment center concept and the validity evidence obtained to that point. Three years later James R. Huck (Huck, 1973) published the results of an extensive review of the assessment center literature. Huck's review, revised and republished in 1977 (Huck, 1977), integrated the results of 50 studies which all showed positive findings. Included in this analysis of the existing research was a comparison of the assessment center approach to more traditional methods of selection. Based on combining 'a series of independent studies conducted over a period of years on different assessment programs . . . ,' Huck states:

> These data allow us to estimate the probability of success, given various methods of selection. . . . the probability of selecting an 'above-average performer' by choosing an individual at random is 15 percent. When management nominates an individual for a supervisory position based on whatever factors are available other than assessment results, the probability of selecting an 'above-average performer' is 35 percent. However, if an individual is recommended by management AND rated 'acceptable' in the assessment center, the probability increases to 76 percent. Thus, by utilizing results of the assessment process, the chance rate is substantially increased and the probability of selecting a 'winner' more than doubles.

By far the most comprehensive summary of the validity of assessment center programs as well as the most complete source on assessment centers, to date, is the Thornton and Byham text, *Assessment Centers and Managerial Performance* (1982).

Research on the validity of the assessment center process as it is now being implemented in thousands of settings, public and private, continues. Unfortunately, the amount of research does not seem to be accelerating as fast as the increase in the use of the process and variations of the methodology. The major entities with the professional commitment and resources who are conducting meaningful research are, in large part, the same entities who conducted the original research studies mentioned above. Smaller organizations it seems, tend to rely on the validity evidence of the larger organizations. Recognizing this trend and potential misunderstanding and misuse of the methodology, professionals using the process drafted and adopted the 'Standards and Ethical Considerations for Assessment Center Operations', the most recent revision of which was adopted by the 7th International Congress on the Assessment Center Method in New Orleans (Moses, 1977).[2] These Standards provide an excellent definition of what an assessment center is and what it is not as well as a number of legal and practical considerations which should be reviewed prior to implementing an assessment center program for selection, promotion or employee development.

[. . .]

What is an assessment center?

While all assessment centers are different they usually have certain elements in common which are governed by ethical standards (Moses, 1977), professional standards (Division of Industrial and Organization Psychologists, 1980), as well as federal guidelines (EEOC, 1978), and case law regarding employee selection procedures.

Assessment centers are often defined as 'a variety of testing techniques designed to allow candidates to demonstrate, under standardized conditions, the skills and abilities most essential for success in a given job'.

A center will usually consist of a series of individual and group exercises designed to simulate the most essential conditions of the job. Candidate behavior is observed by a team of trained raters, called assessors. The assessors are usually 'content experts' drawn from the ranks one or two levels above the target classification. In local government civil service systems the assessors are often from other jurisdictions or other divisions or departments which helps ensure that bias from prior contact with the individual candidates does not interfere with the objective evaluation candidate effectiveness.

The assessors view candidate effectiveness from a common frame of reference under standardized conditions. This frame of reference is established through training the assessors to evaluate behavior relevant to specific performance dimensions (behavioral skill characteristics) determined to be essential through an analysis of the job. The dimensions are observed and evaluated through the standardized job simulation exercises. Finally, after all the exercises have been completed, the assessors meet and pool their observations of each candidate to arrive at an overall estimate of their potential for success at the higher level.

Why are assessment centers used?

Assessment centers are much more time consuming to develop and administer, require more people (personnel staff and evaluators) and as a result cost more than traditional oral interviews. Why then has there been such a dramatic increase in their use? The answer is multidimensional. First, the predictive validity and legal defensibility of unstructured oral interviews have been questioned for years. With the trend toward job relevant testing in recent years, selection interviews have become more job related and structured in format. This change has resulted in improved predictive validity but generally the validity co-efficients achieved are still not as high as those achieved with assessment centers.

Assessment centers allow candidates to demonstrate more of their skills through a number of job-relevant situations. Thus, assessors are able to observe candidates' effectiveness in a variety of realistic settings dealing with typical issues and problems associated with the target job. The results are more accurate primarily because the test is more comprehensive and because the rater can see how effective the candidate is as opposed to the candidate having to convince the panel members orally as is the case in an interview process. Interviews still have a place in the total selection process and are probably best utilized as the final step in the pre-employment or pre-promotion process. It is at this point where the appointing authority can best utilize information on an individual's unique background in relation to the duties and requirements of a specific position or opening.

Past performance undoubtedly holds some value in predicting future success in some situations. The problems which result from using past performance as a predictor usually revolve around measurement problems. First, the conditions and requirements of one's current job are often different than those of the higher level job in the organization. For instance, someone could be an excellent Police Officer, but possess only a few of the skills necessary for being an effective supervisor of Police Officers. If this Officer were promoted based solely on past performance, not only would the department lose a good Officer and gain a poor Sergeant, but the individual would probably suffer from loss of job satisfaction and reduced self-esteem.

Further, even when there is a high correlation between requirements of two jobs, the logical raters in a promotional process, the candidate's immediate supervisors, are often different people with different rating standards. This is further complicated by the fact that the candidates are usually working in different divisions performing different duties which makes meaningful comparisons across candidates extremely difficult.

These issues are dealt with through the assessment center process by having all candidates observed performing the same tasks which are simulations of the job for which they are competing. Also, all candidates are evaluated by raters who have received the same training in behavioral observation and evaluation and are using the same rating standards. To ensure that the same standards are used throughout the process, a final evaluation or integration session is held, usually the day after candidate assessment. During the integration session the assessors meet and review all descriptions of candidate behavior and the tentative ratings they have assigned to each candidate in each exercise on each rating factor. It is through this process that assessors ensure the accuracy and consistency of the ratings that they and each other assessor have assigned.

Another traditional testing instrument, the multiple-choice written test has also begun to take a backseat to assessment centers, especially for the higher management ranks. Actually, well developed written tests are very valuable tools for measuring the technical knowledge requirements of a job. Unfortunately, the higher you go up the organizational chain of command, the less important technical knowledge becomes in relation to supervisory and management skills. Written tests are often still used at the first supervisory level and in some cases the second supervisory or entry-management level as at least part of the examination process. However, the skills such as those often grouped under the labels delegation and management control, decisiveness and quality of decision-making, planning skills, problem solving skills, behavioral flexibility, interpersonal sensitivity and initiative are very difficult to achieve an accurate measure of through a written format which requires choosing the best of several alternatives. Typically, for supervisory and management jobs, the further you advance, the more you will be relying on skills such as those listed above. Similarly, to be valid predictors of success, the higher the position is in the organization the more weight these types of skill factors will have in the selection process.

To summarize, assessment centers are appropriate and likely to result in better predictions, when the target job requires a variety of complex skills, the requirements of the target job vary substantially from those at the next lowest level in the organization or when applicants come from a variety of different backgrounds or locations making it difficult to obtain objective data upon which to make accurate predictions. The assessment center process is most commonly used as a tool for making decisions regarding jobs at the supervisory and management levels. [. . .]

Description of a practical model

[. . .]

Job analysis[3]

The first step in the job analysis is to have all current permanent incumbents complete open-ended Position Description Questionnaires (PDQs). These PDQs are returned to and reviewed by the test developer. Based on this review, preliminary task and Knowledge, Skill, Ability and Behavioral Characteristics (KSAB) inventories are developed.

Concurrent with the development of the preliminary inventories, incumbents of the target job classification select relevant written work samples and complete work sample collection forms. These work samples and the forms describing them are collected by the test developer during a visit to the department for an onsite job analysis workshop. At this workshop, incumbents review and revise, if necessary, the preliminary inventories. After the incumbents agree that the inventories cover all aspects of the classification, the work behavior statements (tasks) are rated on the scales of Essentiality or Importance to successful job performance, Frequency and When Learned. The KSABs are evaluated on the extent to which they are required to perform the previously rated tasks and on a Relation to Performance scale for the extent to which each KSAB differentiates between levels of successful performance on the job.

Once all ratings have been assigned, situational data is collected to supplement the work samples and the results of the task and KSAB statistical analysis. The assembled incumbents respond to open-ended questions designed to elicit information on current issues and problems in the jurisdiction as well as typical frustrations, difficulties and obstacles encountered on the job. This portion of the job analysis is in large part 'overkill' which ensures that sufficient knowledge of the classification and work environment is obtained, while concurrently ensuring that incumbents will not be able to determine exactly which information will be developed into the actual test components. This job analysis workshop process is often completed twice – once with incumbents and once with supervisors.

After the job analysis sessions, the data obtained is statistically analyzed. Tasks which an incumbent could learn after appointment to the class are eliminated from further study as are tasks not rated to be essential to successful job performance. Next, a review of the ratings on the KSABs determines which to delete on the basis of the extent to which they differentiate between levels of effectiveness on the job. Finally, the relationship of the essential tasks which an individual must be able to perform at the time of appointment to the differentiating KSABs is considered. Only KSABs which differentiate between levels of effectiveness on the job are measured in the examination process. If the final list of factors to be evaluated includes technical knowledge areas, a written test may be developed and used as part of the examination process. The remaining skills, abilities and behavioral characteristics which are observable in simulations of essential tasks are the performance dimensions which will be measured through the assessment center.[4]

Exercise development

Working directly from the statistically derived job analysis results, supplemented by the situational data and work samples, three to five exercises are developed which simulate the most essential task areas in the classification. This allows assessors to observe, record, classify and evaluate job relevant behavior in job relevant situations. Using job simulation exercises tailored specifically to the classification as used in the jurisdiction not only increases candidate acceptance and compliance with legal requirements for content validity, but also allows candidates to 'get into' the simulations 'as if' they were real life. In this way, candidates are in the best position to minimize the artificial stress (test anxiety) and demonstrate the extent to which they possess job relevant knowledges, skills, abilities and behaviors.

Listed below are general descriptions of the most common assessment center exercises. It is important to note that these are only examples. Other types of exercises are also used and the specific content of the listed exercises as well as the actual form they take varies considerably depending on the specific job they are designed to simulate.

In-basket exercise

This exercise consists of a variety of materials of varying importance and priority which would typically be handled by an incumbent of the class. Candidates are forced to deal with these materials in a limited amount of time. They are later interviewed by assessors who review with the candidates how they handled the material and their reasoning in doing so.

Leaderless group discussion

This exercise usually takes one of two forms. In the 'unassigned roles' or 'cooperative group discussion' candidates in groups of five to six are given a number of current issues or problems and instructed to formulate specific recommendations or decisions. In the 'assigned roles' or 'competitive group' each candidate is given a different position or recommendation to support and time to make a persuasive presentation to the other members of the group. Then, similar to cooperative groups, candidates are expected to come to a consensus in the time allowed as to which position or recommendation should be adopted. The group interaction is observed by the assessor team, each assessor paying particular attention to one or two of the candidates.

Oral presentation exercise

In this exercise, candidates are allowed a brief time to plan, organize and prepare a presentation on an assigned topic to a specific audience. They then make the presentation and respond to questions and/or challenges. The assessors play the role of the press, board or commission members, community members or other appropriate audience.

Role play exercise

In this exercise, the candidate assumes the role of the incumbent of the position and must deal with a subordinate, irate citizen, member of a community organization, etc., about an issue, problem or complaint. A trained role player is used and responds 'in character' to the actions of the candidate. This interaction is observed and evaluated by the assessors. Depending on the problem, there may be an additional interview with the candidate regarding the handling of the problem.

Written report/analysis exercise

Candidates, in this exercise, are given a job relevant document to analyze or a topic pertinent to the position and are instructed to provide a written report, position statement, outline a new policy, etc. The written document is received and rated independently by two assessors. As in the Role Play Exercise, there may be an additional interview with each candidate responding to their handling of the problem.

Candidate orientation

Candidate orientation is a very important part of any assessment center examination process. In fact, in the author's experience, the few protests that are filed on this type of examination are usually based on a lack of knowledge of the process and suspicions which result from lack of knowledge. Further, a well informed candidate experiences less stress in the examination process and is better able to demonstrate his/her true level of job relevant skills which improves the predictive validity of the process.

One suggested approach to candidate orientation is to send general information to candidates in written form. This information can be enclosed with the notice to appear for the examination. This material addresses typical questions such as the following: What is an assessment center? Who will be at the assessment center? How long will the assessment center last? What will happen? How are the assessors chosen? What information will be used to assess the candidates? What is the role of the assessors? What is the role of the assessment center staff? What will the schedule be? What should the candidate wear? What if I have other questions?

In addition to the written material, all candidates should be provided with a formal orientation session prior to their participation in the first examination test instrument or exercise. During this orientation, candidates are provided with an overview of the entire examination process and answers to all questions asked which do not require a description of the specific content of the examination. This orientation can be a mandatory portion of the examination process which (1) ensures that all candidates receive the same orientation information; (2) allows for an accurate last minute candidate count prior to the administration of the assessment exercises; and (3) allows a time for candidates to be randomly assigned schedules and identification numbers to use through the remainder of their participation in the examination. Further, while all candidates are assembled, any totally written component (i.e., written report exercise) can be administered to all candidates under the same conditions following the orientation session and stored for evaluation by the assessors later in the process.

While potential candidates should become familiar with this type of testing, they should also be warned to avoid training courses which purport to teach candidates how to act in an assessment center. While reading an article or attending a good orientation will help decrease artificial test stress, the types of skills measured are not characteristics which can be learned overnight. Indeed, the best preparation for this type of test is to not prepare for the test at all. Rather, since the assessment center process simulates the job, the best preparation for the serious candidate is to focus on the target job itself and seek out experiences which allow development of the skills required for successful performance on the job. This type of preparation and skills development should begin long before the examination is announced. When the assessment centre is conducted it will matter little which important job tasks are simulated. The well prepared candidate can be confident and draw naturally upon the skills which are necessary to handle each task in the examination and on the job once appointed.

Assessor training

Even though all individuals selected to serve as assessors may have had prior training and experience in evaluating candidates in assessment centers, additional training is necessary due primarily to the custom nature of the examination and the need to standardize scoring tendencies within the specific group of assessors which is assembled. Prior to the onsite assessor training, each assessor receives a comprehensive package of pre-reading materials. These materials include an overview of their involvement in the process, background on the classification as used by the department, and background information on the assessment center process including specific information on the assessor's role, the rating scale and rating process, potential rating errors, the definitions of the dimensions to be measured with summary information linking the dimensions to the job and job simulations as well as copies of all exercise materials, interview guides and rating materials to be used in the process.

Sending out the pre-reading material decreases the time necessary for onsite training to one full day. During this training all background and overview information as well as the test dimensions and rating procedures are first reviewed and any questions or issues raised are resolved. The bulk of the onsite training then focuses on practice and feedback in observing, recording, classifying and evaluating behavior. This training includes observing and practice rating the behaviors of mock candidates in simulations of the assessment exercises. The results of the practice rating sessions, which may include live and video taped examples of candidate performance, are discussed in great detail. Through these discussions the assessors' understanding of the definitions of the dimensions are refined. Similarly, identification and standardization of rating tendencies between assessors occurs through these discussions.

Candidate evaluation

During the assessment center process, each candidate is independently observed and evaluated by two different assessors in each exercise. The process is scheduled such that upon completion of the exercises, each candidate has been evaluated once by each assessor and each assessor has observed some candidates in each type of exercise. One full day is usually required for each 10–12 candidates. It is usually necessary to obtain eight assessors for four exercises. However, when one of the exercises is totally written in format, the process can be scheduled such that every candidate is evaluated once by each of six assessors at the completion of the other three exercises. The written reports or work products are blind rated to ensure that no halo effect occurs from or to the other exercises.

After the candidates have completed their participation in the process, the assessors meet again for the final evaluation or integration session. The procedure for establishing candidate ranking is a combination of cumulative scores on each performance dimension with the addition of an overall evaluation score which the assessors establish by consensus. Each of the performance dimensions may be individually weighted based on and to reflect the extent to which they were determined through the job analysis to differentiate between levels of effective performance on the job. The overall consensus score may be allocated the weight of an additional 10 to 20 percent of each participant's final score. This overall evaluation score (often referred to as the Overall Rating or OAR) allows assessors to assign a score based on a consideration of the total picture of the candidate which is generated by discussing the candidate's performance in all of the exercises. The integration session generally requires 6–8 hours of assessor participation for 10–12 candidates.

[. . .]

Research on scoring

A debate regarding whether statistical (mechanical) or clinical (judgmental) methods for combining scores is superior has been in progress for many years. A comprehensive review of the literature on this issue was provided by Gilbert (1981). Many studies have shown mechanical methods to result in valid predictions. Many other studies have shown the OAR produced by a clinical approach to result in valid predictions. But, insufficient research exists to demonstrate that either method is superior to the other. In fact, the debate is likely to continue for quite some time since the issue of superiority is hard to demonstrate when the correlations between scores produced by the two methods tend to be quite high. For instance, Russell (1983) obtained a correlation co-efficient of .90 between integrated dimension scores and the OAR with 2191 assessees and 71 assessors, Joiner and Carlin (1983) obtained a co-efficient of .89 between integrated dimension scores and the OAR with 52 assessees and 8 assessors and a co-efficient of .98 when correlating pre-integration dimension scores with candidate final scores which included the integrated dimension scores (using the 'practical model' described above) and an OAR with the weight of an additional 10 percent (or a true 9.09 percent).

In a related area of research, it has been discovered that candidate scores on a dimension tend to correlate better with scores on different dimensions in the same exercise than they do with the same dimension in other exercises (Sackett, 1982; Sackett and Dreher, 1982; Sackett and Harris, 1983). While it is suggested that this may be cause of concern, from a content validity point of view the only real concern is that the exercises or test instruments which facilitate this 'method variance' are job relevant simulations of important work situations. If all exercises in an assessment center produced the same ratings for participants on the rating factors or dimensions, there would be no need for multiple simulations.

Most jobs, management and supervisory jobs in particular, require effective performance in a variety of different types of situations, e.g., one on one meetings and meetings with groups, individual presentation to groups, dealing with paperwork, etc. Further, most people tend to be better in some situations than in others. For instance, some people find it difficult to express their ideas in formal settings to large groups while other individuals feel uncomfortable in one on one encounters or small groups. Still others thrive in small groups interactions (staff meetings, quality circles, committees, etc.) but are uncomfortable and less skilled at having to sit at a desk and complete an annual report or analyze the department budget for areas to reduce costs. If the target job requires effective performance in all of these types of situations, then the best test would require participation in simulations of all of them.

If a candidate scores at different ends of the rating scale on Oral Communication Skills in a Formal Presentation Exercise and an Informal Subordinate Counseling Exercise, or the opposite ends of the scale on Problem Solving Skills in a Group Discussion Exercise and an Inbasket simulation, the test administrator should not be alarmed at the thought of method variance but rather should be elated that the examination identified these situational differences in the individual's performance. If the different situations are of equal importance on the job, then the average of the dimension scores across the situations summed should be the best predictor of performance on the job.

What the research of Sackett et al. points out, which is of great importance, is that in an assessment center you are not measuring skills in a vacuum. Rather, you are measuring skills within a specific situation. There-fore, using a content validity approach, it is not sufficient to identify job relevant skills or performance dimensions and then use any method to measure them. The methods or exercises will have considerable impact on the scores attained by candidates and should represent job relevant situations within which the skills you are attempting to measure would be required on the job.

Performance feedback

In addition to developing a rank order list for selection or promotion, another benefit of the assessment center process is the wealth of information gener-ated. This information when viewed across candidates is an excellent source of information for the department or jurisdiction. The group profile from a promotional assessment center is likely to indicate overall areas of strengths and weaknesses within the classification assessed and provide insight into areas of a department's training program to commend or which need revision. The individual candidate profiles can be a source of objective information for individualized department/jurisdiction sponsored training or can be used by candidates for their personally motivated career development efforts.

There are many methods for providing performance feedback to assessment center participants (Slivinski and Bourgeous, 1977; Fitzgerald and Quaintance, 1982; Thornton and Byham, 1982; Spencer, 1984). These methods range from simply providing the one score which reflects the participant's rank on the eligible list to oral or written summaries of the participant's overall effectiveness by exercise and/or performance dimen-sion. The author has found that by far the majority of candidates are receptive to and appreciate performance feedback. Further, most candidates prefer the feedback to be direct and comprehensive as opposed to brief summaries of the data. One unique model for providing candidate feedback was provided by Joiner and Carlin (1983). The procedure involved both oral feedback inter-views and, upon request of the candidates, complete copies of all rating forms, assessor notes and documents related to their performance in the center. Candidate acceptance of this approach was extremely high. Even when the information is not flattering, candidates realize that it is a rare opportunity to receive candid feedback from as many as six to eight professionals in their career field on how they come across in job relevant situations.

Conclusion

This chapter has provided a description of a model for developing and administering content-valid assessment center examinations and has attempted to summarize a great deal of information in a very brief amount of space. The model presented has been used by local government agencies of various sizes for a wide variety of classifications over the last ten years. While there have, as yet, been no court challenges to the methods, procedures or content of these centers, the model was selected for and used successfully under careful scrutiny during the San Francisco Police Captain examination which was administered under a Federal Consent Decree in 1981 (Hurley, Wong and Joiner, 1982). The procedures described appear to be legally defensible and are consistent with the results of the best research available to date.

Well developed and administered assessment centers can greatly improve a selection or promotional process particularly for jobs requiring a variety of skills in a variety of situational contexts. While there are many different models or variations of the concepts expressed in this article, the procedures described are quite typical of those found in local government assessment centers. Legal requirements for the use of job-related examinations and the increased demand for promoting only the very best qualified in these times of shrinking resources continue to reinforce the use of job simulation technology. As a profession we need to continue questioning our methodology and researching the results of unique applications.

Notes

1 Portions of this chapter were adapted from a paper presented at the 1983 Annual Conference of the International Personnel Management Association Assessment Council as part of the paper session, Assessment centers: research and applications, and from a previously published article by the same author, Use of assessment centers in law enforcement promotions, *Journal of California Law Enforcement*, 17(2), 1983. Correspondence related to this article should be addressed to Dennis A. Joiner, Dennis A. Joiner and Associates, P.O. Box 2341, Sacramento, CA 95811-2341.
2 Copies of the Ethical standards and considerations for assessment center operations can also be obtained from other sources including: *The Journal of Assessment Center*

Technology, 2(2), 1979, 19–23; the *Personnel Administrator*, 1980, 25(2), 35–38 and from any professional working with assessment center technology.

3 The approach described here is a content validity approach. For an excellent overview of criterion-related validity see Boehm, V. R., Establishing the validity of assessment centers, Monograph V, Developmental Dimensions International, Pittsburg, PA, 1982.

4 For a more in-depth look at performance dimensions, see Maher, P. T., An analysis of common assessment center dimensions, *Journal of Assessment Center Technology* 6(3), 1983, 1–8, or Byham, W. C., Dimensions of managerial competence, Monograph VI, Developmental Dimensions International, Pittsburg, PA, 1982.

References

[. . .]

Bentz, V. J. The Sears executive model. In W. C. Byham (Chair), *The Assessment Center*. Symposium presented at the Executive Study Conference, New York, 1969.

[. . .]

Bray, D. W. The management progress study. *American Psychologist*, 1964, 19, 419–420.

Bray, D. W. and Campbell, R. J. Selection of salesmen by means of an assessment center. *Journal of Applied Psychology*, 1968, 52 (1), 36–41.

Bray, D. W., Campbell, R. J. and Grant, D. L. *Formative Years in Business: A Long-Term AT&T Study of Managerial Lives*. New York: Wiley & Sons, 1974.

Bray, D. W. and Grant, D. L. The assessment center in the measurement of potential for business management. *Psychological Monographs*, 1966, 80 (17), 1–27.

[. . .]

Byham, W. C. Assessment centers for spotting future managers. *Harvard Business Review*, 1970, 48 (4), 150–160.

Campbell, R. and Bray, D. W. Assessment centers: an aid in management selection. *The Journal of the Society for Personnel Administration*, March/April 1967.

[. . .]

Division of Industrial-Organizational Psychology, American Psychological Association. *Principles for the Validation and Use of Personnel Selection Procedures*, (Second Edition). Berkeley, CA: Author, 1980.

Equal Employment Opportunity Commission, Civil Service Commission, Department of Labor and Department of Justice. Uniform Guidelines on Employee Selection Procedures, in *Federal Register*, 1978, 43, 38290–38315.

Finkle, R. B. and Jones, W. W. *Assessing Corporate Talent: A Key to Managerial Manpower Planning*. New York: Wiley-Interscience, 1970, 248.

[. . .]

Fitzgerald, L. F. and Quaintance, M. K. Survey of assessment center use in state and local government. *Journal of Assessment Center Technology*, 1982, 5 (1), 9–22.

Gilbert, P. J. An investigation of clinical and mechanical combination of assessment center data. *Journal of Assessment Center Technology*, 1981, 4 (2), 1–10.

Hinrichs, J. R. Comparison of 'real life' assessments of management potential with situational exercises, paper-and-pencil ability tests, and personality inventories. *Journal of Applied Psychology*, 1969, 53 (5), 425–432.

Huck, J. R. Assessment centers: a review of the external and internal validities. *Personnel Psychology*, 1973, 26, 191–212.

Huck, J. R. The research base. In Moses, J. L. and Byham, W. C. (eds.), *Applying the Assessment Center Method*. New York: Pergamon Press, 1977.

Hurley, K., Wong, R., and Joiner, D. A. Description of the San Francisco police captain assessment center. *Journal of Assessment Center Technology*, 1982, 5 (1), 23–28.

[. . .]

Joiner, D. A. and Carlin, P. A., Consultant–agency cooperation in conducting research on a promotional assessment center for police lieutenant. Paper presented at the annual conference of the International Personnel Management Association Assessment Council, Washington DC, May 1983.

Kruat, A. I. and Scott, G. S. Validity of an operational management assessment program. *Journal of Applied Psychology*, 1972, 56, 124–129.

[. . .]

MacKinnon, D. W. From selecting spies to selecting managers the OSS assessment program. In Moses, J. L., and Byham, W. C. (eds.), *Applying the Assessment Center Method*, New York: Pergamon Press, 1977.

Meyer, H. H. The validity of the in-basket test as a measure of managerial performance. *Personnel Psychology*, 1970, 23 (3), 297–307.

Moses, J. L. Standards and ethical considerations for assessment center operations. *The Industrial Psychologist*, 1977, 14, 41–45.

Murray, H. A. and MacKinnon, D. W. Assessment of OSS personnel. *Journal of Consulting Psychology*, 1946, 10, 76–80.

OSS, Assessment Staff. *Assessment of Men*. New York: Rinehard, 1948.

Russell, C. J., An examination of internal assessment center processes for compliance with uniform guidelines. Paper presented at the annual conference of the International Personnel Management Association Assessment Council, Washington DC, May 1983.

Sackett, P. R. A critical look at some common beliefs about assessment centers. *Public Personnel Management*, 1982, 11, 140–146.

Sackett, P. R. and Dreher, G. F. Constructs and assessment center dimensions: some troubling empirical findings. *Journal of Applied Psychology*, 1982, 67, 401–410.

Sackett, P. R. and Harris, M., Further examination of constructs underlying assessment center ratings. Paper presented at the 91st annual conference of the American Psychological Association, Anahiem, August 1983.

Slivinski, L. W. and Bourgeous, R. P. Feedback of assessment center results, In Moses, J. L. and Byham, W. C. (eds.), *Applying the Assessment Center Method*. New York: Pergamon Press, 1977.

Spencer, G. M., Feedback and personnel development. Paper presented at the First International Conference on Assessment Centers for Police, Corrections and Fire Services, Miami, April 1984.

Thornton, G. C. III and Byham, W. C. *Assessment Centers and Managerial Performance*. New York: Academic Press, 1982.

Wollowick, H. B. and McNamara, W. J. Relationship of the components of an assessment center to management success. *Journal of Applied Psychology*, 1969, 53, 348–352.

16

Analyzing performance problems
– some selected extracts

R. F. Mager and P. Pipe

What is the performance discrepancy?

■ *Where we are*

We are considering the nature of a performance discrepancy.

Life is studded with discrepancies. There are discrepancies between what people tell you and what you know to be true, between what others believe and what you believe, between the things you want and your ability to pay – and any number of discrepancies between what *is* and what you would like it to be. One such discrepancy is that between people's *actual* performance and the performance *desired* of them. This is a performance discrepancy, the kind of discrepancy with which we will be working.

Examples of performance discrepancies can be found all around you. Sometimes you get too little, sometimes too much. There's the typist who doesn't type accurately enough to suit you, the secretary who organizes your schedule to the point of bossiness; there's the son or daughter who doesn't wash the family car as often as promised, the mechanic who sells you an unneeded oil change; and there are the members of the congregation who don't show up regularly enough to suit the minister and the woman who is unnecessarily bossy with the altar guild.

Many of these discrepancies need not exist. Many of them can be eliminated.

[. . .] One common occurrence that warns you that a performance discrepancy may be lurking around is the announcement that takes some form of 'We've got a training problem'. Someone has detected a difference between what is desired and what is actually happening.

[. . .]

When someone says, 'I've got a training problem', it's like someone going to a doctor and saying, 'I've got an aspirin problem'. It's possible that aspirin will solve his or her problem, but aspirin is the solution, not the problem.

We are careful to use the word *discrepancy* rather than *deficiency*. 'Discrepancy' means only that there is a difference, a lack of balance between the actual and the desired. 'Deficiency' means that a value judgment has been made about a discrepancy and that the discrepancy is bad or in some other way unacceptable. Using the word *discrepancy*, we avoid jumping to conclusions about whether a discrepancy is good or bad; in this way we remember to ask the questions that will give us a solid fix on the importance of the discrepancy.

To recognize a performance discrepancy, ask *why* it occurred to someone to say such things as: 'I've got a training problem.' 'We need a course.' 'He needs a lesson.' Or: 'They oughta wanna be interested.' And even: 'Why can't they ever get it right?'

Each of these statements is only a symptom of a performance discrepancy, not a description of one. And the first step toward eliminating one is understanding its nature. It may be that you noticed people working slower than usual or slower than you desire. It may be that children are leaving more food than you think is reasonable, or that they are using unacceptable language. It may be that someone is less accurate or less careful than desired, or it may be an action as exasperating as that discovered by the manager of a motion picture distribution house – people 'splicing' film with staples and scotch tape.

You'll know you are in the presence of a performance discrepancy when you hear things like this:

'These new supervisors just aren't motivated.'
  'I see. Just what is it they're doing that causes you to say that?'
  'Doing? It's what they *aren't* doing that's the problem.'
  'And what is that?'
  'Well, for one thing, they aren't managing. They spend too much time running the machine they used to run before they were promoted. They shouldn't be doing that; they should be managing.'

The *complaint* was about motivation, but the *event* causing the complaint had to do with time spent operating a machine:

'We've got to teach those kids to have the right attitude.'
  'Just what are they doing or not doing that makes you say that?'
  'Why, they litter the place until you can't see the ground.'
  'I see. So you'd like to reduce the amount of litter?'
  'We sure would.'

The complaint was about attitude, but the performance discrepancy causing the complaint was a difference between what *existed* in the way of littering and what someone *wanted done* about littering. Here's one more:

'They just don't have the right attitude about their jobs.'

'Who doesn't have the right attitude?'

'Our salespeople. They just won't use the sales aids that we provide them.'

The complaint was about attitude, but the discrepancy had to do with not using sales aids.

It's difficult to select a course of action to fix a situation when it is described in such broad (fuzzy) terms as 'attitude problem', or 'training problem', or 'motivation problem'. You *can*, however, plan a course of action when you know that the discrepancy to be influenced is clear and specific.

The first step is to ask yourself, '*Why* do I say something is not the way it ought to be? Why do I say there is a "training" problem? What *event* causes me to say that changes must be made?'

What to do

Identify the *nature* of the discrepancy. Once its nature has been identified, the importance of the discrepancy can be considered.

How to do it

Ask these questions:

- Why do I think there is a training problem?
- What is the difference between what is being done and what is supposed to be done?
- What is the event that causes me to say that things aren't right?
- Why am I dissatisfied?

[. . .]

Is it important?

■ Where we are

A performance discrepancy has been identified.

People see things differently. Some will perceive a joke to be the funniest thing they've ever heard, while others will wonder what the chuckling was all about. Some will perceive a sunset to be spectacular, while others will say 'Ho hum'. Some will consider certain behaviors to be a shocking breach of common courtesy, while others may find the same behaviors more than acceptable.

There is no question that there are different perceptions of the same event. That goes for performance discrepancies, too. Some people will feel that a particular discrepancy is urgently in need of fixing, while others will wonder what the fuss is about.

[. . .]

Many discrepancies often exist only in the eyes of the beholder. They are simply personal biases about what is 'right' or a blind preference for 'the way we've always done it'. If you insist that a discrepancy is serious, be sure at least to ask, 'Is it likely that the effort of searching for a solution will be justified by the results?'

The elimination of discrepancies can be approached from two directions. You can change what you are getting (the actual performance), or you can change your expectations (the desired performance). Or, of course, you can change both.

Changing the expectations is something that you can do on *your* side of the fence, and it may be the easiest way out. As far as the 'performer' (the employee, the student, the child) is concerned, the effect is that the discrepancy has been ignored.

What to do

Having identified a performance discrepancy that you or someone else feels is important to eliminate, be sure to find out how much the discrepancy is 'costing' before taking action. To estimate the size or value (and thus the importance) of the discrepancy:

(a) List all the consequences (outcomes) caused by the discrepancy.
(b) Calculate the cost of each outcome wherever possible.
(c) Total the costs.
(d) Answer the question, 'What would happen if I left it alone?'

If the result of letting it alone would be negligible, drop it there. If the result is substantially larger than nothing, go to the next steps of the analysis.

How to do it

Ask these questions:

● Why is the discrepancy important? (What is its cost?)
● What would happen if I left the discrepancy alone?
● Could doing something to resolve the discrepancy have any worthwhile result?

Now we begin to determine the *cause* of the discrepancy, so that an appropriate remedy can be selected or designed. This is a pivotal point in your checklist of questions, because the answer to this next question determines which of two sequences of questions you will follow.

In this step you must decide whether the performance discrepancy is due to a *skill deficiency*. In essence, are nonperformers not performing as desired because they *don't know how* to do it? If their lives depended on it, would they still not perform?

If there is a genuine skill deficiency, then the primary remedy must be either to change an existing skill level by teaching new skills or to change what people are required to do.

On the other hand, if people are able to perform but don't, the solution lies in something other than enhancement of skills. 'Teaching' what is already known isn't going to change anyone's skill level. The remedy in these cases is to change the conditions under which people are expected to do that which they already know how to do.

[. . .]

After all, there are different 'forms' of skill deficiencies. Sometimes people can't do it today because they have forgotten how, and sometimes because they never knew how. Solutions for these situations are different. And sometimes people don't do the job because they can't – perhaps they lack the mental capacity or the physical strength. Again, a different solution is called for.

[. . .]

It is not a skill deficiency

They could do it if they wanted to

Could nonperformers perform if they had to? This pivotal question was asked immediately after we determined that we were looking at an important performance discrepancy [. . .]. To this point, we've looked at several solutions that apply when the answer is plainly 'No. Even if their lives depended on it, they couldn't do it.' Now we're going back to the question to see what happens when the answer is something other than that unequivocal 'no'.

When you know or suspect that a person could perform if he or she really had to, it's probably plain that something other than instruction is needed. In general, the remedy is that of *performance management*. Rather than modify the person's skill or knowledge (since it's likely that the ability already exists), you will have to modify the conditions associated with the performance, or the consequence or result of that performance. Rather than change what the person *can* do, change something about the world in which he or she does it so that doing it will be more attractive, or less repulsive, or less difficult.

[. . .]

There are four general causes of such nonperformance:

1 It is punishing to perform as desired.
2 It is rewarding to perform other than as desired.
3 It simply doesn't matter whether performance is as desired.
4 There are obstacles to performing as desired.

17

Staff appraisal – theory, concepts and experience in other organizations and problems of adaptation to education

Brian Fidler

Introduction

Much of the writing on appraisal by educationalists has more of the flavour of accountability, assessment and evaluation about it than is the current practice in other organizations. It is possible that this reflects a stereotypical view of the assumed authoritarian style used by managers in industry and commerce. Whereas in fact what is quite striking, when looking at the theory of appraisal and its practice in well-managed industry, commerce and other public services, is that appraisal is quite positive and developmental. Many of the anticipated problems of applying appraisal to educational situations, have also been experienced in other organizations and there is a great deal that can be learned from their experience which will enable managers in education to avoid the same mistakes. Unless we study and learn from the experience of others we shall find ourselves with either a cosy system which achieves little and lacks public credibility, or a system which is Draconian in its application and similarly achieves little because of the hostile reaction it provokes. Almost all of the concepts of appraisal in other organizations can be taken over into an educational context. The one feature which may have no parallel in other organizations is any requirement to observe systematically the work performance of the appraisee. Thus there appears to be no equivalent of observation of teaching performance.

[. . .]

Terms

Staff appraisal is the term used in this chapter for the process by which an employee and his or her superordinate meet to discuss the work performance of the employee. There is a huge variety of terms used – performance appraisal, performance review, performance evaluation, staff review, staff reporting and more especially teacher appraisal, teacher assessment – which have no accepted difference of meaning. Staff development, on the other hand, as the name implies, is wholly concerned with the increase of knowledge, skill or experience of staff without the evaluative connotation associated with appraisal.

Increasingly, however, staff appraisal has been concerned with staff development. Recently staff appraisal has concentrated on improving individual performance at work and so the two terms have become closer.

Another related process is institutional evaluation. Inevitably school and college evaluation reflect on an individual teacher's performance and in many schemes of institutional review there are self-appraisal or self-review documents for staff to complete. However, in this chapter the focus is upon staff appraisal as a managerial activity whereby a manager engages in an appraisal process with a subordinate for whom he or she is, in some sense, accountable.

Appraisal system and interview

It is helpful to differentiate between the appraisal interview and the whole system of which it is a part. The system comprises all the papers and procedures involved in appraisal.

The GRIDS handbooks (McMahon *et al.*, 1984) envisage self-review of individual teachers for internal development purposes as leading to a staff development programme, whilst if the focus were on formal external accountability then this would lead to a staff appraisal scheme. This implies a neat conceptualization which identifies appraisal with accountability but not with development. As we shall see [. . .] in non-educational organizations, appraisal is concerned with both individual development and accountability or evaluation and it is precisely this combination which gives appraisal such central importance and which also makes it so difficult to accomplish.

In designing a particular appraisal system it is important to be quite clear about the extent to which it is intended to be evaluative and the extent to which it should lead to individual development. It may be useful conceptually to try to mark the position of a particular system on a display which has evaluation and development as axes (Figure 17.1). An appraisal system could be placed anywhere between the axes depending on its particular balance between evaluation and development.

We shall later return to the fundamental contradiction inherent in using appraisal for both evaluative and developmental functions.

[. . .]

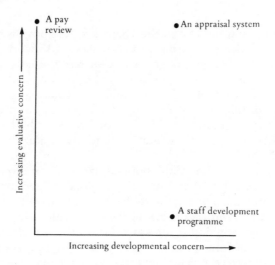

Figure 17.1   Display of evaluative and developmental contributions of appraisal

Management by objectives

Although the concept is generally attributed to Peter Drucker, it was Douglas McGregor who allied it to performance appraisal (Strauss, 1972). MBO is seen by many as a device for ensuring that employees in an organization are all engaged on work which is consistent with the organization's overall objectives as identified by the most senior personnel in the organization. Others have seen MBO as emphasizing employee participation, better communication and enhanced motivation through clearly identified goals and the achievement of results (Giegold, 1978).

Schuster and Kindall (1974) have identified three structural elements to MBO:

1 Performance goals or targets initiated periodically by the employee.
2 Mutual agreement on a set of goals by the employee and his superior after discussion.
3 Periodic review by the employee and his superior of the match between goals and achievements.

These are the features of MBO which changed the nature of the appraisal process. The appraisal process is then concerned with the performance of employees as demonstrated by the extent to which they have achieved targets to which they were committed. Some appraisal systems use MBO explicitly whilst others concentrate on performance and may talk about targets and results without taking on all the features of an MBO approach. Clearly in appraisal interview has a very clear rationale under MBO and so this approach has been very pervasive.

Appraisal and management

Whether appraisal is on classical lines or part of MBO it is quite clear as Freemantle (1985) says in *Superboss*, that 'appraisal is an integral part of management, not a system external to it'. Beer (1986) also points out 'performance evaluation is an important element in the information and control system of most complex organisations'.

Appraisal has implications for the appraisee, the appraiser, central planning and control of the organization, and the outside world. It is an all-embracing process. Since generally there is a concentration of attention on the appraisee and appraiser, it is worthwhile to state the range of purposes which appraisal may serve for central planning and control of an organization. Stewart and Stewart (1977) list the following:

(a) manpower skills audit;
(b) manpower forecasting;
(c) assessment of employee potential;
(d) succession planning;
(e) salary planning;
(f) training planning;
(g) equity between subordinates;
(h) downward transmission of company objectives;
(i) problem and grievance detection and handling.

For a public service organization accountability to the outside world is also an important purpose of an appraisal system.

Goals of performance appraisal

In an excellent recent review article, Beer (1986) has identified the main theoretical issues in performance appraisal.

(i) For the manager (and the organization)

In addition to providing data to the central planning and control function in the organization, appraisal is of direct benefit to the manager. It is a 'major tool for changing individual behaviour' (Beer 1986). The goals cover both evaluation and development. Beer lists eight:

1 evaluation goals
   (a) To give feedback to subordinates so they know where they stand.
   (b) To develop valid data for pay and promotion decisions and to aid communication of these.
   (c) To provide a means of warning subordinates about unsatisfactory performance.

2 development goals
   (a) To counsel and coach subordinates so that they will improve their performance and develop future potential.

(b) To develop commitment to the organization through discussion of career opportunities and career planning.
(c) To motivate subordinates through recognition of achievements and support.
(d) To strengthen supervisor–subordinate relations.
(e) To diagnose individual and organizational problems.

Categorizing these goals as evaluation or development emphasizes that some of them are in conflict. The appraisal relationship required for the evaluation goals will be inimical to the trusting open relationship required for development. It is important for appraisal systems to recognize this problem. Decisions on pay and promotability can be separated in time from more developmental activities whilst within the appraisal interview there may be a sequencing of activities which seeks to minimize the potential conflict [. . .].

(ii) For the individual employee

Individuals have a number of possible goals which they may achieve by taking part in appraisal. Six major benefits can be identified.

1 To receive feedback on their performance and progress.
2 To discuss their present job and amend their job description if changes are agreed.
3 To identify opportunities for professional personal development.
4 To identify training opportunities.
5 To discuss their aspirations and career plans.
6 To discuss problems in the organization and their relationship with their manager.

When feedback is positive and is consistent with the employee's own self image, the inherent conflicts in the process are minimized; however, when the feedback is critical of poor performance, a defensive reaction from an employee may set up barriers which inhibit acceptance of this feedback and prevent open discussion of how performance might be improved.

Beer (1986) identifies the most fundamental conflict as that between the individual and the organization.

> The individual desires to confirm a positive self image and to obtain organisational rewards of promotion or pay. The organisation wants individuals to be open to negative information about themselves so that they can improve their performance. As long as individuals see the appraisal process as having an important influence on their rewards (pay, recognition), their career (promotions and reputation), and their self image they will be reluctant to engage in the kind of open dialogue required for valid evaluation and personal development.
>
> (p. 289)

Clearly this conflict is at its most acute when dealing with poor performers. Inevitably an appraisal system which covers all employees will throw up a small minority whose performance is below an acceptable standard. This is known to happen in all organizations and there is a great temptation to avoid the issue by both parties in the name of good relations. This is at best a palliative and at worst undermines the whole appraisal system and leads to no improvement for the individual. This is a problem to which we shall return.

Reducing the fundamental conflict

Beer identifies a number of measures which tend to lessen the fundamental conflict.

(i) Separating evaluation and development

As far as possible these purposes should be separated. Any concern with pay or promotion should be removed from the main developmental appraisal process. Separating these purposes in time by six months is often suggested.

(ii) Choosing appropriate performance data

Performance data has to be related to the job being done. A systematic approach to this (Stenning and Stenning, 1984) requires

(a) A clear comprehensive and accurate job description.
(b) A statement of the results expected of the job holder which are as objective and measurable as possible.
(c) A clear description of the abilities, skills, knowledge and personal characteristics of effective job performers.
(d) Data systematically assembled over the review period.

A comprehensive approach would suggest that each element of a job description should have an associated standard of performance attached to it. However, this approach suffers from two major disadvantages. One is that job descriptions typically have a large number of individual tasks and each of these would require a standard of performance. The second problem is that a multi-element job description provides no indication of the priority which should be attached to each individual element.

The MBO approach is to select a limited number of important parts of the job description and to designate these 'key results areas' (Morrisey 1976). These five to ten specific areas then have objectives or measurable results associated with them. In addition to these work objectives which ensure the efficient operation of the organization, there would be personal development objectives which were intended to ensure growth and development of the individual (in areas not incompatible with organizational objectives).

An alternative approach suggested by Odiorne (Morrisey, 1983) where much of the work is ongoing and repetitive is to identify three levels of objectives. The basic level of *regular or routine objectives* assumes that there are already well established levels of performance for most of an individual's work activities. To deal with problems which have been identified in the routine work there would then be *problem-solving objectives*. Finally, there would be *innovative objectives* which represent a major change or development in the work of an individual which would benefit the organization. The personal development objectives could involve both problem-solving and innovation. This latter approach may be worthy of consideration in trying to appraise the work of teachers.

The appraisal interview provides an opportunity to review periodically the job description and to amend it to ensure that it is a faithful record of the current job.

Clarity can be achieved and defensiveness minimized if feedback on performance refers to specific behaviours and actual incidents as exemplars of more general behaviour. This data, however, must be collected over a substantial period and not only refer to incidents in the preceding week or two otherwise it will lack credibility in the eyes of the appraisee.

On the other hand any problems should be discussed with the employee as they happen and not stored up only to be discussed at the appraisal interview. Supervision and coaching should be continuous, as should any modification of targets and objectives arising from new circumstances. The appraisal interview should summarize and recap such events during the year – not add new evidence.

Whilst an MBO approach focuses on accomplishments which are tangible, it is less concerned with how they are achieved and there may have been organizational reasons which precluded success and are no reflection on the performance of the appraisee. It is suggested that behavioural ratings on the way objectives were achieved should supplement the MBO performance data as these would be useful for development purposes.

(iii) Recognizing individual differences in system designs

Beer suggests that not all employees should be appraised with the same frequency. Some, particularly the upwardly mobile, may need more feedback on performance whilst those who are competent but have reached the peak of their capabilities should only be appraised every two or three years.

(iv) Upward appraisal

Allowing an employee to rate the performance of his or her manager can help to break down barriers and may give the manager useful feedback on how his or her performance is perceived. It can generate a dialogue and allow the manager to demonstrate the open non–defensive behaviour which it is hoped the employee may also show.

(v) Using an appropriate interview style

Maier (1976) has characterized three interview styles as '*Tell and Sell*', '*Tell and Listen*' and '*Problem-Solving*'. These may be appropriate for different interview situations. In the 'Tell and Sell' method, the manager directs the interview and gains the acceptance of the appraisee to take steps to improve performance. The 'Tell and Listen' style requires the manager to give authentic feedback but then to allow the appraisee to respond. Communication and understanding may be much improved. Changes in performance, however, depend upon a change of attitude following improved communication.

The 'Problem-Solving' style as the name implies requires both appraiser and appraisee jointly to acknowledge problems and to work on them together.

Beer suggests that a mixed-mode interview moving from the 'Problem-Solving' style to the 'Tell and Sell' or 'Tell and Listen' may be appropriate for a variety of situations. This would permit open-ended discussion of problems and possible solutions before moving to an agreed plan, but would also allow the manager to ensure that difficult issues are faced if they are not raised by the appraisee.

[. . .]

Management and poor performance

A point worth emphasizing is that the appraisal interview is the one formal occasion in the year when employee and manager sit down to discuss work performances; but there should be informal on-going discussions particularly if improvement needs guiding and monitoring. The appraisal interview may need supplementing with a counselling interview either if intensive help is needed or a neutral exploration of issues is required. For cases of extreme and persistent underperformance, a separate disciplinary interview may be required.

Steinmetz (1985) has presented a useful analysis of reasons for unsatisfactory performance. These are characterized as:

(a) managerial or organizational shortcomings,
(b) individual personal shortcomings of the employee, and
(c) outside influences.

[. . .]

Reason for failure	Whose problem	Remarks
Can't do	Management	1 Training
		2 Provide resources
		3 Remove obstacles
Won't do	Individual	Change attitude
Doesn't know what he/she should be doing	Management	Improve communication

Figure 17.2 The causes and correction of performance failure (adapted from Steinmetz, 1985)

Organizational culture

The final point is that the appraisal system must be consistent with the organizational culture. If the organization is participative, dynamic, and has a clear sense of direction, then the appraisal system should reflect this by following a target-setting, problem-solving approach. If, however, the organization is more authoritarian and hierarchical, then the appraisal system should mirror this more evaluative approach. Mixed messages are more likely to be confusing than successful. As Long (1986) reported after studying 300 appraisal systems 'ready made' systems imported from other organisations rarely function satisfactorily, partly because of organisational cultural differences'.

Experience of appraisal in non-educational organizations

Fletcher and Williams (1985) in their book *Performance Appraisal and Career Development* describe the history of appraisal practice and give an 'Identikit picture' of a British appraisal system. They look at problems and issues encountered in operating appraisal systems and also try to foresee future developments.

A feature of appraisal systems is that they are constantly being changed and reviewed. Long (1986) found that one third of the systems in his survey had been in operation for three years or less. It is, therefore, somewhat difficult to describe adequately this moving picture. However, from two recent surveys by the Institute of Personnel Managers in 1977 and 1986 some trends are clear (Gill, 1977; Long, 1986).

Purpose of appraisal

In each sample of around 300 organizations, over 80% had performance appraisal systems and very few had abandoned appraisal. *By 1986 most systems were primarily concerned with improving current performance rather than future potential.* Other important purposes were to set performance objectives and to assess training and development needs. Although not directly using MBO, almost two thirds of schemes used a results-oriented approach to appraisal.

Appraisal documents

Appraisal forms generally consisted of a combination of rating scales and open-ended questions. Fletcher and Williams (1985) describe a typical appraisal form as having four sides. The first has biographical details of the job holder and a job description. The final page, which is not generally seen by the job holder, has an assessment of the job holder's promotability and long-term potential. Whereas all previous sections are completed by the appraiser, this page has a section for the manager's manager to comment. The middle two pages written by the manager list the objectives which the appraisee has been concentrating on in the past year and comments on the extent to which these have been achieved. The manager outlines possible future improvements in performance and associated training and development needs. The manager gives an overall performance rating typically on a seven-point scale from 'poor' to 'outstanding'.

There is a space at this point for the appraisee to sign the report and to add any comments which he or she wishes (knowing that these will be read by the manager's manager). However, Long reported that only half the organizations had a formal appeals mechanism.

Interview

Over 80% of organizations had an interview preparation form for appraisees. The interview was reported to be generally problem-oriented with a joint problem-solving style of operation rather than being evaluative and judgemental. Almost all organizations provided notes of guidance for appraisees and almost 80% provided appraisal interview training. The practice of combining reviews of performance and potential has declined in the later survey.

Main weaknesses reported

There were three main weaknesses reported by Long's survey respondents.

1 Unequal standards of assessment amongst different appraisers.
2 Some lack of commitment to the process among line managers.
3 Some lack of follow-up action on training and development plans.

There was growing recognition that a successful appraisal system has to attempt to meet the needs of individuals, line managers and the organization.

Some particular systems

Fletcher and Williams (1985) provide (anonymous) case studies of appraisal systems in a variety of organizations. The Civil Service has published a trainer's resource pack (1985) which both describes its system and prepares appraisers and appraisees to use the system. It contains a training manual, a video and an audio tape (available from CFL Vision, Chalfont Grove, Gerrards Cross, Bucks SL9 8TN). This marks a major change of emphasis in the Civil Service appraisal system towards improvement of current performance and uses a results-oriented approach. This is a major attempt by a non-profit making service organization to use this approach.

The appraisal system at the Plant Protection Division of ICI is described in the proceedings of a BEMAS appraisal conference (Laycock, 1987). This division of ICI employs a large number of professional scientists engaged in research and development work. Although part of a commercial organization, this particular division has the problem of professionals engaged in work where it is not easy to assess results, and particularly where some of them may be very long term. The Civil Service and this division of ICI appear to offer closer parallels to the situation in educational organizations than most other industrial and commercial organizations.

Other appraisal experience is described by Everard (1986b) and Hayes (1984). Everard mainly describes experience at ICI, whilst Hayes chronicles the introduction of appraisal at Nicholas International. The Suffolk study (1985) describes some general industrial and commercial experience. Richardson (1987), writing from an industrial perspective, examines the training and development policies of large multinational companies and considers their applicability to a 'mass public service profession' such as education.

In a recent article Whyte (1986) surveys some management literature on appraisal mainly between 1980 and 1984 to look for implications for teacher appraisal. The article interposes US and British non-educational appraisal practice and has a section which deals with possible gender bias in appraisal.
[. . .]

Adaptation to education

When studying the theory of appraisal and its application in other organizations it is clear that there are substantial differences in the context and climate compared to publicly funded educational institutions. I have identified seven problem areas which are discussed here, concerned with adapting this experience to schools and colleges and suggest some ways forward. Two particular issues arising which are further explored are the nature of 'line management' in education and the appraisal of heads of institution. Finally, I list the features of an appraisal scheme which seem to be most important from the foregoing theory and experience.

Problem areas

(i) *Management of professionals*

The management of professionals poses a basic problem. Handy (1984) describes many professionals as independent operators and in this model, management and appraisal are inappropriate. However, as organizations become more complex, co-ordination of some kind is required and for larger organizations some form of management is essential, particularly in turbulent times. With the gradual acceptance of management in education, a balance has to be struck between management approaches and professionalism. This is a situation met in some other spheres where appraisal is used.

(ii) Results unclear

When the purpose of the whole organization is somewhat unclear, then appraisal of the leader is particularly problematic and this is also true of others in the organization. The problem of assessing institutional performance is in three parts: the first is to decide on the purposes or objectives of the institution. These are generally many and complex. The second is to find ways of assessing how well those objectives have been met. Some may be assessed quantitatively but most can only be assessed qualitatively. The third is how to make valid comparisons between institutions when the nature of the output in terms of educated students is crucially dependent on the level of ability and other characteristics of the students on entry, and over which the school or college has little direct control. Even at the level of examination performance comparisons between schools can be radically transformed when adjustments are made for the quality of the intake (Gray, 1982). This is also the case when the results of an individual school are compared over time (Glogg, 1986). Such adjustments can be done in a quantitative way for exam results. How much more difficult then to make such adjustments conceptually for those measures of output which can only be assessed qualitatively. For a discussion of recent research on school effectiveness see Reynolds (1985). Finally, when the success of the institution can be assessed, there is a further problem associated with assessing the contribution of the leader to that success.

Institutions need to be clear about their purpose even if the purpose may be difficult to assess except in qualitative terms. A statement of objectives provides the yardstick against which to assess performance. All other organizations have a multiplicity of objectives and need internal performance measures. Many of these are difficult to assess. Commercial firms have other objectives in addition to overall profitability.

(iii) Rewards uncertain

Industrial and commercial organizations generally have rewards which they are able to bestow after assessing work performance. Thus financial and other benefits are connected with appraisal. The connection may not be direct – it may be staggered in time – but there is a relationship. There is no way in educational practice of directly rewarding good work in any financial sense. Sir Keith Joseph, one of the most fervent disciples of relating payment and performance, came to accept that merit pay or annual increments should not be related to annual appraisal procedures (DES 1986). Although there are no such annual merit awards in education, data collected through appraisal could be reflected in references and promotion some time in the future. However, personal and professional recognition of achievement should not be underestimated in its motivating potential.

(iv) Difficulty of assessing teaching

Assessing the work of a teacher is particularly difficult. There are no universally agreed criteria for good teaching and more fundamentally the relationship between teaching and learning is not direct. [. . .] It may well be that assessing teaching performance, let alone pupil learning, may not be defensible in any research sense but if it is part of a management process then the test to be applied to the assessment is one of 'fitness for purpose'. It is then important to decide on realistic standards of performance. As Ray Sumner (1988) observes, 'the utility of taking an ideal as the standard for judging performance seems highly questionable'. Yet that is what tends to happen when describing teaching performance. A counsel of perfection is not an adequate baseline for judgement. If a realistic standard of competent performance on various aspects of the teacher's job can be agreed, then the assessment of teaching performance might reduce to an overall acceptable/ unacceptable judgement. Remedial measures will be needed for those judged unacceptable whilst for the overwhelming majority who are judged acceptable there may be individual elements of performance which need raising in standard and which could be set as targets for the coming year. For the *acceptable* the dialogue between appraiser and appraisee would be a professional dialogue intended to stimulate reflection and new ideas. A danger of a checklist approach to assessing teaching performance as observed by Peaker (1986) after a visit to the USA, is that it tends to encourage 'safe' teaching, i.e. static and didactic teaching. Whilst measuring the work of teaching presents problems, so does measuring the work performance of intermediate level personnel in other organisations and particularly those in service functions within the organization.

No other organization observes the work performance of its personnel in ways which resemble classroom observation.

(v) Too many bosses

For headteachers and most teachers in secondary schools there is no direct superordinate. The head has a number of people and groups to whom he or she is accountable. Equally, those in secondary schools with both subject and pastoral duties have at least two people to whom they are accountable. This more complicated form of organization is usually referred to as a matrix structure and has been more usually associated with further and higher education (Fidler, 1984). The pastoral–academic matrix organization of the secondary school does have counterparts in other organizations (Morrisey, 1983), but generally there is a strong arm of the matrix which is close to line management and through which the major elements of appraisal proceed. Problems of co-ordination and communication between the two people to whom an individual is accountable have been noted. Schools will need to consider such problems and ensure that data on performance in other tasks is fed into a designated main appraisal chain.

(vi) Lack of time

Appraisal carried out properly in any organization takes a lot of time. This poses acute problems in education where generally the time allowed for management is too small (Handy, 1984). Other organizations accept the importance of appraisal and regard the time taken by the process as an efficient use of time. In education a combination of not giving a full appraisal to every teacher every year and finding extra management time to carry out appraisal will have to be used to tackle the time problem.

Various estimates of the time required for appraisal have been made. The second Suffolk report (Suffolk Education Department, 1987) assumed that an appraisee would appraise only seven teachers and involve three periods of classroom observation for each of them. This would take 5.25 hours for each teacher. In addition there would be initial and on-going time required for training in appraisal skills. There would also be a need for extra administrative and clerical staff. The costs are assessed at £125 per teacher and £600–£1,100 per headteacher.

(vii) Lack of infrastructure in LEAs

Well managed organizations recognize that there are service functions which need to be provided to those carrying out the direct work of the organization. Two of these directly link with appraisal – personnel and training. Personnel oversees the whole process of appraisal and co-ordinates such work across the organization. It ensures that action is taken as a result of appraisal, be this training, a job change, career progression, or whatever. Training looks at training needs across the organization and either provides or purchases training to meet these needs. Whilst some aspects of both these may be carried out at school level by a professional tutor type appointment, there is a need for both these functions to be co-ordinated right across an LEA. This would provide a unit of ample size and scope for both these functions to be carried out effectively and efficiently. But this will pose new manpower needs for every LEA.

Appraisal and line managers

In other organizations line managers play a key role in the appraisal process because appraisal is an integral part of the management process not an unrelated activity.

It is line managers who control and direct the activity of subordinates, are accountable for their performance and control resources which may support and improve their performance. These activities go on throughout the year and an appraisal interview is the formal stage in the year for taking stock of these activities.

Although the term *line manager* may conjure up the vision of an authoritarian figure barking out orders, the term also applies to a leader operating within a team in a participative, problem-solving mode. The term here is used to identify the person who is accountable for the operation of a section of the organization and who has human and other resources available to achieve results. It is a matter of style how the manager operates in order to achieve these results. In an organization largely staffed by professionals the successful approach is more likely to involve leadership and teamwork than a bureaucratic authoritarian style.

However, from the point of view of accountability and control of resources, the team leader has the attributes of a line manager and this is the term other organizations use. If this term jars, then the reader should replace it with the term *team leader* when thinking about appraisal in education.

Line managers in education

In educational institutions the identification of a line manager has hardly been considered. In a primary school it is clear that the headteacher occupies a position equivalent to a line manager from the point of view of a teacher within the school, although where there are team leaders they may exercise a middle management role. In a secondary school, on the other hand, the position is much less clear. First, in a typical secondary school, there are too many teachers for the headteacher to exercise a direct line management function. Second, there are two sets of middle managers in the pastoral–academic matrix structure as has already been remarked. The most stable grouping is the academic or subject grouping and so this is probably the most appropriate to identify with line management-type functions. It may be that if heads of department are required to appraise staff within their department, this will bring about a more managerial outlook from such middle managers [. . .]. As line managers these middle managers are both appraised and also appraise others. The main thrust of the appraisal of this group should probably concentrate on their managerial function rather than their class-room performance since their key role is to manage their departments or pastoral teams and thereby contribute to the overall work of the school. However, their teaching performance should not be neglected. Appraisals should be carried out by this group of middle managers before they them-selves are appraised since the appraisal reports which they write provide information on their management performance. This is the sequencing of appraisals practised at ICI (Laycock, 1987).

Colleges with a matrix structure will similarly have to identify middle managers who are to carry the main appraisal function.

Heads of institutions

Other organizations have most difficulty in appraising senior management. In the case of educational organizations, difficulties are compounded by the fact tht heads of institutions do not have an equivalent of a line manager. Legally they are accountable to their governing bodies and in employment terms they are employed by a local authority which has other more senior positions within it – both line (education officers) and staff (inspectors/advisers).

Proposals to deal with this situation have ranged from introducing a line manager for heads into the educational system (Trethowan, 1987), to allowing heads to appraise each other by peer group review, with many suggestions between these two extremes (Hawe, 1987).

The requirements of providing public credibility, being part of the management process and enjoying the confidence of heads cannot all be met. A compromise which has attracted much support is for a triumverate of an education officer, an adviser and a fellow head to play a part in the appraisal process (Suffolk Education Department, 1987).

Summary

Essential features of an appraisal system

- It should be part of the managerial process.
- It should be positive and developmental whilst still maintaining credibility as a check on quality.
- It should ultimately improve the learning experiences of pupils and students.
- It should be combined with some element of career development and progression.
- It should formulate training needs and professional development opportunities.
- It should provide a two-way dialogue by which the appraisee gives feedback on the manager's performance and is able to raise organizational problems.
- It should have an infrastructure to provide the back-up to plan and deliver training and co-ordinate professional development through experience in other parts of the organization.

References

Beer, M. (1986) 'Performance Appraisal' in Lorsch, J. W. (Ed) *Handbook of Organizational Behaviour*, Prentice Hall Inc, Englewood Cliffs, NJ (pp. 286–300).
[. . .]
Civil Service (1985) Staff Appraisal: Trainer's Resource Pack, CFL Vision, Gerrards Cross, Bucks.
[. . .]
DES (1986) *Better Schools – Evaluation and Appraisal Conference*, HMSO, London.
[. . .]

Everard, K. B. (1986b) 'Staff Appraisal: Lessons from Industry' in *Coombe Lodge Reports*, 18(8) (pp. 393–401).
[. . .]
Fidler, B. (1984) 'Leadership in Post-Compulsory Education' in Harling, P. (Ed) *New Directions in Educational Leadership*, The Falmer Press, Lewes.
[. . .]
Fletcher, C. & Williams, R. (1985) *Performance Appraisal and Career Development*, Hutchinson, London.
[. . .]
Freemantle, D. (1985) *Superboss: The A–Z of Managing People*, Gower Press, Aldershot.
[. . .]
Giegold, W. C. (1978) *Performer Appraisal and the MBO Process: A Self-Instructional Approach*, McGraw Hill Book Co, New York.
Gill, D. (1977) *Appraising Performance*, Institute of Personnel Management, London.
[. . .]
Glogg, M. P. (1986) *Examination Results in a Mid-Hants Comprehensive: An Investigation into Management Effectiveness*, unpublished MEd dissertation, Bulmershe College of Higher Education, Reading.
Gray, J. (1982) 'Publish and Be Damned? The Problems of Comparing Exam Results in Two Inner London Schools' in *Educational Analysis*, 4(3) (pp. 47–56).
[. . .]
Handy, C. (1984) *Taken for Granted? Understanding Schools as Organizations*, Longman, London.
[. . .]
Hawe, M. (1987) *The Outward Signs of Inward Grace: The Appraisal of Headteachers in Berkshire*, Bulmershe College Mimeo, Reading.
Hayes, M. (1984) 'One Company's Experience with Performance Appraisal' in Kakabadse, A. and Mukhi, S. (Eds), *The Future of Management Education*, Gower, Aldershot.
[. . .]
Laycock, N. (1987) 'Appraisal at ICI Plant Protection Division' in Cooper, R. & Fidler, B. (Eds) *Appraisal in Schools and Colleges 'What can be learned?' and 'The Way Forward?'*, Crewe and Alsager College, Alsager.
[. . .]
Long, P. (1986) *Performance Appraisal Revisited*, IPM, London.
[. . .]
McMahon, A., *et al.* (1984) *Guidelines for Review and Internal Development in Schools (GRIDS): Primary School Handbook; Secondary School Handbook*, Longman, London.
Maier, N.R.F. (1976) *The Appraisal Interview: Three Basic Approaches*, University Associates Inc., La Jolla, California.
[. . .]
Morrisey, G. L. (1976) *Management by Objectives and Results in the Public Sector*, Addison-Wesley Publishing Co, Reading, Mass.
Morrisey, G. L. (1983) *Performance Appraisals in the Public Sector*, Addison-Wesley Publishing Co, Reading Mass.
[. . .]
Peaker, G. (1986) 'Teacher Management and Appraisal in two School Systems in the Southern USA' in *Journal of Education for Teaching*, 12(1) (pp. 77–83).

[. . .]

Reynolds, D. (Ed.) (1985) *Studying School Effectiveness*, The Falmer Press, Lewes.

Richardson, W. (1987) 'A Perspective from Industry: Industrial Staff Training and Career Development Panacea or Pitfall?' in *School Organization*, 7(1) (pp. 13–18).

[. . .]

Schuster, F. E. & Kindall, A. F. (1974) 'Management by Objectives – Where We Stand Today' in *Human Resource Management*, 13(1) (pp. 8–11).

[. . .]

Steinmetz, L. L. (1985) *Managing the Marginal and Unsatisfactory Performer* (Second Ed.), Addison-Wesley, Reading, Mass.

Stenning, W. I. & Stenning, R. (1984) 'The Assessment of Teachers' Performance: Some Practical Considerations' in *School Organization and Management Abstracts*, 3(2) (pp. 77–90).

Stewart, V. & Stewart, A. (1977) *Practical Performance Appraisal*, Gower, Aldershot.

Stewart, V. & Stewart, A. (1983) *Managing the Poor Performer*, Gower, Aldershot.

Strauss, G. A. (1972) 'Management by Objectives: A Critical View' in *Training and Development Journal*, 26(4) (pp. 10–15).

[. . .]

Suffolk Education Department (1985) *Those Having Torches: Teacher Appraisal: A Study*, Suffolk LEA, Ipswich.

Suffolk Education Department (1987) *In the Light of Torches: Teacher Appraisal: A Further Study*, The Industrial Society, London.

Sumner, R. (1988) 'Formal teacher appraisal: Why and how, not if' in *Staff Appraisal in Schools and Colleges*, Longman, Harlow.

[. . .]

Trethowan, D. M. (1987) *Appraisal and Target Setting: A Handbook for Teacher Development*, Harper and Row, London.

[. . .]

Whyte, J. B. (1986) 'Teacher Assessment: A Review of the Performance Appraisal Literature with Special Reference to the Implications for Teacher Appraisal' in *Research Papers in Education*, 1(2) (pp. 137–163).

[. . .]

Author index

Subject index